Teach Yourself

VISUALLY ™

Photoshop® Elements 8

WITHDRAWN

Visual

by Mike Wooldridge

WILEY

Wiley Publishing, Inc.

Teach Yourself VISUALLY™ Photoshop® Elements 8

Published by
Wiley Publishing, Inc.
10475 Crosspoint Boulevard
Indianapolis, IN 46256
www.wiley.com

Published simultaneously in Canada

Library of Congress Control Number: 2009937843

ISBN: 978-0-470-56690-9

Manufactured in the United States of America

10 9 8 7 6 5 4 3 2 1

Trademark Acknowledgments

Contact Us

For general information on our other products and services please contact our Customer Care Department within the U.S. at 877-762-2974, outside the U.S. at 317-572-3993 or fax 317-572-4002.

For technical support please visit www.wiley.com/techsupport.

Permissions

Brianna Stuart
http://www.stuartphotography.net

Wiley Publishing, Inc.

Sales

Contact Wiley
at (877) 762-2974 or
fax (317) 572-4002.

Praise for Visual Books

"Like a lot of other people, I understand things best when I see them visually. Your books really make learning easy and life more fun."

John T. Frey (Cadillac, MI)

"I have quite a few of your Visual books and have been very pleased with all of them. I love the way the lessons are presented!"

Mary Jane Newman (Yorba Linda, CA)

"I just purchased my third Visual book (my first two are dog-eared now!), and, once again, your product has surpassed my expectations.

Tracey Moore (Memphis, TN)

"I am an avid fan of your Visual books. If I need to learn anything, I just buy one of your books and learn the topic in no time. Wonders! I have even trained my friends to give me Visual books as gifts."

Illona Bergstrom (Aventura, FL)

"Thank you for making it so clear. I appreciate it. I will buy many more Visual books."

J.P. Sangdong (North York, Ontario, Canada)

"I have several books from the Visual series and have always found them to be valuable resources."

Stephen P. Miller (Ballston Spa, NY)

"Thank you for the wonderful books you produce. It wasn't until I was an adult that I discovered how I learn — visually. Nothing compares to Visual books. I love the simple layout. I can just grab a book and use it at my computer, lesson by lesson. And I understand the material! You really know the way I think and learn. Thanks so much!"

Stacey Han (Avondale, AZ)

"I absolutely admire your company's work. Your books are terrific. The format is perfect, especially for visual learners like me. Keep them coming!"

Frederick A. Taylor, Jr. (New Port Richey, FL)

"I have several of your Visual books and they are the best I have ever used."

Stanley Clark (Crawfordville, FL)

"I bought my first Teach Yourself VISUALLY book last month. Wow. Now I want to learn everything in this easy format!"

Tom Vial (New York, NY)

"Thank you, thank you, thank you...for making it so easy for me to break into this high-tech world. I now own four of your books. I recommend them to anyone who is a beginner like myself."

Gay O'Donnell (Calgary, Alberta, Canada)

"I write to extend my thanks and appreciation for your books. They are clear, easy to follow, and straight to the point. Keep up the good work! I bought several of your books and they are just right! No regrets! I will always buy your books because they are the best."

Seward Kollie (Dakar, Senegal)

"Compliments to the chef!! Your books are extraordinary! Or, simply put, extra-ordinary, meaning way above the rest! THANK YOU THANK YOU THANK YOU! I buy them for friends, family, and colleagues."

Christine J. Manfrin (Castle Rock, CO)

"What fantastic teaching books you have produced! Congratulations to you and your staff. You deserve the Nobel Prize in Education in the Software category. Thanks for helping me understand computers."

Bruno Tonon (Melbourne, Australia)

"Over time, I have bought a number of your 'Read Less - Learn More' books. For me, they are THE way to learn anything easily. I learn easiest using your method of teaching."

José A. Mazón (Cuba, NY)

"I am an avid purchaser and reader of the Visual series, and they are the greatest computer books I've seen. The Visual books are perfect for people like myself who enjoy the computer, but want to know how to use it more efficiently. Your books have definitely given me a greater understanding of my computer, and have taught me to use it more effectively. Thank you very much for the hard work, effort, and dedication that you put into this series."

Alex Diaz (Las Vegas, NV)

Credits

Executive Editor
Jody Lefevere

Project Editor
Christopher Stolle

Technical Editor
Dennis Cohen

Senior Copy Editor
Kim Heusel

Editorial Director
Robyn Siesky

Editorial Manager
Cricket Krengel

Business Manager
Amy Knies

Senior Marketing Manager
Sandy Smith

Vice President and Executive Group Publisher
Richard Swadley

Vice President and Executive Publisher
Barry Pruett

Project Coordinator
Patrick Redmond

Graphics and Production Specialists
Carrie A. Cesavice
Andrea Hornberger
Jennifer Mayberry
Christine Williams

Quality Control Technician
John Greenough

Proofreading and Indexing
Cindy Lee Ballew/
Precisely Write
Potomac Indexing, LLC

Screen Artist
Ana Carrillo
Jill A. Proll

Illustrators
Ronda David-Burroughs
Cheryl Grubbs
Mark Pinto

About the Author

Mike Wooldridge is a Web developer in the San Francisco Bay area. He has authored more than 20 books for the Visual series.

Author's Acknowledgments

Mike thanks Brianna Stuart for the use of her beautiful photographs in some examples and for her help in preparing the hundreds of screenshots for the book. He thanks Christopher Stolle for his top-notch project editing, Dennis Cohen for his knowledgeable technical editing, Kim Heusel for his careful copyediting, and Ronda David-Burroughs, Cheryl Grubbs, and Mark Pinto for all their clever illustrations. This book is dedicated to Mike's wife Linda and son Griffin.

Table of Contents

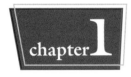
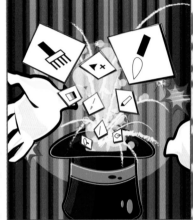

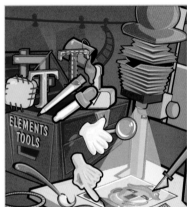

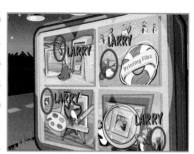

Table of Contents

chapter 5 Image-Editing Basics

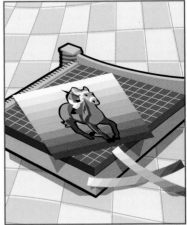

chapter 6 Selection Techniques

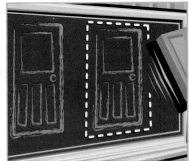

chapter 7 Manipulating Selections

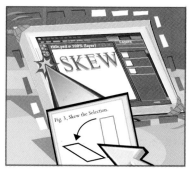

chapter 8 Layer Basics

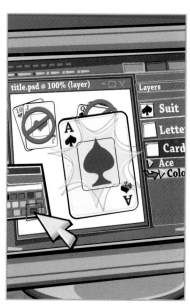

Table of Contents

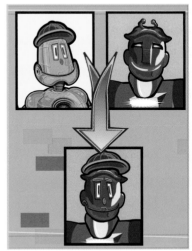
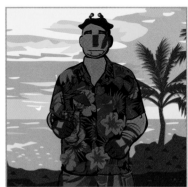

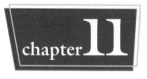

chapter 11 · Enhancing Colors

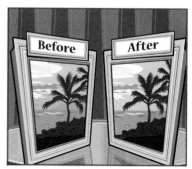

chapter 12 · Painting and Drawing on Photos

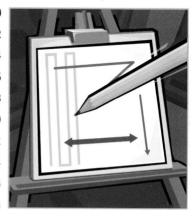

Table of Contents

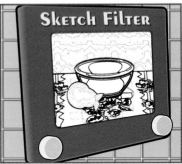

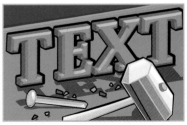

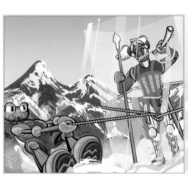

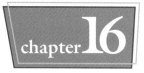

chapter **16** **Presenting Photos Creatively**

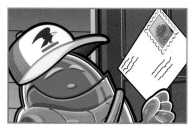

chapter **17** **Saving and Sharing Your Work**

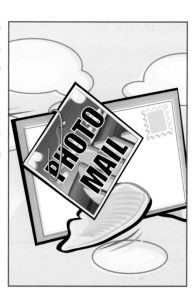

How to use this book

Do you look at the pictures in a book or newspaper before anything else on a page? Would you rather see an image instead of read about how to do something? Search no further. This book is for you. Opening Teach Yourself VISUALLY Photoshop Elements 8 allows you to read less and learn more about *Photoshop Elements 8*.

Who Needs This Book

This book is for readers who have never used image-editing software and want to learn how to work with digital photos on their computers. It is also for more computer-literate individuals who want to expand their knowledge of the different features that Photoshop Elements 8 has to offer.

Book Organization

Teach Yourself VISUALLY Photoshop Elements 8 has 17 chapters.

Chapter 1, **Getting Started**, introduces you to the two main parts of Photoshop Elements 8: the Editor and the Organizer. In the Editor, you can change the look of your photos, combine different parts of images into one using layers, and correct imperfections in your photos. The Organizer allows you to categorize the photos in your collection so you can easily find them later and use them in projects.

In Chapter 2, **Acquiring and Storing Digital Images**, you learn how to import digital photos into the Elements environment as well as how to open and save your work.

Chapter 3, **Organizing Your Photos**, covers the Elements Organizer, which lets you browse your collection of images, view them at full screen or as a slide show, and caption your photos.

Chapter 4, **Advanced Organizing Tools**, teaches you how to categorize your photos with keyword tags, automatically recognize faces, and place your photos on a map.

Chapter 5, **Image-Editing Basics**, shows you how to resize your photos in the Elements workspace and undo changes when you make mistakes.

Chapter 6, **Selection Techniques**, introduces you to the many different tools for selecting objects in your photos.

Chapter 7, **Manipulating Selections**, teaches you how to change the shape and orientation of objects in your photos after you have selected the objects.

Chapter 8, **Layer Basics**, gives you extensive information about Elements layers, which allow you to separate objects in your photo from one another and then style the objects independently.

Chapter 9, **Retouching Photos**, shows you how to eliminate imperfections by performing automatic fix commands, cloning from other parts of a photo, or cropping out unneeded content.

Chapter 10, **Enhancing Contrast and Exposure**, covers some of the many lighting commands and tools in Photoshop Elements 8.

Chapter 11, **Enhancing Colors**, introduces features for changing hues in your photos, correcting colorcasts, and converting photos to black and white.

Chapter 12, **Painting and Drawing on Photos**, covers the different brush tools, which enable you to paint both color and special effects onto your photos. It also introduces tools that allow you to overlay shapes.

Chapter 13, **Applying Filters**, gives you a look at some of the more than 100 filters in Photoshop Elements 8, which are tools for adding special effects to photos or objects within a photo.

Chapter 14, **Adding Text Elements**, teaches you how to apply stylized lettering to your photos to inform or decorate.

In Chapter 15, **Applying Styles and Effects**, you learn about the customizable features available in the Effects panel. These features let you quickly apply color or 3-D effects to your photos.

Chapter 16, **Presenting Photos Creatively**, covers some of the photo-based projects you can complete in Photoshop Elements 8. You can make slide shows, combine several photos into a panorama, create greeting cards, and more.

Chapter 17, **Saving and Sharing Your Work**, shows you how to save your photos after you have customized or optimized them and then share your photos with friends or family by e-mail. It also introduces the sharing and backup services available at Photoshop.com.

Chapter Organization

This book consists of sections, all listed in the book's table of contents. A *section* is a set of steps that show you how to complete a specific computer task.

Each section, usually contained on two facing pages, has an introduction to the task at hand, a set of full-color screen shots and steps that walk you through the task, and a set of tips. This format allows you to quickly look at a topic of interest and learn it instantly.

Chapters group together sections with a common theme. A chapter may also contain pages that give you the background information needed to understand the sections in a chapter.

What You Need to Use This Book

To install and run Photoshop Elements 8, you need a computer with the following:

- An Intel or compatible processor running at 2 GHz or faster
- Microsoft Windows XP with Service Pack 2 or 3, Windows Vista, or Windows 7
- Color monitor with a 1024x768 or greater resolution
- 1GB of RAM
- 1.5GB of available hard-drive space

You may find the following useful for capturing digital photos to use in Elements:

- Digital camera
- Image scanner
- Digital camcorder

The program's Web features require an Internet connection and a Web browser. The following browsers are supported:

- Microsoft Internet Explorer 6, 7, and 8; Firefox 1.5, 2, and 3; and Safari 2.0

Using the Mouse

This book uses the following conventions to describe the actions you perform when using the mouse:

Click

Press your left mouse button once. You generally click your mouse on something to select something on the screen.

Double-click

Press your left mouse button twice. Double-clicking something on the computer screen generally opens whatever item you have double-clicked.

Right-click

Press your right mouse button. When you right-click on anything on the computer screen, the program displays a shortcut menu containing commands specific to the selected item.

Click and Drag and then Release the Mouse

Move your mouse pointer and hover it over an item on the screen. Press and hold down the left mouse button. Now, move the mouse to where you want to place the item and then release the button. You use this method to move an item from one area of the computer screen to another.

The Conventions in This Book

A number of typographic and layout styles have been used throughout Photoshop Elements 8 to distinguish different types of information.

Bold

Bold type represents the names of commands and options that you interact with. Bold type also indicates text and numbers that you must type into a dialog box.

Italics

Italic words introduce a new term, which is then defined.

Numbered Steps

You must perform the instructions in numbered steps in order to successfully complete a section and achieve the final results.

Bulleted Steps

These steps point out various optional features. You do not have to perform these steps; they simply give additional information about a feature.

Indented Text

Indented text tells you what the program does in response to your following a numbered step. For example, if you click a certain menu command, a dialog box may open or a window may open. Indented text may also tell you what the final result is when you follow a set of numbered steps.

Notes

Notes give additional information. They may describe special conditions that may occur during an operation. They may warn you of a situation that you want to avoid — for example, the loss of data. A note may also cross-reference a related area of the book. A cross-reference may guide you to another chapter or to another section within the current chapter.

Icons and Buttons

Icons and buttons are graphical representations within the text. They show you exactly what you need to click to perform a step.

You can easily identify the tips in any section by looking for the TIPS icon. Tips offer additional information, including tips, hints, and tricks. You can use the TIPS information to go beyond what you have learned in the steps.

Operating System Difference

The screenshots used in this book were captured by using the Windows Vista operating system. The features shown in the tasks may differ slightly if you are using Windows 7, Windows XP, or an earlier operating system. For example, the default folder for saving photos in Windows Vista is named "Pictures," whereas the default folder in Windows XP for saving photos is named "My Pictures." The program workspace may also look different based on your monitor resolution setting and your program preferences.

CHAPTER 1

Getting Started

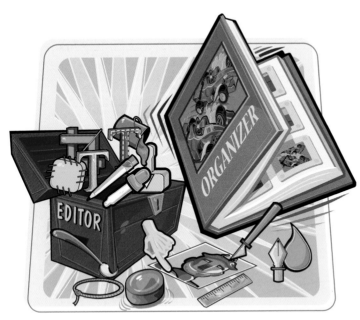

Are you interested in working with digital images on your computer? This chapter introduces you to Adobe Photoshop Elements 8, a popular software application for editing and creating digital images.

Introducing Photoshop Elements 8

Photoshop Elements is a popular photo-editing program you can use to modify, optimize, and organize digital images. You can use the program's Editor to make imperfect snapshots clearer and more colorful as well as retouch and restore older photos. You can also use the program's Organizer to group your photos into albums, assign descriptive keyword tags, and create slide shows, online galleries, and more.

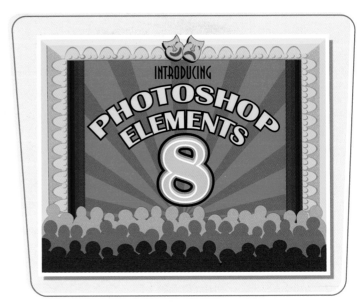

Manipulate Photos

As its name suggests, Photoshop Elements excels at letting you edit elements in your digital photographs. The program includes numerous image-editing tools and commands you can apply to manipulate the look of your photos. Whether you import photos from a digital camera or a scanner, you can apply a wide variety of editing techniques to your images — from subtle adjustments in color to elaborate filters that make your snapshots look like paintings. See Chapter 7 for more on manipulating selected parts of your photos. See Chapter 12 for more on painting and drawing, and see Chapter 13 for more on using filters.

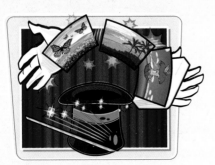

Retouch and Repair

You can use Photoshop Elements to edit new photos to make them look their best as well as retouch and repair older photos that suffer from aging problems. For example, you can restore a faded photo by using saturation controls to make it more vibrant or you can use the Clone Stamp tool to repair a tear or stain. You can also use the program's exposure commands to fix lighting problems as well as edit out unwanted objects with the Healing Brush. See Chapter 9 for more on retouching your photos.

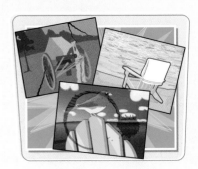

Add Decoration

The painting tools in Photoshop Elements make the program a formidable illustration tool as well as a photo editor. You can apply colors or patterns to your images with a variety of brush styles. See Chapter 12 to discover how to paint and draw on your photos. In addition, you can use the application's typographic tools to integrate stylized letters and words into your images. See Chapter 14 for more on adding text elements.

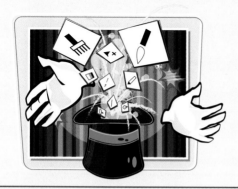

Create a Digital Collage

You can combine parts of different images in Photoshop Elements to create a collage. Your compositions can include photos, scanned art, text, and anything else you can save on your computer as a digital image. By placing elements on separate layers, you can move, transform, and customize them independently of one another. See Chapter 8 for more on layers. You can also merge several side-by-side scenes into a seamless panorama, which is covered in Chapter 16.

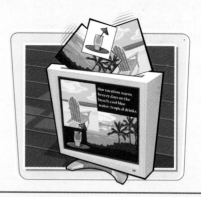

Organize and Catalog

As you bring photos into Photoshop Elements, the program keeps track of them in the Organizer. In the Organizer, you can place groups of photos into theme-specific albums, tag your photos with keywords that describe where they were taken or who is in them, and search for specific photos based on a variety of criteria. See Chapters 3 and 4 for more on the Organizer.

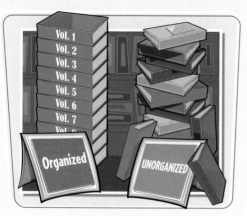

Put Your Photos to Work

After you edit your photographs, you can use them in a variety of ways. Photoshop Elements lets you print your images, save them for the Web, or bring them together in a slide show. You can e-mail your photos with the Photo Mail feature. You can also create greeting cards, calendars, and other projects. For more on creating and printing your photo projects, see Chapters 16 and 17.

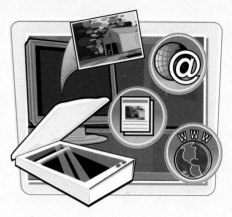

Understanding Digital Images

To work with photos in Photoshop Elements, you must first turn them into a digital format. This section introduces you to some important basics about how computers store images in digital form.

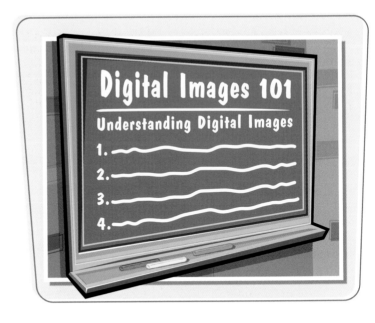

Acquire Photos

You can acquire photographic images to use in Photoshop Elements from a number of sources. You can download photos to Photoshop Elements from a digital camera, memory card, or photo CD. You can scan photographs, slides, or artwork and then import the images directly into the program. You can also bring in photos that you have downloaded from the Web. For more on importing photos, see Chapter 2.

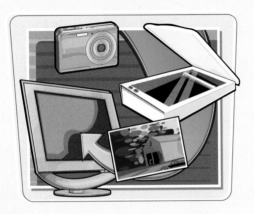

Understanding Pixels

Digital images that you download from a camera consist of tiny, solid-color squares called *pixels*. Photoshop Elements works its magic by rearranging and recoloring these squares. You can edit specific pixels or groups of pixels by selecting the area of the photo you want to edit. If you zoom in close, you can see the pixels that make up your image. Chapter 5 covers the Zoom tool.

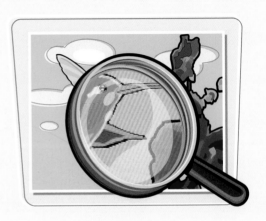

Bitmap Images

Images that are composed of pixels are known as *bitmap images* or *raster images*. The pixels are arranged in a rectangular grid, and each pixel includes information about its color and position. Most of the time when you are working in Photoshop Elements, you are working with bitmap content.

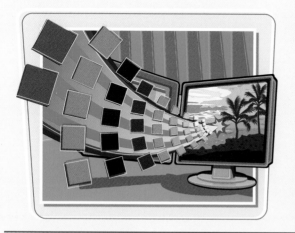

Vector Graphics

The other common way of displaying pictures on your computer is with vector graphics. Vector graphics encode image information by using mathematical equations rather than pixels. Unlike raster images, vector graphics can change size without a loss of quality. When you add shapes or text to your photos in Elements, you are working with vector graphics.

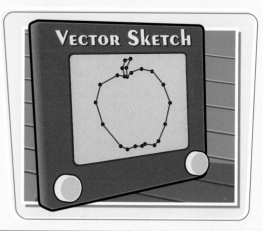

Supported File Formats

Photoshop Elements supports a variety of file types you can both import and export. Popular file formats include BMP, PICT, TIFF, EPS, JPEG, GIF, PNG, and PSD, which stands for Photoshop Document. Files that you save in the PSD format can be shared with other Adobe programs, such as Photoshop and Illustrator. For images that are published on the Internet, JPEG, GIF, and PNG are the most common formats.

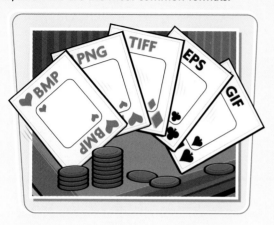

File Size

File formats such as PSD and TIFF tend to take up more space on your computer because they faithfully save all the information that was originally captured by your camera or other device. Those formats can also include multiple layers. JPEG, GIF, and PNG files are built to be sent over the Internet and usually sacrifice some quality for the sake of compactness.

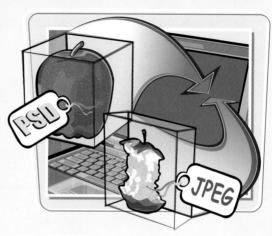

Start Photoshop Elements

You can now start Photoshop Elements to begin creating and editing digital images.

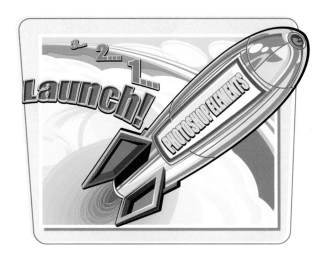

1 Click **Start**.

2 Type **Elements** in the search box.

Windows displays a list of search results.

3 Click **Adobe Photoshop Elements 8.0**.

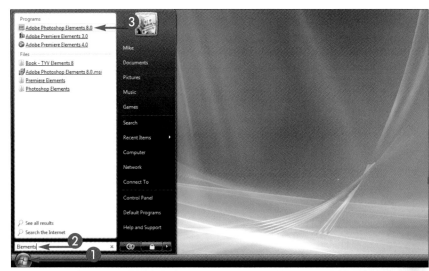

The Photoshop Elements welcome screen opens.

The welcome screen displays clickable buttons that take you to different workspaces in Photoshop Elements.

4 Click **Edit**.

The Photoshop Elements Editor opens.

● You can click **Organize** to open the Organizer.

● You can also log in to or sign up for Adobe's photo-sharing and backup services. See Chapter 17 for more.

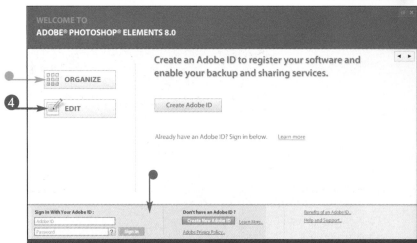

In the Photoshop Elements Editor, you can use a combination of tools, menu commands, and panel-based features to open and edit your digital photos. The main Editor pane displays the photos that you are currently modifying. This section gives you a preview of the interface elements in the Editor.

To open the Editor, click Edit on the welcome screen.

● **Image Window**

Displays each photo you open in Photoshop Elements.

● **Layout Button**

Opens a menu that lets you select from a variety of image window arrangements.

● **Image Tabs**

Clickable tabs for switching between open images in the Editor.

● **Photoshop.com Links**

Clickable links for signing in to Photoshop.com for managing your photos online.

● **Organizer Button**

Clickable button for switching to the Organizer interface, where you can catalog your photos.

● **Task Tabs**

Clickable tabs for switching between workflows in the Editor.

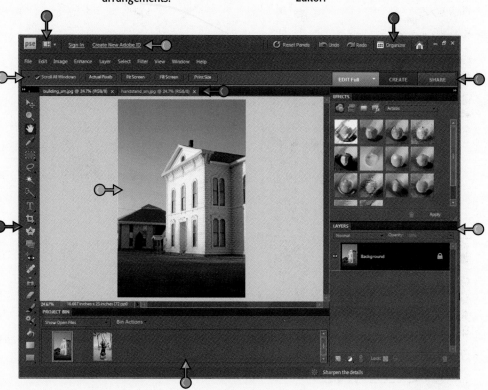

● **Panel Bin**

A storage area for panels, which are the resizable windows that hold related commands, settings, and other information.

● **Project Bin**

Enables you to open and work with multiple photos.

● **Toolbox**

Displays a variety of icons, each representing an image-editing tool.

● **Options Bar**

Displays controls that let you customize the selected tool in the Toolbox.

The Organizer Workspace

In the Photoshop Elements Organizer, you can catalog, view, and sort your growing library of digital photos. The main Organizer pane shows miniature versions of the photos in your catalog. This section gives you a preview of the interface elements in the Organizer.

To open the Organizer, click Organize on the welcome screen.

Photo Browser

Displays miniature versions, or *thumbnails*, of the photos in your catalog.

Toolbar

Displays buttons and other options for modifying and sorting photos in the Photo Browser.

Photoshop.com Links

Clickable links for signing in to Photoshop.com for managing your photos online.

Display Menu

Contains commands for switching to different views in the Organizer.

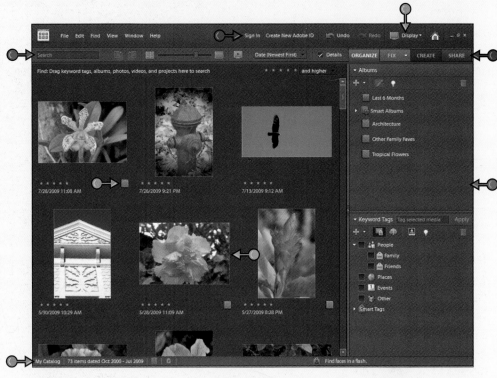

Task Tabs

Clickable tabs for switching between workflows in the Organizer.

Panel Bin

A storage area for panels, which are the resizable windows that hold related commands, settings, and other information.

Tag Icon

Shows which tags have been applied to a photo.

Status Bar

Displays the name of the currently open catalog, how many photos are in the catalog, and other summary information.

Switch between the Editor and the Organizer

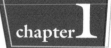
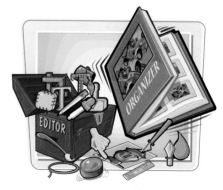

Photoshop Elements has two main views: the Editor and the Organizer. The Editor enables you to modify, combine, and optimize your photos, while the Organizer lets you browse, sort, share, and categorize photos in your collection. You can easily switch between the two views.

Switch between the Editor and the Organizer

① Start Photoshop Elements in the Editor view.

Note: See the section "Start Photoshop Elements" for more on starting the program.

You can open and edit a photo in the Editor.

② Click **Organizer**.

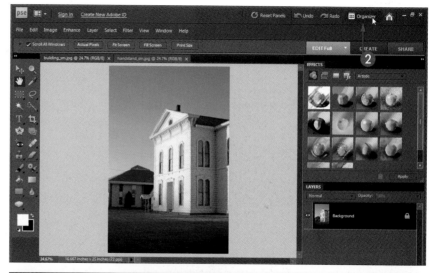

The Organizer appears.

● You can click **Fix** and then **Full Photo Edit** to return to the Editor.

● A lock icon (🔒) appears on any Organizer photos that are currently being edited in the Editor.

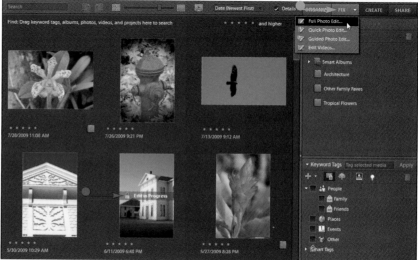

Anatomy of the Photoshop Elements Toolbox

Photoshop Elements offers a variety of specialized tools that let you edit your image. Take some time to familiarize yourself with the Toolbox tools.

You can select tools by clicking buttons in the Toolbox or by typing a keyboard shortcut key. Keyboard shortcut keys are shown in parentheses.

● **Move (V)**

Moves selected areas of an image.

● **Zoom (Z)**

Zooms your view of an image in or out.

● **Hand (H)**

Shows unseen parts of larger images.

● **Eyedropper (I)**

Samples color from an area of an image.

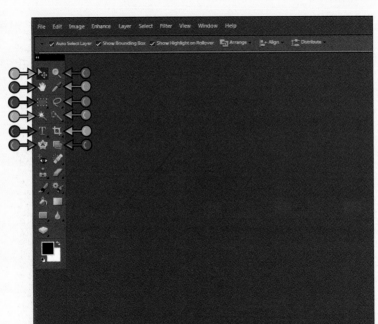

● **Lasso (L)**

Selects pixels by drawing a free-form shape around the area you want to edit.

● **Magic Wand (W)**

Selects pixels of odd-shaped areas based on similar pixel color.

● **Marquee (M)**

Selects pixels by drawing a box or ellipse around the area you want to edit.

● **Quick Selection Brush (A)**

Selects pixels by using brush shapes.

● **Type (T)**

Adds type to an image.

● **Crop (C)**

Trims an image to create a new size.

● **Cookie Cutter (Q)**

Crops your image into shapes.

● **Straighten (P)**

Straightens tilted images.

12

Red-Eye Removal (Y)

Corrects red-eye problems.

Spot-Healing Brush (J)

Quickly fixes slight imperfections by cloning nearby pixels.

Clone Stamp (S)

Duplicates an area of the image.

Eraser (E)

Erases pixels.

Brush (B)

Paints strokes of color.

Smart Brush (F)

Simultaneously selects objects and applies color adjustments.

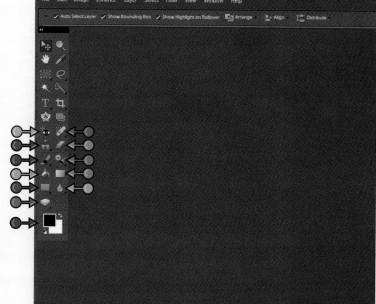

Paint Bucket (K)

Fills areas with color.

Gradient (G)

Creates blended color effects to use as fills.

Custom Shape (U)

Draws predefined shapes.

Blur (R)

Blurs objects in your image.

Sponge (O)

Adjusts color saturation or intensity.

Foreground and Background Color

Sets foreground and background colors to use with tools.

Work with Toolbox Tools

You can use the tools in the Photoshop Elements Toolbox to make changes to an image. After you click to select a tool, the Options bar displays controls for customizing how the tool works. Some tools include a tiny triangle in the bottom-right corner to indicate hidden tools you can select. For example, the Marquee tool has two variations: Rectangular and Elliptical.

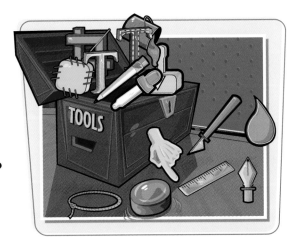

Work with Toolbox Tools

Select a Tool

1 Position the mouse pointer over a tool.

● A screen tip displays the tool name and shortcut key. You can click the tool name to access Help information about the tool.

2 Click a tool to select it.

● The Options bar displays customizing options for the selected tool.

3 Specify any options you want for the tool.

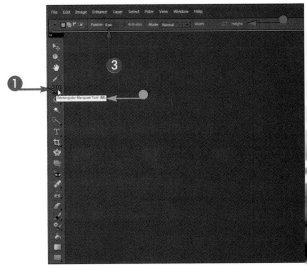

Select a Hidden Tool

1 Click a tool that has a triangle in its corner.

2 Press and hold the mouse button.

● A menu of hidden tools appears.

You can also right-click on a tool to show hidden tools.

3 Click the tool you want to use.

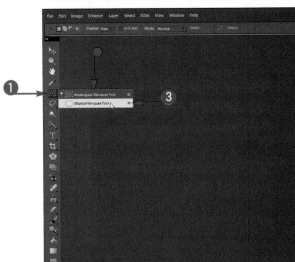

Configure the Toolbox

1 At the top of the Toolbox, click ▶▶.

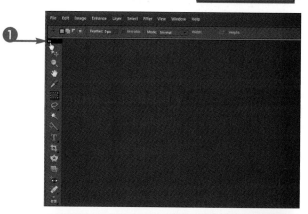

The Toolbox changes configurations.

In this example, the one-column Toolbox changes to a two-column Toolbox.

● You can click ◀◀ to switch back to the previous configuration.

Both the one-column and two-column configurations are used in the examples in this book.

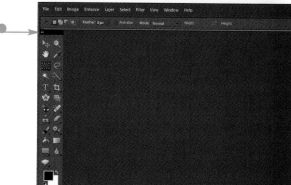

 TIP

How can I float the Toolbox?
You can float the Toolbox over the workspace to make it convenient to select tools as you work.

1 Position the mouse over the top of the Toolbox.

2 Click and drag the Toolbox to a different part of the workspace.

3 Release the mouse button.

Photoshop Elements displays the Toolbox as a floating panel.

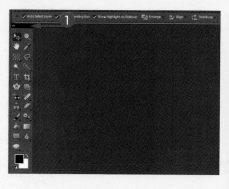

● You can drag the Toolbox back to the left side of the workspace to unfloat it.

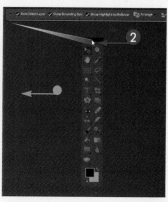

Work with Panels

In the Photoshop Elements Editor, you can open resizable windows called *panels* to access different Photoshop Elements commands and features. By default, most panels open in the Panel Bin located on the right side of the Photoshop Elements workspace. You can float panels over the program workspace to give yourself easy access to commands.

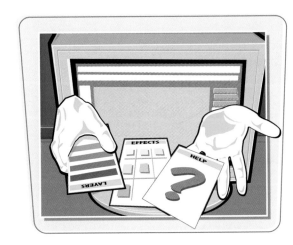

Work with Panels

Open and Close a Panel

① Open the Photoshop Elements Editor.

Note: *For more on opening the Editor, see the section "Start Photoshop Elements."*

② Click **Window**.

③ Click a panel name.

A check mark (☑) next to the panel name indicates the panel is already open.

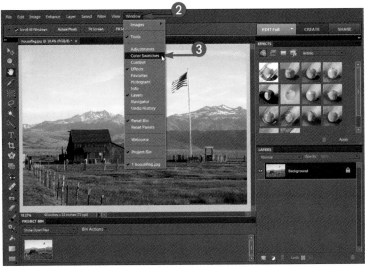

The chosen panel opens.

● You can hide or show a panel by double-clicking its title tab.

④ Click the panel menu.

A menu with panel commands opens.

⑤ Click **Close**.

The panel closes.

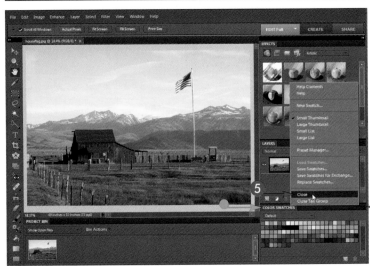

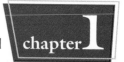

Float a Panel

1. Click and drag the title tab of a panel to the work area.

2. Release the mouse.

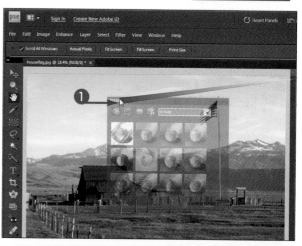

The panel opens as a free-floating window.

- You can resize a floating panel by clicking and dragging its corner ().

- To close a floating panel, click the **Close** button (⊠).

- To reset the Photoshop Elements panels to their default arrangement, click **Reset Panels**.

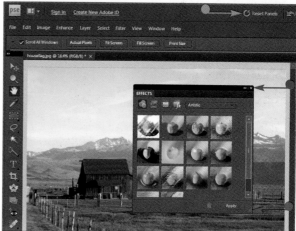

TIP

How do I rearrange panels in the Panel Bin?

1. Position the mouse over the title tab of a panel.

2. Click and drag the panel to a different part of the Panel Bin.

- Photoshop Elements highlights the area to which the panel will be moved.

3. Release the mouse button.

Photoshop Elements moves the panel.

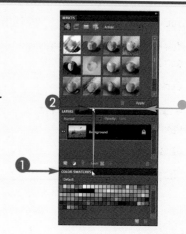

Set Program Preferences

The Preferences dialog box lets you change default settings and modify how the program looks. You can set preferences in both the Editor and Organizer workspaces to customize the program to match how you like to work.

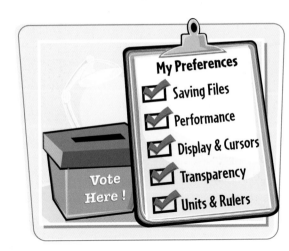

In the Editor

1 In the Editor, click **Edit**.

Note: For more on opening the Editor, see the section "The Editor Workspace."

2 Click **Preferences**.

3 Click **General**.

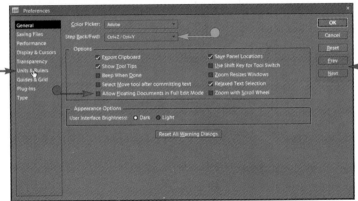

The Preferences dialog box opens and displays General options.

4 Select any settings you want to change.

● For example, you can specify the shortcut keys for stepping backward and forward through your commands.

● You can click here to open images in floating windows instead of tabbed windows.

5 Click a different preference category.

● You can also click **Prev** and **Next** to move back and forth between categories.

In this example, the Preferences dialog box displays Units & Rulers options.

⑥ Select any settings you want to change.

● For example, you can specify the default units for various aspects of the program.

⑦ Click **OK**.

Photoshop Elements sets the preferences.

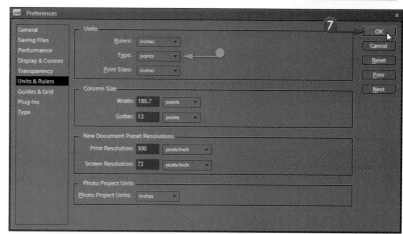

In the Organizer

① In the Organizer, click **Edit**, **Preferences**, and then **General**.

Note: *For more on opening the Organizer, see the section "The Organizer Workspace."*

The Preferences dialog box opens.

② Select any settings you want to change.

● For example, you can specify date ordering and formatting preferences.

③ Click **OK** to close the dialog box.

Photoshop Elements sets the preferences.

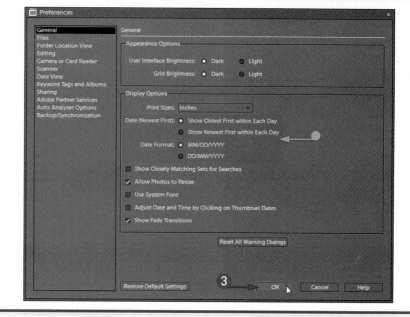

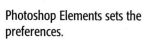

What type of measurement units should I use?

You should use the units most applicable to the type of output you intend to produce. Pixel units are useful for Web imaging because monitor dimensions are measured in pixels. Inches, picas, centimeters, and millimeters are useful for print because those are standards for working on paper. You can find measurement settings in the Units & Rulers preferences.

How do I allocate extra memory for opening more files?

The Performance preferences show how much memory you have available and how much of it Photoshop Elements is using. You can make changes to these settings to enhance the program's performance. The Scratch Disks preferences enable you to allocate extra memory on your hard drive, called *scratch disk space*, to use if your computer runs out of RAM.

View Rulers and Guides

You can turn on rulers and create guides to help place elements accurately in your image. Rulers appear on the top and left sides of the image window and enable you to measure distances within your image. Guides are lines that help you position different elements in your image. These lines do not appear on the printed image.

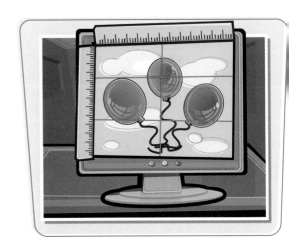

View Rulers and Guides

① Click **View.**

② Click **Rulers.**

Note: To change the units of the rulers, see the section "Set Program Preferences" in Chapter 1.

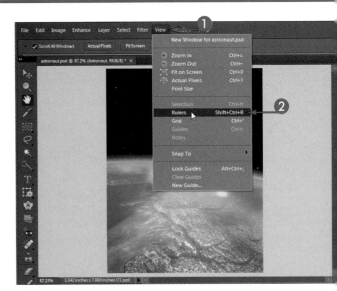

● Photoshop Elements adds rulers to the top and left edges of the image window.

③ Click one of the rulers and drag the cursor into the window (⇧ changes to ⊹).

Drag the top ruler down to create a horizontal guide.

Drag the left ruler to the right to create a vertical guide.

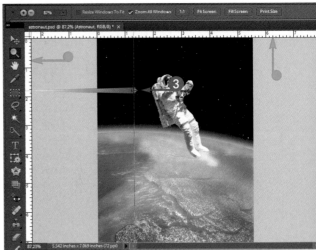

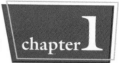

- A thin, colored line called a guide appears.

- You can also click **View** and then **New Guide** to add a guide.

  You can use guides to align objects in the different layers of an image.

Note: See Chapter 8 for more about layers.

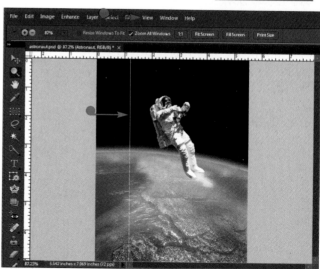

Move a Guide

1. Click the **Move** tool (⬩).

2. Place the cursor over a guide (⬩ changes to ⬩⬩) and then click and drag.

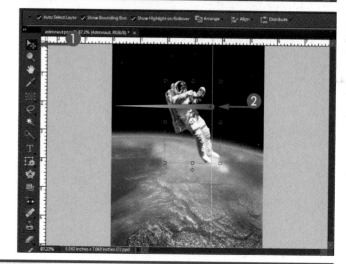

TIPS

How do I make objects in my images "snap to" my guides when I move those objects?

The "snap to" feature is useful for aligning elements in a row or a column.

1. Click **View**.

2. Click **Snap To**.

3. Click **Guides**.

When you move an object near a guide, Photoshop Elements automatically aligns it with the guide.

Note: For more about layers, see Chapter 8.

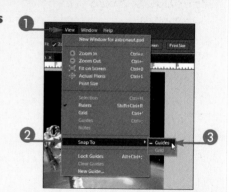

CHAPTER

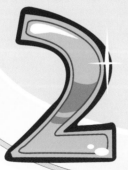

Acquiring and Storing Digital Images

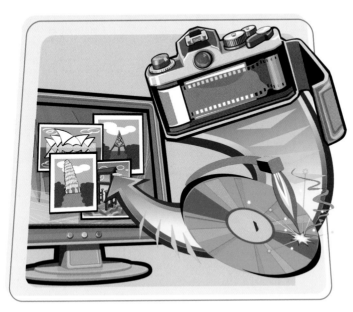

Before you can start working with photos in Photoshop Elements, you must first import them from a camera, scanner, or another digital device or from folders on your computer. This chapter shows you how to import photos into the Photoshop Elements Organizer and then open them in the Photoshop Elements Editor.

Get Photos for Your Projects

To work with images in Photoshop Elements, you must first acquire the images. You can get raw material for Photoshop Elements from a variety of sources.

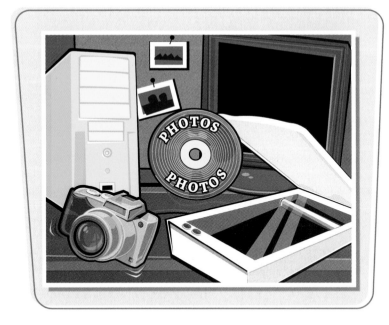

Digital Cameras

A digital camera is probably the most common way to take photographs and then import them into your computer. Most digital cameras save their images as JPEG or TIFF files, both of which you can open and edit in Photoshop Elements. You can transfer images directly from a camera by using a USB cable or you can transfer images by using a card reader, which is a device that reads your camera's memory card.

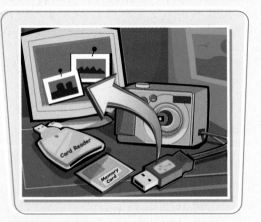

Scanned Photos and Art

A scanner gives you an inexpensive way to convert existing paper-based content into a digital form. You can scan photos and art into your computer, retouch and stylize them in Photoshop Elements, and then output them to a color printer. You can also use a slide attachment to digitize slides by using a scanner. For tips on automatically straightening scanned photos, see Chapter 5.

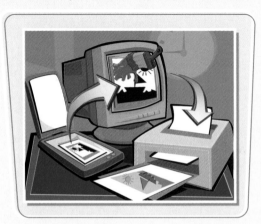

Web Images

If you have photos or art stored on the Web, you can easily save those image files to your computer and then open them in Photoshop Elements. In Internet Explorer on the PC, you can save a Web image by right-clicking on it and then choosing Save Picture As. Inexpensive stock photo Web sites, such as iStockphoto, offer professional-grade images for download. On photo-sharing sites, such as Flickr, users often allow noncommercial use of their photos.

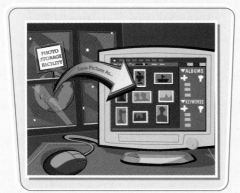

Start from Scratch

You can also create your Photoshop Elements image from scratch by opening a blank canvas in the image window. You can then apply colors and patterns with the painting tools in Photoshop Elements or you can cut and paste parts of other images to create a composite. See the section "Create a Blank Image" for more on opening a blank canvas.

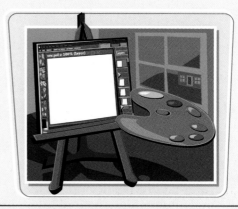

Film Photos

If you have a film camera, you can have your photos burned to a CD during film processing. Then, you can import the photos from the CD just as you would import photos from a folder on your computer. See the section "Import Photos from a Folder" for more.

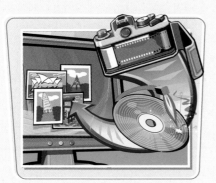

Working with Imported Photos

When you import images into Photoshop Elements, they are stored in the program's Organizer. There, you can browse miniature versions of your photos, called *thumbnails*, sort them, group them into albums, and assign keyword tags to them. You can edit your photos by opening them in the Photoshop Elements Editor. You can open them in the Editor from the Organizer or open them directly from folders on your computer. See Chapter 1 for more on the Editor and the Organizer workspaces.

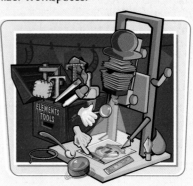

Import Photos from a Digital Camera or Card Reader

You can import photos into Photoshop Elements from a digital camera or directly from the camera's memory card. Most cameras and card readers manufactured today connect to a computer through a USB port. A typical PC comes with multiple USB ports. Make sure the device is properly connected before you begin. Also, some computers have special media slots that accept memory cards for transferring photos and other files.

Every camera and card reader works differently. Consult the documentation that came with your device for more information.

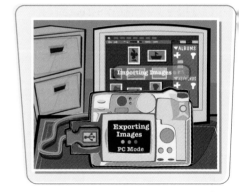

Import Photos from a Digital Camera or Card Reader

① In the Organizer, click **File**.

Note: For more on using the Organizer, see Chapter 3.

② Click **Get Photos and Videos**.

③ Click **From Camera or Card Reader**.

The Photo Downloader dialog box opens. Photo Downloader may automatically open when you connect your device to your computer, depending on the settings in Photoshop Elements.

④ Click here to choose your camera or memory card from the Get Photos from menu.

By default, Photoshop Elements downloads your photos into dated subfolders inside your Pictures folder.

● You can click **Browse** to select a different download location.

● You can click here to choose a different naming scheme for the subfolders.

⑤ Click here to choose a naming scheme for your files.

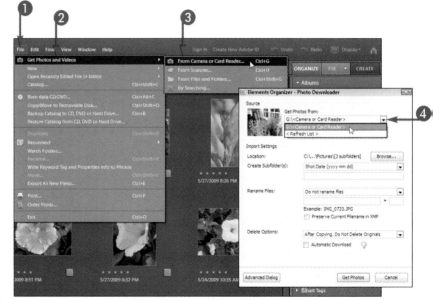

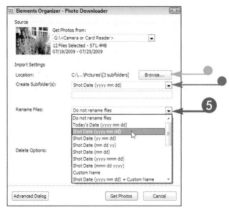

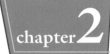

6 Click here to choose whether to keep your photos on the device or delete them after downloading.

● You can click this check box to enable Photoshop Elements to download your photos automatically by using the current settings whenever a photo device is connected to your computer (☐ changes to ☑).

7 Click **Get Photos**.

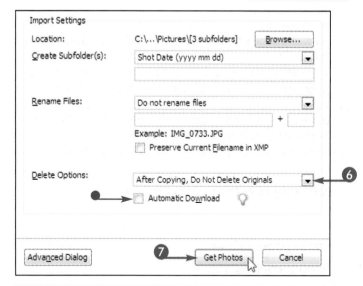

Photoshop Elements downloads the photos from the device.

After downloading the photos, Photoshop Elements adds them to the current Organizer catalog. There, you can add the photos to albums and perform other functions.

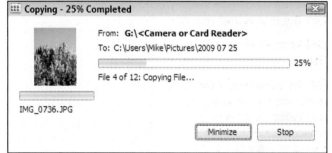

TIP

What is the Advanced dialog box in the Photo Downloader?

The Advanced dialog box gives you access to additional import features.

1 Click **Advanced Dialog** in the bottom-left corner of the Photo Downloader to open the Advanced dialog box.

2 Click the check box for each photo you want to import from your device (☐ changes to ☑).

3 Click this check box to turn on red-eye correction (☐ changes to ☑).

4 Type creator and copyright details to be applied to all the imported photos.

5 Click **Get Photos**.

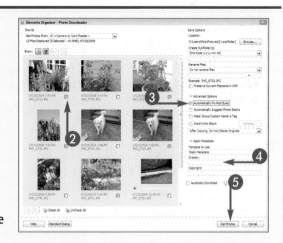

Import Photos from a Scanner

You can import a photo into Photoshop Elements through a scanner attached to your computer. You can scan black-and-white and color photos to import into Photoshop Elements. To scan an image, make sure the scanner is properly connected before you begin. Some scanners include slide or film attachments that enable you to also digitize slides or film.

Every scanner works differently. Consult the documentation that came with your scanner for more information.

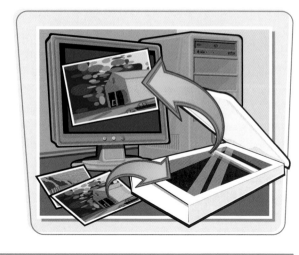

Import Photos from a Scanner

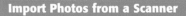

① In the Organizer, click **File**.

Note: For more on using the Organizer, see Chapter 3.

② Click **Get Photos and Videos**.

③ Click **From Scanner**.

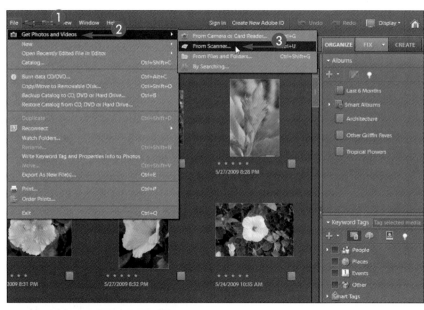

The Get Photos from Scanner dialog box opens.

④ Click here to choose your scanner.

By default, Photoshop Elements saves scanned photos in the Adobe folder inside your Pictures folder.

● You can click **Browse** to choose another location.

⑤ Click here to choose a file format. For more on file formats, see Chapter 17.

● If you are importing as a JPEG, it is typically best to import at a high-quality setting.

⑥ Click **OK**.

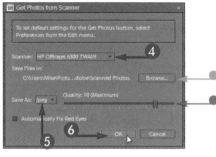

The software associated with your scanner opens. The window can look significantly different depending on the scanner's make and model.

7 Change your scanning settings as needed. You may need to specify whether the photo is black and white or color. You may also get to preview the scan.

8 Click a button to scan your photo by using the scanner software.

The image is scanned and added to the current catalog in the Organizer.

● Photoshop Elements displays the imported photo by itself.

9 Click **Show All** to view your entire catalog of photos.

Note: To crop or straighten a scanned image, see Chapter 5.

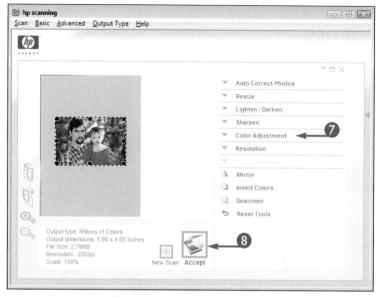

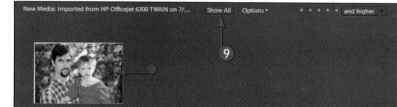

TIP

How can I adjust the default settings for importing photos?

You can adjust the default settings for importing photos from a scanner or another device in the Preferences dialog box.

1 Click **Edit**, **Preferences**, and then **Scanner**.

The Scanner preferences dialog box opens.

2 Adjust the default settings in the Scanner pane.

3 Click **OK**.

Photoshop Elements displays the updated settings the next time you scan a photo.

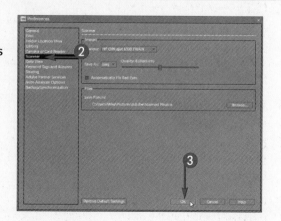

Import Photos from a Folder

You can use the Organizer program in Photoshop Elements to import images from a folder on your computer or a disc. You may find this useful if you already have an archive of digital photos on your PC or on photo CDs.

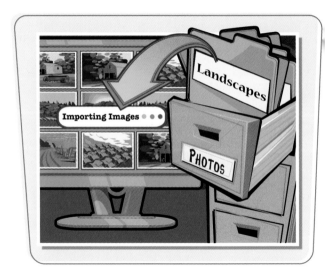

Import Photos from a Folder

① In the Organizer, click **File**.

Note: For more on using the Organizer, see Chapter 3.

② Click **Get Photos and Videos**.

③ Click **From Files and Folders**.

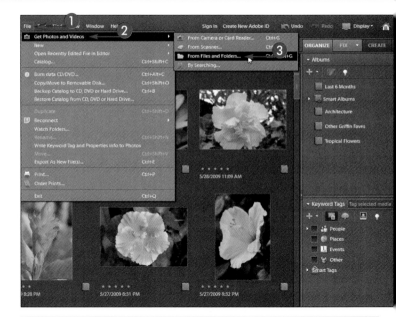

The Get Photos from Files and Folders dialog box opens.

④ Click here to choose the folder containing your photos.

⑤ Ctrl +click to select the photos you want to import. You can press Ctrl + A to select all the photos in the folder.

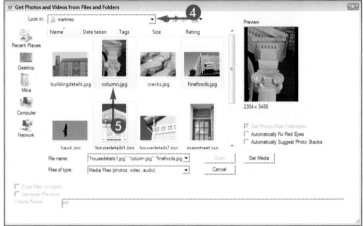

● Click this check box to have Photoshop Elements automatically fix red-eye (☐ changes to ☑).

● You can import different types of files, such as PDF documents or Photoshop Elements projects, by clicking here.

Note: For more on creating projects in Photoshop Elements, see Chapter 16.

6 Click **Get Media**.

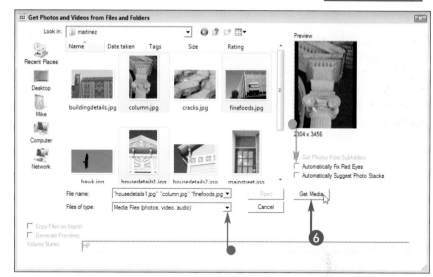

Photoshop Elements downloads the selected photos from the folder.

● Photoshop Elements displays the imported photos by themselves in the Organizer.

7 Click **Show All** to view your entire catalog of photos.

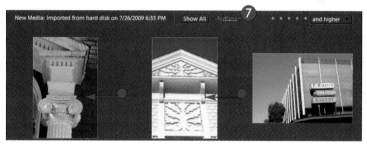

 TIP

How can I quickly search my entire computer for photos to import?

1 Click **File**, **Get Photos and Videos**, and then **By Searching**.

The Search dialog box opens.

2 Click here to choose all hard drives, a single hard drive, or a folder.

Storage devices such as USB flash-memory drives are considered hard drives by Photoshop Elements.

3 Click **Search**.

● Photoshop Elements performs a search and displays a list of folders that contain photos.

4 Select one or more folders and then click **Import Folders** to get the photos. You can Ctrl +click to select multiple folders.

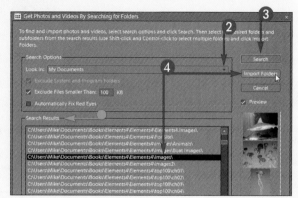

Watch a Folder for New Images

Photoshop Elements can watch certain folders on your computer for the addition of new photos. You can have Photoshop Elements notify you when it recognizes new photos or you can have it import those photos automatically. The imported photos are added to your Organizer catalog.

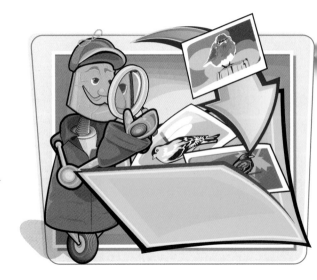

Watch a Folder for New Images

1 In the Organizer, click **File**.

Note: For more on using the Organizer, see Chapter 3.

2 Click **Watch Folders**.

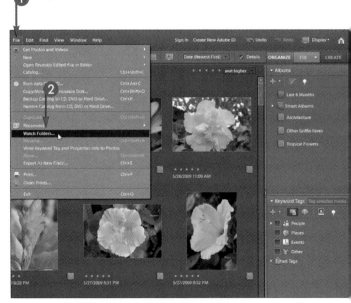

The Watch Folders dialog box opens.

3 Click **Add**.

The Browse For Folder dialog box opens.

4 Choose a folder to watch.

5 Click **OK**.

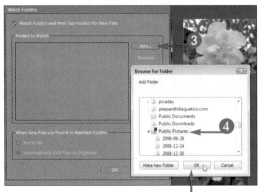

The folder appears in the watch list.

● You can click this check box to watch subfolders inside your watched folders (■ changes to ✓).

● You can choose whether to receive alerts about new images or have Photoshop Elements add photos to the Organizer automatically (● changes to ○).

6 Click **OK**.

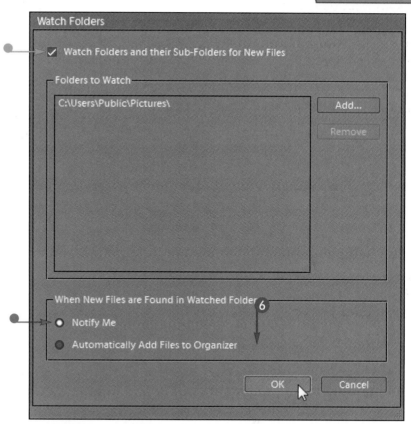

Receive a Watch Notification

1 Exit Photoshop Elements and then add new photos to a watched folder on your computer.

Note: To get new photos, see some of the other tasks in this chapter.

2 Start Photoshop Elements and then open the Organizer.

● Photoshop Elements alerts you about new photos in your watched folders.

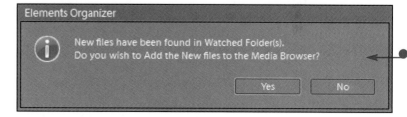

How can I adjust the brightness of the interface?

1 In the Editor or the Organizer, click **Edit**, **Preferences**, and then **General**. This example shows changing preferences in the Organizer.

The General Preferences dialog box opens.

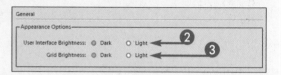

2 Click here to adjust the overall brightness of the interface (● changes to ○).

3 Click here to adjust the brightness of the photo grid in the Organizer (● changes to ○).

4 Click **OK**. Photoshop Elements applies the brightness levels.

Open a Photo

You can open a photo in the Editor to modify it or use it in a project. You can also open photos from the Organizer for editing in the Editor.

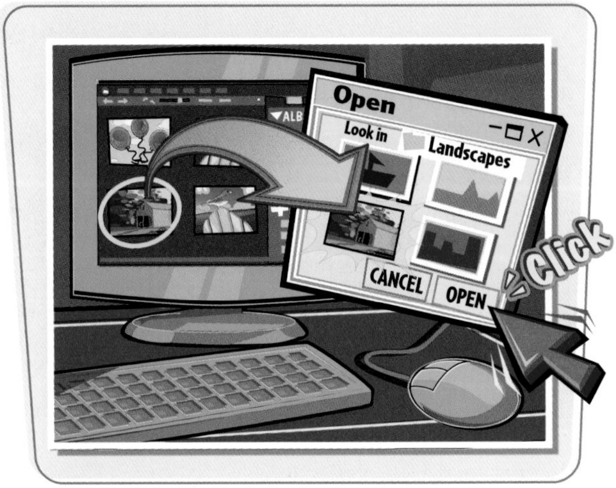

Open a Photo

Open a Photo from a Folder

1. In the Editor, click **File**.

Note: *For more on opening the Editor, see Chapter 1.*

2. Click **Open**.

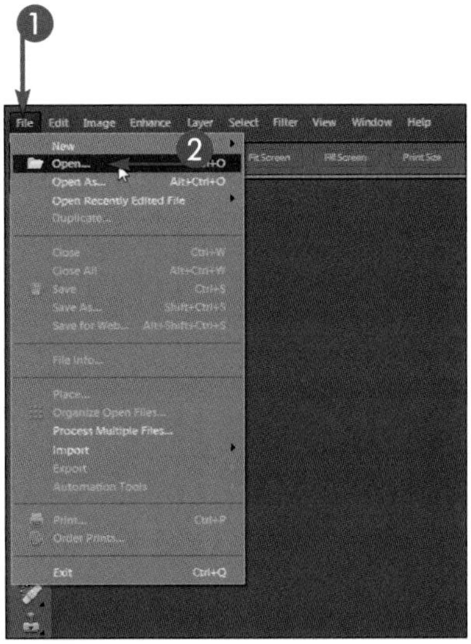

The Open dialog box opens.

3. Click here to navigate to the folder that contains the file you want to open.
4. Click the photo you want to open.

- A preview of the image appears.

5. Click **Open**.

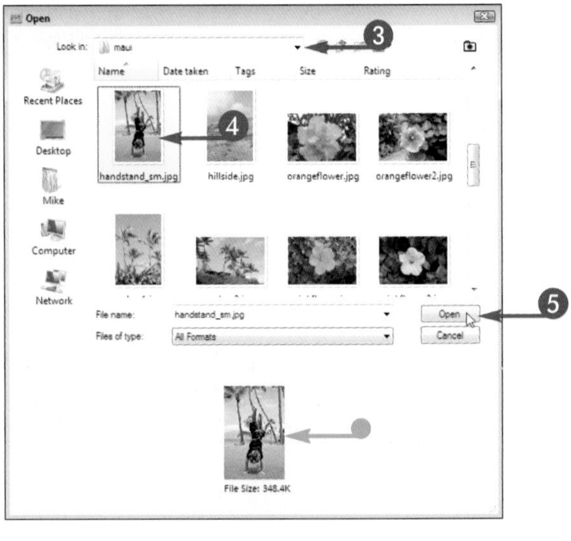

Photoshop Elements opens the image.

● The file name and zoom value appear in the tab for the image.

Note: *The image may also open in a floating window depending on how your program preferences are set.*

● If the Project Bin is open in the Editor, the image also appears in the bin.

● If you open multiple photos at once, you can click **Window** to view a list of the open photos.

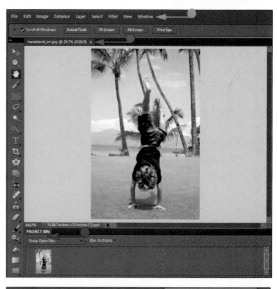

Open an Organizer Photo for Editing

① In the Organizer, right-click on the photo you want to edit.

② In the menu that appears, click **Edit with Photoshop Elements**.

Photoshop Elements opens the photo in the Editor.

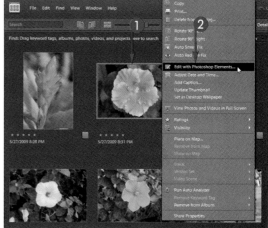

What types of files can Photoshop Elements open?
Photoshop Elements can open most of the image file formats in common use today. Some of the more popular ones are:

BMP (Bitmap)	The standard Windows image format
TIFF (Tagged Image File Format)	A popular format for print
EPS (Encapsulated PostScript)	Another print-oriented format
JPEG (Joint Photographic Experts Group)	A format for Web images
GIF (Graphics Interchange Format)	Another format for Web images
PNG (Portable Network Graphics)	Yet another format for Web images
PSD (Photoshop Document)	Photoshop's native file format

Create a Blank Image

You can start a Photoshop Elements project by creating a blank image and then you can add photographic, textual, and other content to the blank image.

You can add content from other images as separate layers. For more on layers, see Chapter 8.

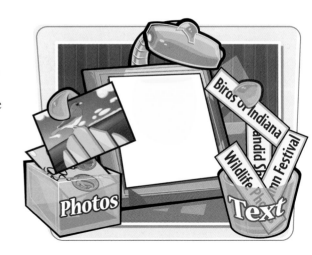

Create a Blank Image

① In the Editor, click **File**.

Note: For more on opening the Editor, see Chapter 1.

② Click **New**.

③ Click **Blank File**.

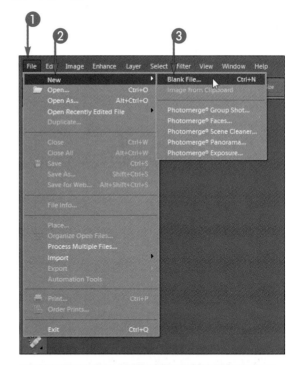

The New dialog box opens.

④ Type a name for the new image.

⑤ Type the desired dimensions and resolution or choose a preset dimension and resolution from the pop-up menu.

● You can click here to change the background of the blank canvas.

⑥ Click **OK**.

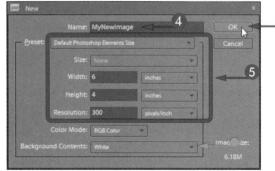

Photoshop Elements creates a new image window at the specified dimensions.

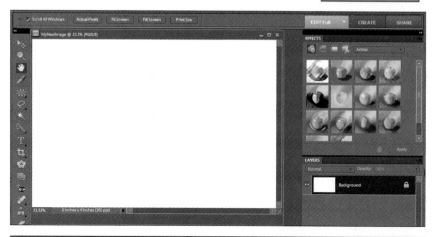

⑦ Use Photoshop Elements tools and commands to edit the new image.

● In this example, parts of other photos are cut and pasted onto the blank image.

Note: See Chapter 7 for more on how to copy and paste into a blank image.

● The parts appear in different layers in the Layers panel.

Note: See Chapter 8 for more on layers.

Note: To save your image, see the section "Save a Photo."

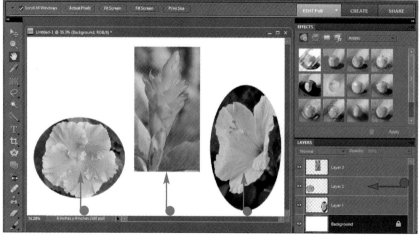

 TIPS

What should I choose as a resolution for a new image?
The appropriate resolution depends on how you plan to use the image. For Web or multimedia images, select 72 pixels/inch — the standard resolution for on-screen images. If you are printing black-and-white images on regular paper by using a laser printer, 150 pixels/inch will probably suffice. For full-color magazine or brochure images, you should use a higher resolution — at least 250 pixels/inch.

How do I open a frame from a video clip?
You can open a video frame in Photoshop Elements by clicking **File**, **Import**, and then **Frame from Video**. A dialog box opens, enabling you to browse for and open a video clip, scan through the clip, and then import a frame into the Editor. You can then edit the frame as you would any other photo. Photoshop Elements supports importing from WMV, MPEG, and AVI video files, although some types of MPEG files are problematic. It does not support importing from MOV files.

Save a Photo

You can save a photo in Photoshop Elements to store any changes that you made to it. PSD is the default file format for Photoshop Elements. Photoshop Elements supports a variety of other image file formats, including the popular JPEG, GIF, and PNG formats often found on the Web.

You can have multiple versions of the same image saved as a version set in the Organizer.

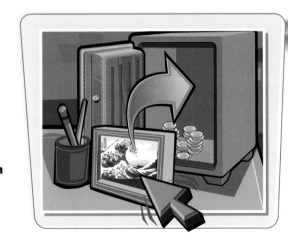

Save a Photo

Save a new photo

1 In the Editor, click **File**.

Note: For more on opening the Editor, see Chapter 1.

2 Click **Save As**.

*Note: For photos that you have previously saved, you can click **File** and then **Save**.*

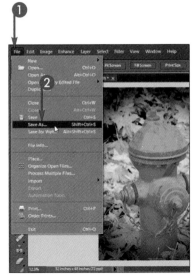

The Save As dialog box opens.

3 Type a name for the file.

● You can click here to choose another folder or drive in which to store the file.

● You can click here to choose another file format.

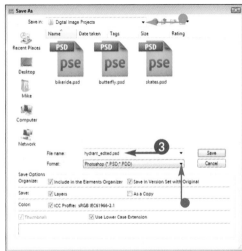

38

4 Click this check box to include the saved file in the Organizer (☐ changes to ☑).

5 Click this check box to save the edited file with other versions of the same file in the Organizer (☐ changes to ☑).

You can save a photo into a version set only when the photo already exists as a version in the Organizer.

6 Click **Save**.

Photoshop Elements saves the file.

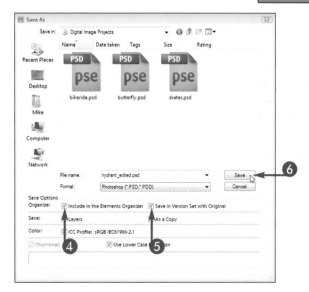

View a Version Set in the Organizer

1 In the Organizer, find a version set. Version sets have light gray boxes around them and are marked with a 🖼 icon.

Note: For more on using the Organizer, see Chapter 3.

● You can use the scrollbar to browse photos.

2 Click here to expand (◀▶) the version set so you can view all the photos in that set.

Photoshop Elements expands the set.

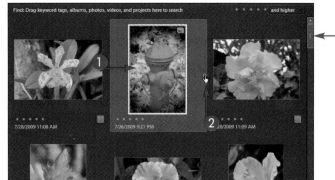

In the Editor, how can I save all my open photos as an album in the Organizer?

1 In the Editor, open the photos you want to save as an album.

2 In the Project Bin, click **Bin Actions**.

3 Click **Save Bin as an Album**.

4 Type a name for the album.

5 Click **OK**.

The photos are saved as a new album in the Organizer. For more on albums, see Chapter 3.

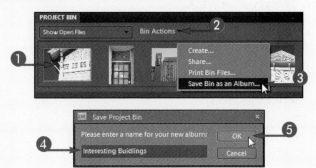

Duplicate a Photo

In the Editor, you can duplicate a photo to keep an unchanged copy while you continue to work on the duplicate. Photoshop Elements puts the duplicate in its own window.

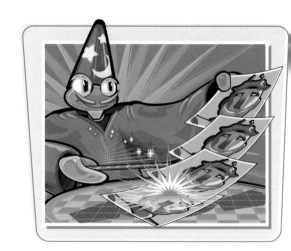

1 In the Editor, click **File**.

Note: *For more on opening the Editor, see Chapter 1.*

2 Click **Duplicate**.

The Duplicate Image dialog box opens.

● Photoshop Elements displays an editable name for the duplicate.

3 Click **OK**.

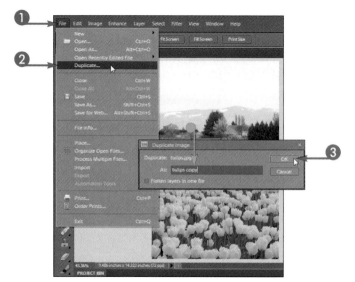

● Photoshop Elements opens a duplicate of the photo as another tabbed window.

Note: *For more on working with images by using tabs, see Chapter 1.*

● The name and zoom value appear in the tab.

Note: *See the section "Save a Photo" for more on how to save the duplicate.*

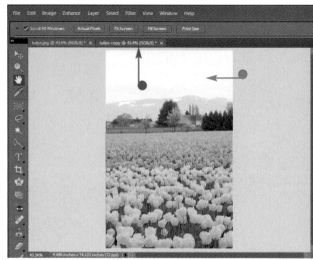

Close a Photo

You can close a photo after you finish editing it. Although you can have more than one photo open at a time, closing photos you no longer need can speed up your computer's performance.

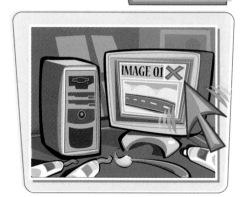

Close a Photo

1 In the Editor, click **File**.

Note: For more on opening the Editor, see Chapter 1.

2 Click **Close**.

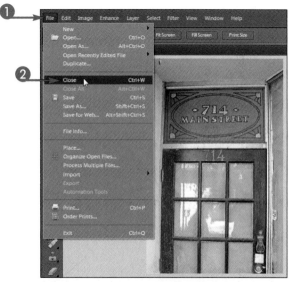

● You can also click ✕ to close a photo.

● If you have made any changes to the file and have not saved them, Photoshop Elements prompts you to do so before closing the file. Click **Yes** to save your work.

Note: See the section "Save a Photo" for more on how to save files.

After saving, if needed, Photoshop Elements closes the photo. The program remains open.

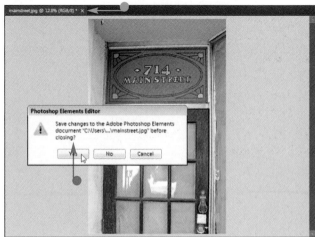

Organizing Your Photos

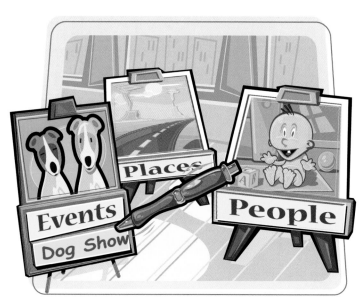

Are you ready to organize your digital photos? You can catalog, view, and sort photo files by using the Organizer. A complement to the Editor in Photoshop Elements, the Organizer helps you manage your growing library of digital pictures by categorizing them in a variety of ways. This chapter shows you how to take advantage of the many photo-management features in the Organizer.

Introducing the Organizer

You can use the Organizer program to manage your growing library of digital photos. As you import or save photos in Photoshop Elements, they are automatically added to the Organizer catalog. In the Organizer, you can sort and filter your photo collection in different ways. You can also group photos into albums, tag them with descriptive keywords, and even place them on a geographic map.

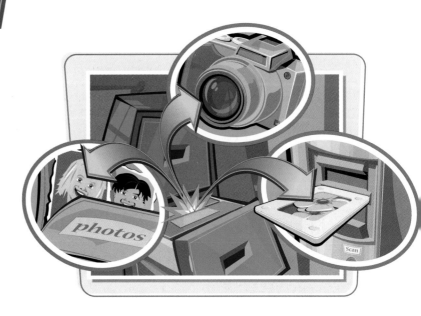

Virtual Browser

The Organizer acts as a virtual browser, enabling you to view *thumbnails,* or miniature versions, of your pictures. The thumbnails you see in the Organizer are merely pointers to the original file locations. The images remain intact in their original location unless you decide to delete them. The Organizer enables you to view your photos from one convenient window. See the sections "View Photos in the Media Browser" and "View Photos by Date" to learn more.

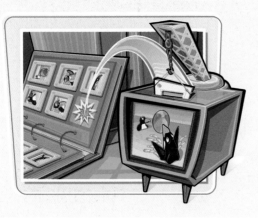

Catalog

When you bring photo files into the Organizer, the program adds them to your catalog of images. Images are cataloged by date. You can keep all your photos in one catalog or you can store them in separate catalogs. If you want to group your photos further, you can place them into albums or stacks. See the sections "Create a Catalog" and "Work with Albums" for more on these topics. For more on stacking photos, see Chapter 4.

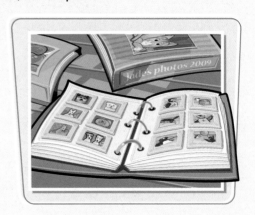

Keyword Tags

You can use keyword tags to help you sort and track your photos. A *keyword tag* is a text identifier you assign to a photo. After you assign tags, you can search for photos that match certain tags and also sort your photos in tag order. You can assign any of the preset tags that come with the Organizer or you can create your own. The Organizer's presets include tags for people, places, events, and more. You can also assign multiple tags to the same photo. For more on keyword tags, see Chapter 4.

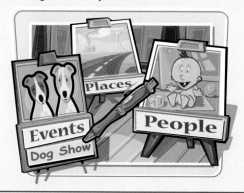

Map Photos

Have you ever wanted to pull up photos that were taken in a particular location, such as a favorite vacation spot or where you used to live? The Organizer helps you associate your photos with certain places by letting you put them on a geographic map. Once you map your photos, the photos appear as red pins on the map. You can navigate through your collection by scrolling and zooming to different countries, cities, and streets. For more on mapping photos, see Chapter 4.

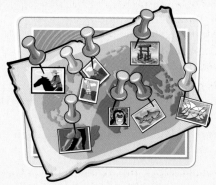

Find Photos

As your photo collection grows, being able to quickly find photos becomes critically important. Although filtering photos by album or keyword tag offers one way to find photos, the Organizer also includes full-featured searching tools. You can search your catalog by date, file name, caption, camera model, map location, and more. You can even mix multiple search criteria to create more powerful searches. See the section "Find Photos" for more information.

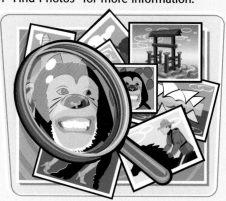

Creations

Because it lets you easily organize and find photos in your collection, the Organizer is an important first step in completing various Photoshop Elements projects. For example, you can display your favorite photos in the Organizer and then create a custom slide show to distribute to friends and family. You can also create online photo galleries, greeting cards, postage stamps, and more. See Chapter 16 for photo projects you can build in Photoshop Elements.

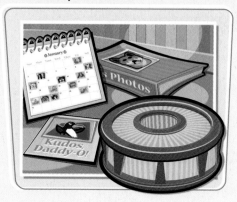

Open the Organizer

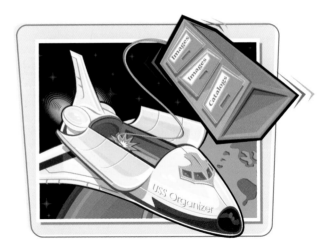

You can organize and manage your digital photos in the Organizer in Photoshop Elements. The Organizer works alongside the Editor to help you keep track of the digital photos and other media you store on your computer. You can open the Organizer from the welcome screen that appears when you first start up Photoshop Elements or switch to it from the Editor.

Open the Organizer

From the Welcome Screen

1. Start Photoshop Elements.

   Note: See Chapter 1 for more on starting Photoshop Elements.

   The welcome screen appears.

2. Click **Organize** to open the Organizer.

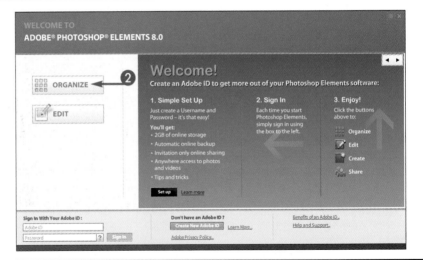

The Organizer opens.

To import photos into the Organizer workspace, see Chapter 2.

To create a new catalog with which to organize your photos, see the section "Create a Catalog."

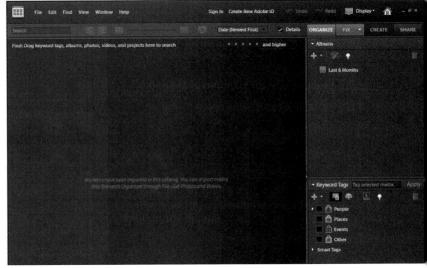

From the Editor

① Start Photoshop Elements.

② From the welcome screen that appears, click **Edit** to open the Editor.

③ Click **Organizer**.

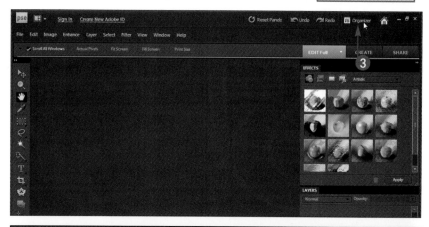

The Organizer opens.

● To return to the Editor, click **Fix** and then click **Full Photo Edit**.

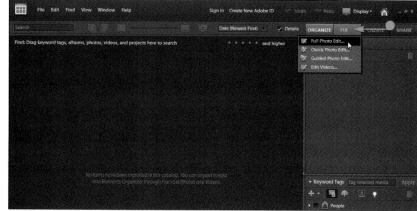

TIP

Can I edit photos from within the Organizer?

Yes. The Organizer offers basic editing commands under the Fix tab. The commands can save you from having to switch to the Editor to optimize your photos.

① In the Organizer, click **Fix**.

The editing buttons appear.

② Click a thumbnail to select a photo to edit.

③ Click an Auto button to optimize the color or lighting of your photo.

● You can click **Crop** to open an image for cropping. See Chapter 5 for more on cropping.

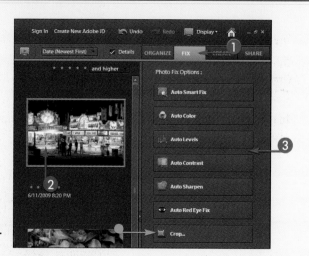

Create a Catalog

The photos you manage in the Organizer are stored in catalogs. You can keep your photos in one large catalog or separate them into smaller catalogs. When you start the Organizer, Photoshop Elements creates a default catalog for you called My Catalog.

You can organize your photos within a catalog into smaller groups called albums. See the section "Work with Albums" for more information.

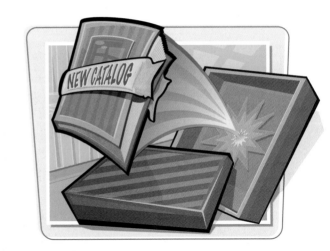

Create a Catalog

1. In the Organizer, click **File**.

2. Click **Catalog**.

● You can restore a catalog you have previously backed up by clicking **Restore Catalog from CD, DVD or Hard Drive**. See Chapter 17 for more on backing up photos.

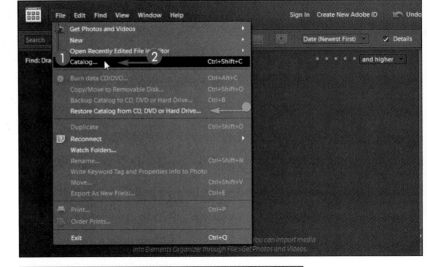

The Catalog Manager dialog box opens.

Photoshop Elements lists the available catalogs.

3. Click **New**.

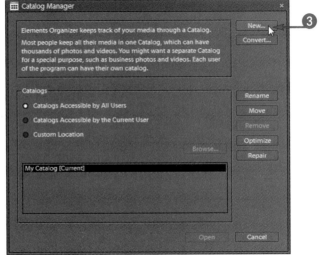

④ Type a name for the new catalog.

⑤ Click **OK**.

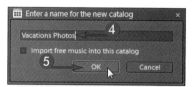

Photoshop Elements creates the new catalog and opens it.

● Photoshop Elements displays the name of the current catalog.

● The number of files in the catalog and the range of dates for the files are displayed here.

Note: To add photos to your catalog, see chapter 2.

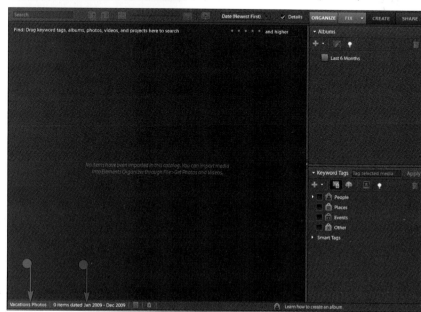

TIPS

How do I switch to a different catalog in the Organizer?

Open the Catalog Manager by following steps **1** and **2** on the previous page. Select the catalog that you want to open in the catalog list and then click **Open**. You can open only one catalog at a time in the Organizer.

How can I protect the photos in the Organizer from viewing by others?

You can edit a catalog so that only the user who is currently logged in to your computer can access it. Open the Catalog Manager by following steps **1** and **2** on the previous page. From the list that appears, select the catalog that you want to protect and then click **Move**. A dialog box opens to let you change the accessibility of the catalog.

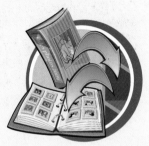

View Photos in the Media Browser

After you add photos to your catalog, you can view them by using the Organizer's Media Browser. The Media Browser displays thumbnails, or miniature versions, of your photos, along with details about those photos. You can filter, sort, and change the size of the thumbnails.

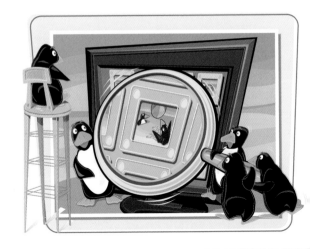

① Open the Organizer.

The Media Browser displays the photos in the Organizer catalog.

● Photos are sorted from newest to oldest by default.

② Click and drag the thumbnail size slider (▦) to the right.

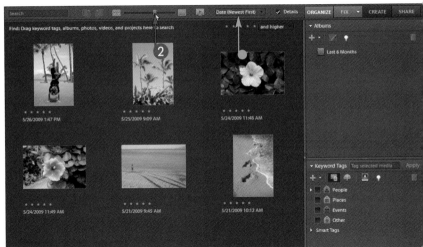

● The thumbnails enlarge. You can click ▦ to maximize the thumbnails.

Dragging the slider (▦) to the left decreases the size of the thumbnails. You can click ▦ to minimize the thumbnails.

● You can use the scrollbar to browse other available thumbnails in the Media Browser.

③ Click here and then click **Date (Oldest First)**.

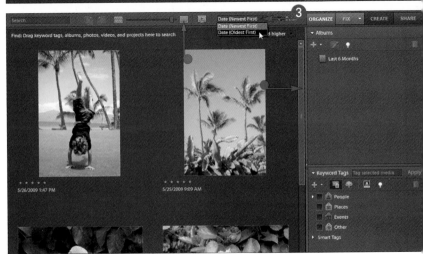

The sorting order reverses in the Media Browser, with the oldest photos at the top.

● The star rating and date details appear below each photo.

Note: *See the section "Rate Photos" for more on star ratings.*

④ Click **Details** (☑ changes to ■).

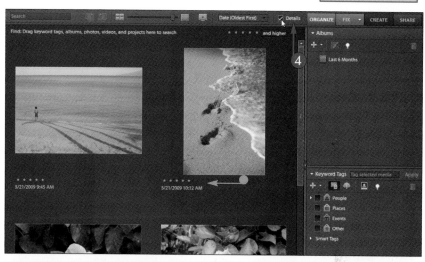

Photoshop Elements hides the photo details.

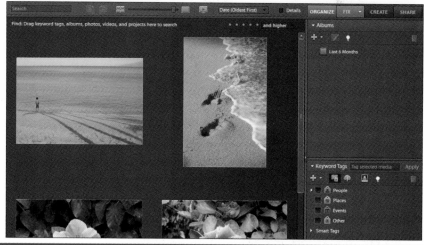

TIP

How can I hide certain file types in the Media Browser?

The Media Browser can help you organize photos, videos, audio files, projects built in Photoshop Elements, and PDF files. You can filter the file types that appear in the Media Browser.

① In the Organizer, click **View**.

② Click **Media Types**.

Media types that are shown are checked.

③ Click a checked media type. Photoshop Elements hides the media type in the Media Browser.

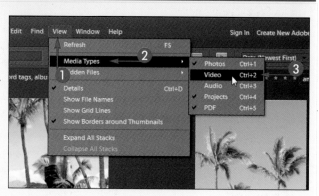

View Photos in Full Screen Mode

You can switch to Full Screen mode in the Organizer to get a clearer view of your photos. Photoshop Elements expands the photos to fill the workspace and displays special panels for applying commands.

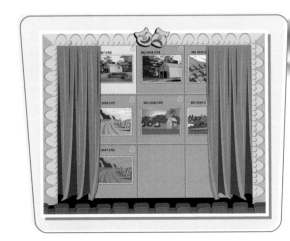

① In the Organizer, click the photo you want to view in Full Screen.

② Click 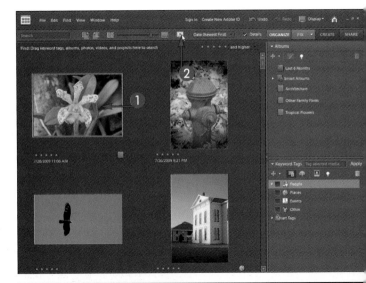.

Photoshop Elements opens the photo in Full Screen.

● A Quick Edit panel for performing image edits is shown.

● A Quick Organize panel for adding images to albums and applying keyword tags is shown.

Note: See the section "Work with Albums" for more on albums. See Chapter 4 for more on applying edits and applying keyword tags.

● The panels automatically hide if not used. You can click Auto Hide ( ) to turn hiding on and off.

● Controls for viewing different photos and managing panels appear here.

③ Click to go to the next photo in the Organizer. You can also press .

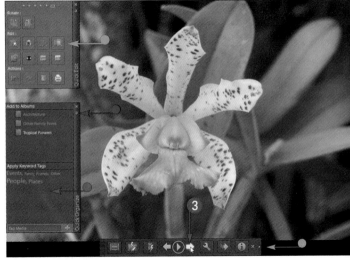

Photoshop Elements displays the next photo.

4 Click Toggle Film Strip ().

● The Film Strip opens, displaying thumbnail versions of your images.

5 Click a thumbnail.

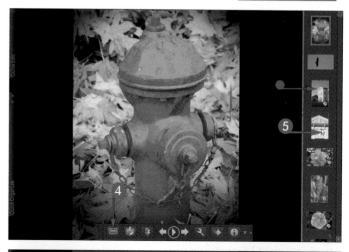

Photoshop Elements displays the photo.

6 Click ⊠ or press Esc to exit Full Screen mode.

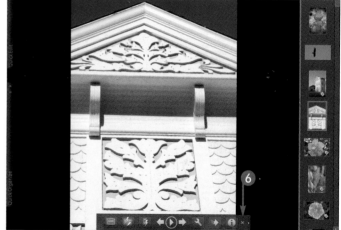

TIP

How do I view detailed areas of my photos in Full Screen?

You can view details by zooming and panning with the mouse.

1 While in Full Screen mode, roll the mouse wheel forward.

● The image zooms in and displays the zoom percentage.

You can roll the mouse wheel backward to zoom out.

2 Click and drag the image with the mouse. The image pans.

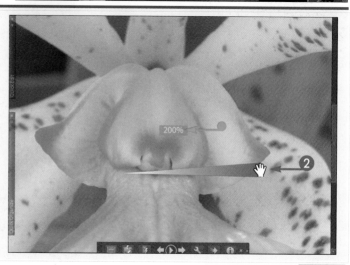

View a Slide Show in Full Screen

You can play a slide show in Full Screen mode to cycle through large versions of your images. You can choose background music and transition effects to accompany the slides.

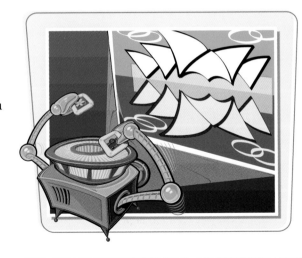

① In the Organizer, display the images you want to view as a slide show in the Media Browser.

● You can click an album to display photos from an album as a slide show.

② Click 🖼.

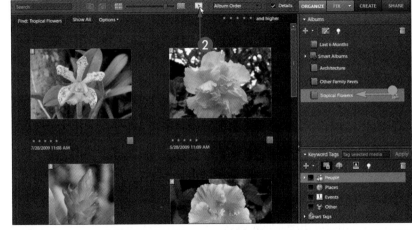

Photoshop Elements displays the first image in Full Screen mode.

③ Click the **Open Settings Dialog** button (🔧).

The Full Screen View Options dialog box opens.

④ Click here to choose background music.

● You can click Browse to look for music on your computer to use as background music.

⑤ Click **OK** to close the dialog box.

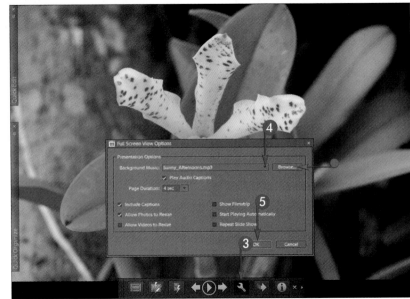

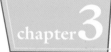

6 Click the **Transitions** button (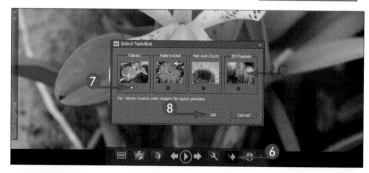).

The Select Transition dialog box opens.

7 Click a transition effect to display between slides in the slide show.

● You can roll your mouse over an option to preview an option.

8 Click **OK** to close the dialog box.

9 Click the **Play** button (⊙) or press Spacebar.

Photoshop plays the slide show, cycling through the images at full screen.

You can click the Play button again to pause the slide show.

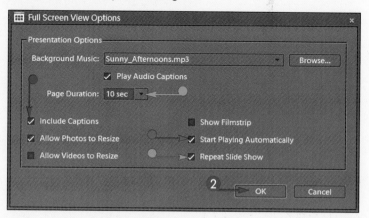

TIP

How else can I customize my slide show?
You can customize your slide show in the Full Screen View Options dialog box.

1 Click **Open Settings Dialog** (🔧).

The Full Screen View Options dialog box opens.

● You can choose a slide duration here.

● Click here to automatically start the slide show when you open Full Screen mode (■ changes to ✓).

● Click here to display captions for photos that have them (■ changes to ✓).

● Click here to repeat the slide show after it finishes (■ changes to ✓).

2 Click OK to save the settings.

View Photo Properties

You can view the properties for any photo in your catalog. The Properties box displays a photo's general information, which includes the file name, file size, image size, and location. You can also view any associated tags, file history, and metadata information. Metadata, also known as EXIF data, is detailed information about how a digital photo was taken; it includes camera settings, such as exposure time and f-stop.

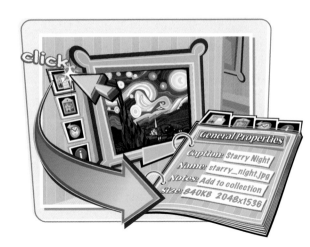

1 In the Organizer, right-click on a photo.

2 Click **Show Properties**.

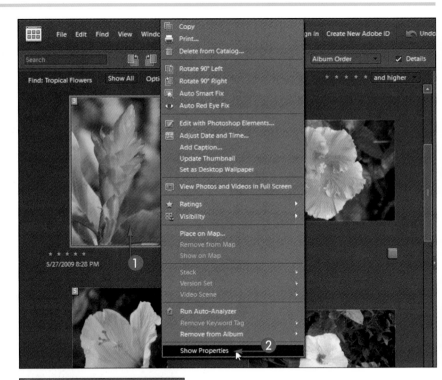

The Properties dialog box opens.

The General properties appear by default.

● You can add or edit a caption for the photo here.

● The rating, size, capture date, and other information for the photo are shown here.

3 Click the **Metadata** button (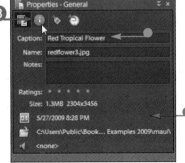).

The Metadata properties appear. This includes the camera model and settings if the photo came from a digital camera.

● You can click here to display the complete metadata for a photo (● changes to ○).

④ Click the **Keyword Tags** button (🔖).

The Keyword Tags properties appear.

Photoshop Elements displays any keyword tags or albums associated with the photo. You can right-click on a tag or album to remove it from the photo.

● You can click the **History** button (🔄) to view Organizer statistics for the photo.

⑤ Click ✖ to close the Properties dialog box.

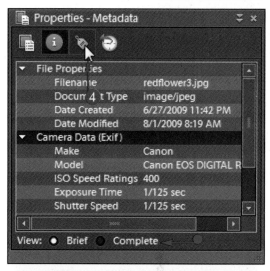

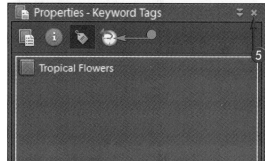

TIP

How do I change a photo's date and time?

① Right-click on the photo you want to edit.

② Click **Adjust Date and Time**.

The Adjust Date and Time dialog box opens.

③ Click the **Change to a specified date and time** radio button (● changes to ○).

④ Click **OK**.

⑤ In the Set Date and Time dialog box, set the new date and time.

⑥ Click **OK**.

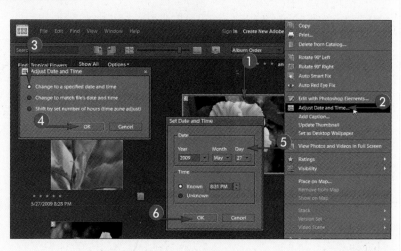

Add a Caption

In the Organizer, you can add captions to your photos to help you remember important information about the images you catalog. For example, you can add captions to your vacation pictures with details about the location or subject matter. Captions appear below a photo when the image is viewed in Single Photo View.

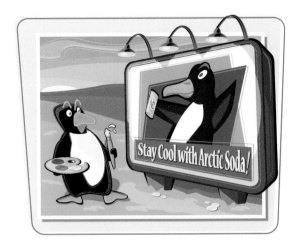

① In the Organizer, right-click on the photo you want to caption.

② Click **Add Caption**.

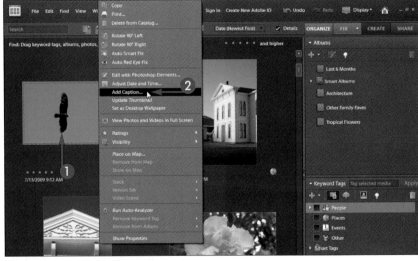

The Add Caption dialog box opens.

③ Type a caption for the photo.

④ Click **OK**.

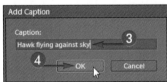

The Organizer adds the caption to the photo.

⑤ Click the **Single Photo View** button ().

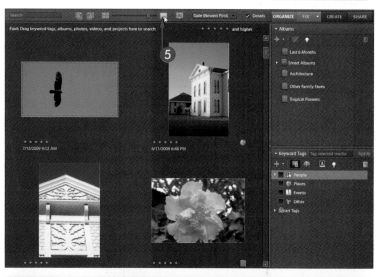

A large thumbnail of the photo appears.

● The caption appears below the photo.

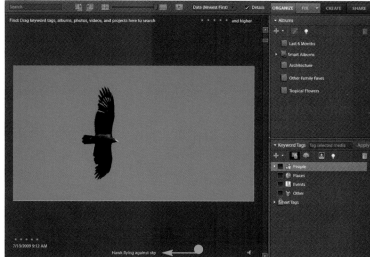

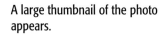

TIPS

Are there other ways to add captions to my photos?

Yes. You can also add captions to your photos by using the Properties box. See the section "View Photo Properties" for more.

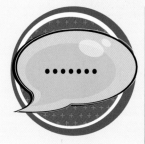

How do I edit a caption?

To edit a caption, view the photo in Single Photo View in the Media Browser window, click the caption, and make your changes. You can delete the caption completely, type a new caption, or make changes to the existing caption text. Press Enter to save your changes.

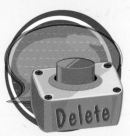

Work with Albums

Albums are a way to organize your photos within an Organizer catalog. For example, you can take photos shot at a particular time or place and group them as an album. This makes it easier to find the photos later.

You can also organize photos in a catalog by using keyword tags. See Chapter 4 for more information.

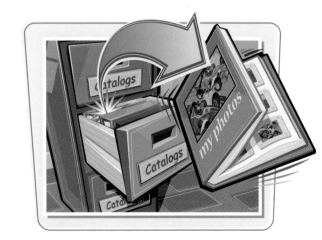

Work with Albums

Create a New Album

1 In the Organizer, open the catalog within which you want to create an album.

Note: For more on catalogs, see the section "Create a Catalog."

2 Open the Albums panel in the Panel Bin.

3 Click the plus sign (![+]) and then click **New Album**.

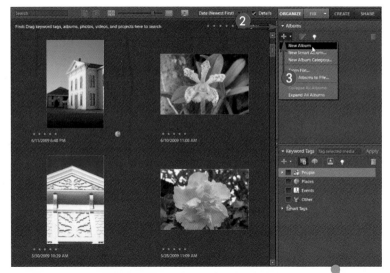

The Album Details panel opens.

4 Type a name for the album.

● You can assign the album to an album category.

● If logged in, you can click here to enable Photoshop Elements to back up your album photos by using the Photoshop.com service (![ ] changes to ![✓]).

Note: For more on Photoshop.com, see Chapter 17.

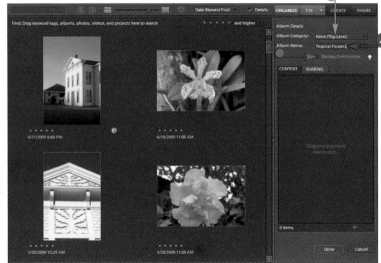

⑤ Click and drag a photo from the Media Browser to the Items list.

The Organizer adds the photo to the album.

⑥ Repeat step **5** for all the photos you want to add to the album.

Alternatively, you can **Ctrl** +click to select multiple photos and then click and drag to add them all to the album.

⑦ Click **Done** to close the Album Details panel.

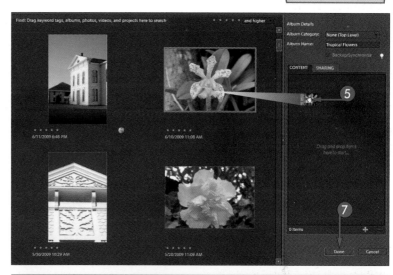

View an Album

① Click the album name in the Albums panel.

The Organizer displays all the photos in the album.

● Photos assigned to an album are marked with an Album icon.

● You can click **Show All** to return to the entire catalog.

● You can click the trash icon (🗑) to delete the album.

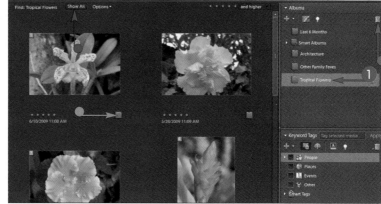

TIP

How do I remove a photo from an album?

① Under the photo in the Media Browser, right-click on the Album icon for the album.

② In the menu that appears, click **Remove from *Name* Album**.

The Organizer removes the photo from the album. The Album icon under the photo disappears.

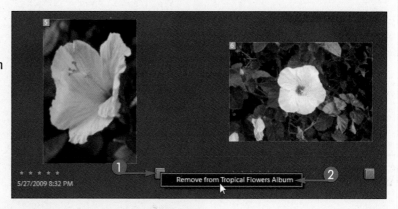

View Photos by Date

To help you keep track of your photos, the Organizer can sort your images by date and display those that were taken during a specific date range. You can also view the images for a particular date range as a slide show.

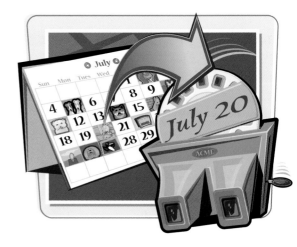

① In the Organizer, click **Display**.

② Click **Date View**.

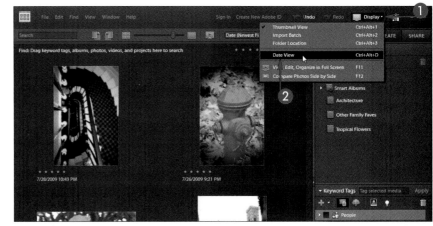

The Organizer displays a calendar view of your catalog.

● You can view your photos by year, month, or day. In this example, the Month view is displayed.

● To see a different month, click the **Previous Month** (◉) or **Next Month** (◉) button.

③ Click the date for the photos you want to view.

● The first photo in the group appears here.

④ Click the **Play** button (◉).

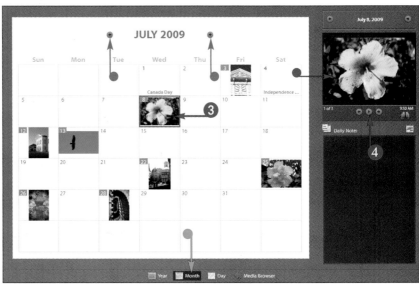

The Organizer starts a slide show, displaying each photo from the date you selected.

● To pause or stop the sequence, click the **Pause** button ( ).

To view the previous image, click the **Previous Item** button ( ).

To view the next image, click the **Next Item** button ( ).

⑤ Click the **Find in the Media Browser** button ( ).

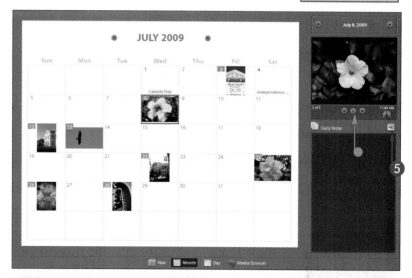

● The Media Browser appears with the photo from the Date View selected.

You can also get to the Media Browser from the Date View by clicking **Display** and then **Media Browser**.

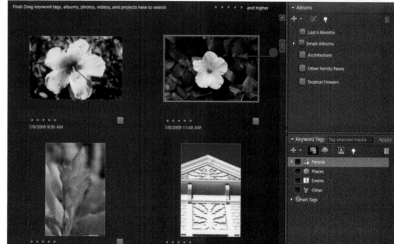

TIP

What is the Organizer timeline?
In the Media Browser, you can browse photos by date by clicking and dragging along a timeline.

① Click **Window**.

② Click **Timeline**.

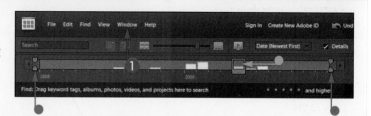

The timeline opens at the top of the Media Browser.

● You can click and drag the slider to move to a different photo date in the Media Browser.

● You can click and drag the endpoints to limit the range of dates displayed in the Media Browser.

Find Photos

The Organizer offers a variety of methods for finding particular photos in your catalog. You can search for photos by date, file name, tags, text, and more.

In this example, you search for photos taken during a specific date range and by text.

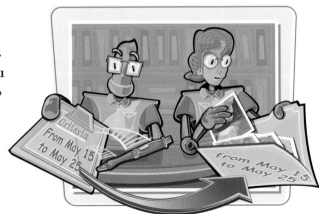

Find Photos by Date

1. In the Organizer, click **Find**.

2. Click **Set Date Range**.

   The Set Date Range dialog box opens.

3. Select the start date for the date range you want to search.

4. Select the end date for the date range you want to search.

5. Click **OK**.

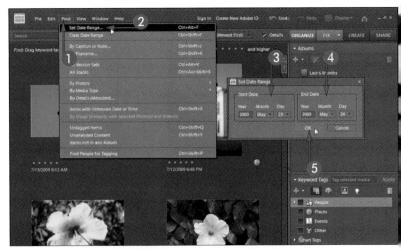

The Organizer displays any matching photos in the Media Browser.

● A summary appears at the bottom of the Media Browser.

You can reset the date search by clicking **Find** and then **Clear Date Range**.

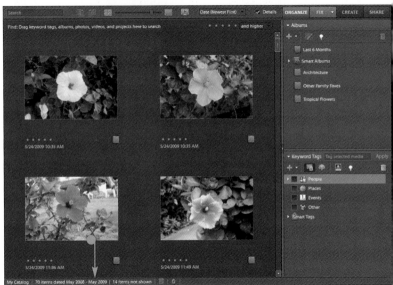

Find Photos by Text

1 Type one or more keywords in the search box.

Photoshop Elements searches the file names, captions, keyword tags, album names, and other text associated with your photos.

● Photoshop Elements displays photos associated with the text as you type.

If you type multiple keywords, photos must be associated with all the keywords to match.

2 Click **Show All**.

Photoshop Elements cancels the search and displays all the photos.

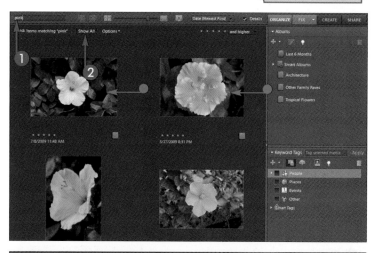

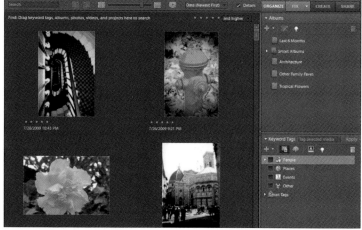

What other search methods can I use?	By Caption or Note	Looks for photos based on the text of the notes and captions you have added to a photo
Here are some of the other ways to search the photos in the Organizer. You can access them from the Find menu.	By Filename	Searches the catalog for a particular file name
	By History	Looks up a photo based on when it was printed or e-mailed or by other criteria
	By Media Type	Searches for creations, photos, and audio or video files in your catalog
	Items with Unknown Date or Time	Looks for photos lacking date or time data
	By Visual Similarity with Selected Photo(s) and Video(s)	Finds photos whose colors are similar to those of a selected photo
	Untagged Items	Searches for photos without assigned tags
	Items Not in Any Album	Displays items that are not associated with an album

Rate Photos

You can add star ratings to your photos in the Organizer to distinguish which ones are interesting and suitable for editing or projects. After you rate your photos, you can filter them by rating.

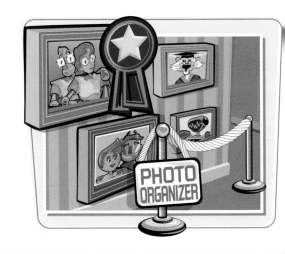

Apply a Rating

1 Click a star rating icon (■) below a photo in the Media Browser.

You can add a star rating from 1 to 5 by clicking the icons from left to right.

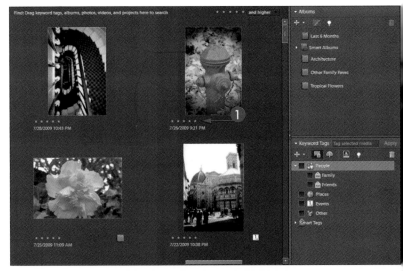

● Photoshop Elements assigns the rating, and gold stars (★) appear.

You can also apply ratings in the Properties box in the General section. See the section "View Photo Properties" for more.

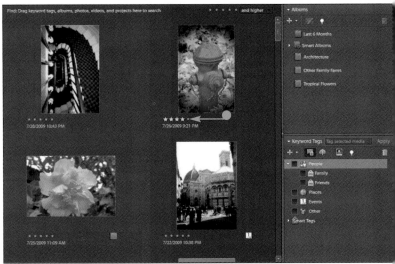

Filter by rating

1 Click a star rating here.

2 Click here and then choose **and higher**, **and lower**, or **only**.

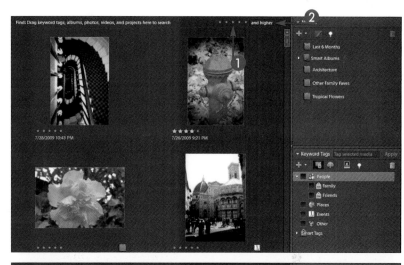

Photoshop Elements displays photos that meet the rating criteria.

● You can click **Show All** to remove the rating filter.

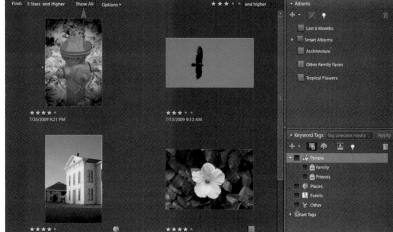

TIP

How do I apply the same rating to multiple photos?

1 Ctrl +click to select the photos you want to rate.

2 Apply a star rating to one of the selected photos.

● The rating is applied to all the selected photos.

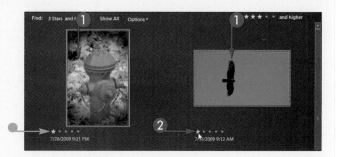

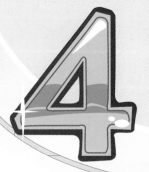

Advanced Organizing Tools

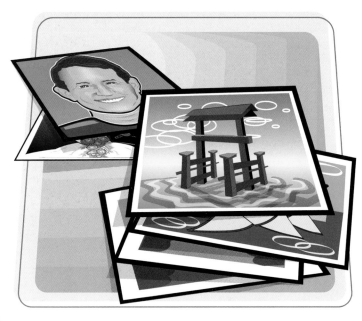

Photoshop Elements gives you a number of advanced tools for managing the images in a collection. For example, you can create Smart Albums that automatically group photos that meet certain criteria. You can associate special terms, known as keyword tags, with photos to help you identify their content. You can also locate photos on a geographic map to associate them with the places they were shot.

Create a Smart Album

A Smart Album has special criteria that determine what Photoshop Elements adds to the album. You can create Smart Albums for particular dates, tags, camera models, file sizes, and more.

The Organizer starts with a default Smart Album that contains all photos taken in the past six months.

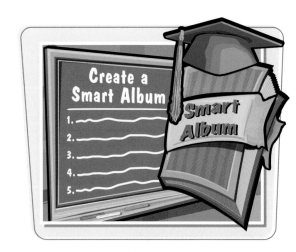

Create a Smart Album

① Open the Albums panel in the Organizer bin.

② Click the plus sign (![plus]) and then click **New Smart Album**.

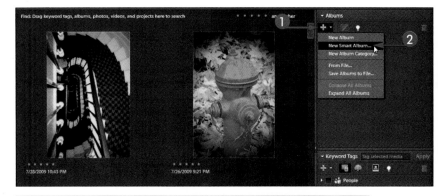

The New Smart Album dialog box opens.

③ Type a name for your Smart Album.

④ Click here to choose a photo attribute.

⑤ Click here to choose a limiting factor.

⑥ Choose or type the criterion for the attribute.

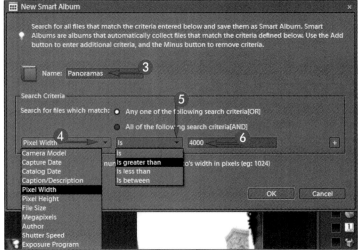

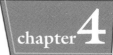

- You can click the plus sign () to add additional criteria.

- If your Smart Album includes more than one criterion, you can specify whether the album requires any or all of the criteria to be met.

7 Click **OK**.

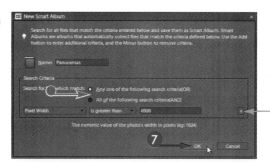

Photoshop Elements automatically adds photos that meet the criteria to the Smart Album and then displays the album in the Photo Browser.

As you add more photos to your catalog, photos that meet the criteria are automatically added to the Smart Album.

- You can click **Options** and then **Modify Search Criteria** to change the Smart Album settings.

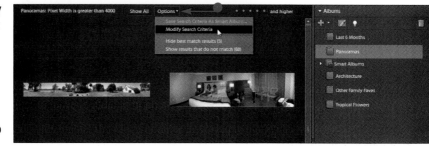

TIP

How do I create an album category?
You can organize similar albums in your Organizer into album categories.

1 Click the plus sign () and then click **New Album Category**.

The Create Album Category dialog box opens.

2 Type a name for the album category.

3 Click **OK**.

Photoshop Elements creates a new album category in the Albums panel. You can add albums to the category when you create them.

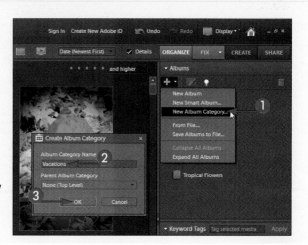

Work with Keyword Tags

Keyword tags help you categorize and filter your photos. You can assign the Organizer's preset tags or use tags that you have created. You can also assign more than one tag to a photo.

Preset tags include those for people, family, friends, places, and events. You can assign tags to categories and subcategories.

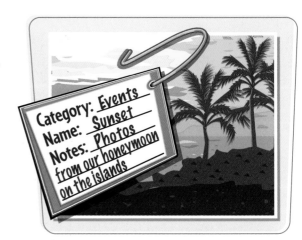

Work with Keyword Tags

Create a Keyword Tag

① In the Organizer, open the **Keyword Tags** panel in the Organizer bin.

② Click the plus sign (▐) and then click **New Keyword Tag**.

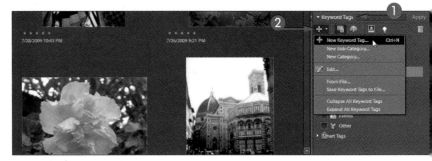

The Create Keyword Tag dialog box opens.

③ Click here to choose a category for the new tag.

④ Type a name for the keyword tag.

● You can add a note about the keyword tag here.

⑤ Click **OK**.

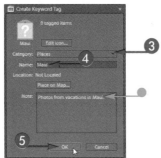

chapter 4

Assign Tags

6 Click and drag the tag from the Keyword Tags panel and then drop it on the photo that you want to tag.

The Organizer assigns the keyword tag.

You can also drag a thumbnail image from the Media Browser to a keyword tag to assign a tag.

● A keyword tag icon indicates that the photo has a tag assigned to it.

7 Type text for a tag in the Keyword Tags search box.

Photoshop Elements suggests tags with that text.

8 Click a tag in the list that appears.

9 `Ctrl` +click to select photos you want to tag.

10 Click **Apply**.

● Photoshop Elements applies the tag to the selected photos.

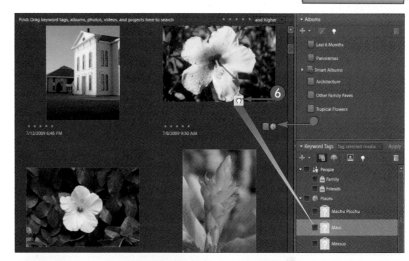

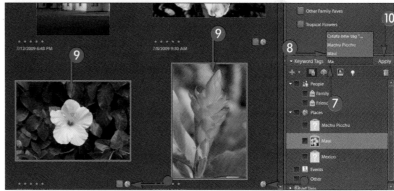

 TIP

How do I edit a keyword tag?

1 Right-click on the keyword tag and then choose **Edit *name* keyword tag**.

The Edit Keyword Tag dialog box opens.

2 Type a new keyword tag name or make other edits to the tag.

3 Click **OK**.

Photoshop Elements applies the changes. Any images that have the keyword tag applied are updated.

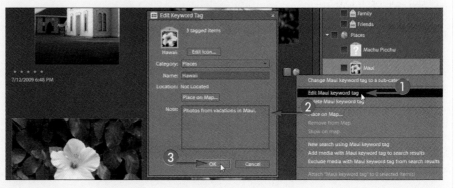

continued

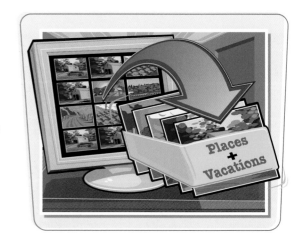

After you assign keyword tags, you can filter your catalog to show only those photos that have certain tags. For example, you can filter your photos to show only photos of people or events. You can also simultaneously filter multiple keyword tags.

Work with Keyword Tags *(continued)*

Filter By Tags

1 Open the Keyword Tags panel if it is not already displayed.

2 Click the check box next to the keyword tag on which you want to filter (■ changes to ✓).

● You can click here (▶) to expand a tag category.

● You can click here (▼) to collapse a tag category.

To filter by more than one keyword tag, you can click additional tags.

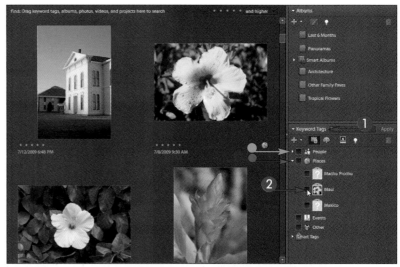

● The Organizer displays the photos that share the keyword tag.

If you selected multiple tags, only photos that have all the tags appear.

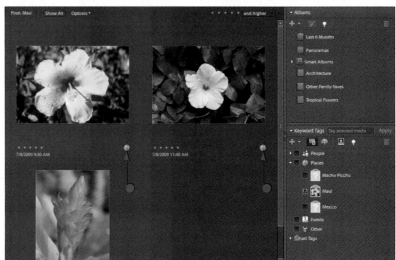

Remove a Tag from a Photo

1 Right-click on the photo containing the tag you want to remove.

2 Click **Remove Keyword Tag**.

3 Click the keyword tag you want to remove.

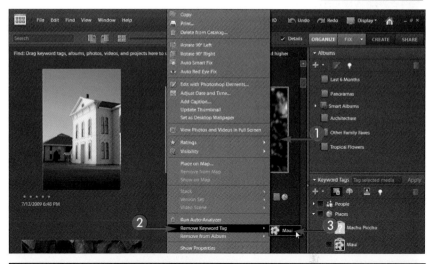

The Organizer removes the keyword tag from the photo.

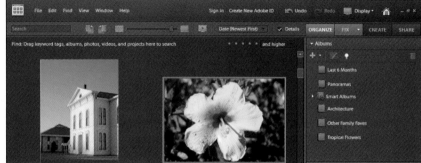

TIP

How can I use keyword tags when I use the regular search box?

The regular search box will suggest keyword tags as you type search terms.

1 Type text in the search box.

● Photoshop Elements displays any keywords that match that text.

2 Click the keyword tag to display tagged photos with that keyword.

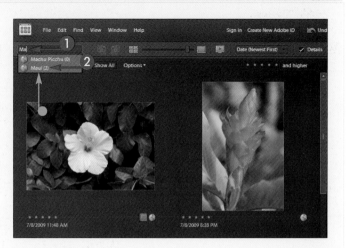

View a Tag Cloud

You can view your keyword tags as a tag cloud, which organizes tags alphabetically and sizes them by the number of times applied. You can click tags in the tag cloud to filter the photos in the Media Browser.

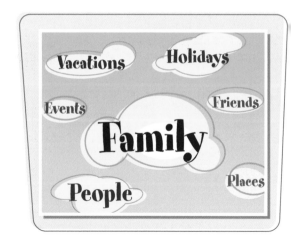

1 In the Organizer, open the Keyword Tags panel if it is not already displayed.

● The default view is Keyword Tag Hierarchy View, which lists tags categorically.

2 Click the **View Keyword Tag Cloud** button (⬆).

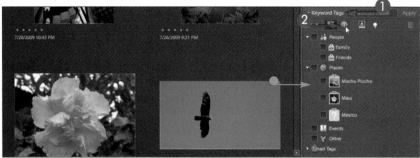

Photoshop Elements displays a tag cloud.

● A tag cloud displays tags in alphabetical order and sizes the terms according to the number of times they are used.

3 Click a keyword tag.

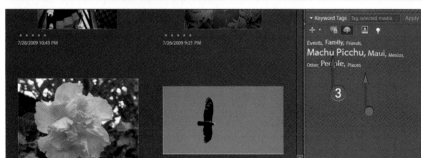

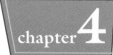
● Photoshop Elements highlights the term.

○ Only the photos tagged with that term are shown in the Media Browser.

Only one tag in the tag cloud may be selected at a time.

④ Click the keyword tag again.

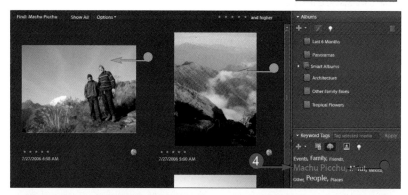

● Photoshop Elements removes the highlighting.

The view in the Media Browser is reset.

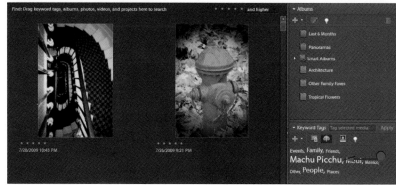

TIP

How can someone else use the keyword tags that I have created?
You can export your keyword tags as an XML file. You can then send the file to someone else to import the file into Photoshop Elements.

① In the Organizer, open the Keyword Tags panel if it is not already displayed.

② Click the plus sign ( ).

③ Click **Save Keyword Tag(s) to File**.

● To import tags from a file, you can click From File.

④ In the dialog box, click **Export All Keyword Tags** (● changes to ○).

⑤ Click **OK**.

A Save dialog box opens, allowing you to save the keyword tags.

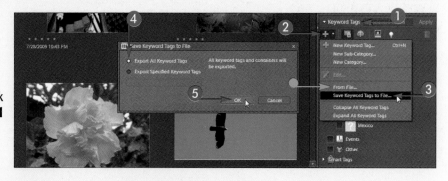

Tag Faces

You can use the Organizer's face-recognition feature to pinpoint the faces in your photos for easy tagging. Photoshop Elements automatically scans photos in the Organizer for the colors and structures that are characteristic of human faces.

As you tag recognized faces, Photoshop Elements creates custom keyword tags in the People category for the friends and family members whose faces appear often in your photos.

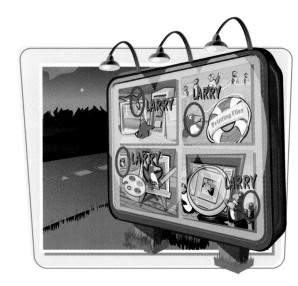

Tag Faces

1. In the Organizer, open the Keyword Tags panel if it is not already displayed.

2. **Ctrl** + click to select the photos in which you want to recognize faces.

   If you do not select any photos, Photoshop Elements searches all the photos.

3. Click the **Start People Recognition** button (▣).

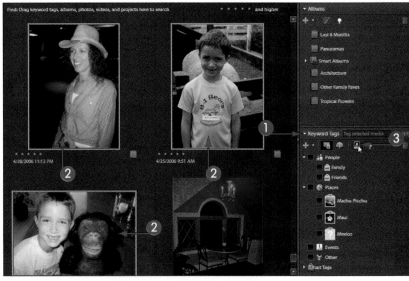

Photoshop Elements searches for faces and displays the results in a People Recognition dialog box.

● Recognized faces are highlighted with a box.

4. Click here to type a descriptive tag, such as a name for the face.

5. Press **Enter**.

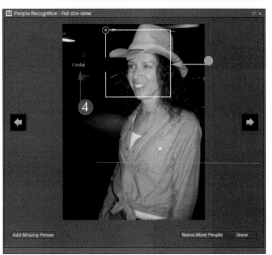

Photoshop Elements tags the face.

● A new keyword tag is created under the People tag category.

Note: For more on using tags to filter photos, see the section "Work with Keyword Tags."

⑥ Click here to cycle through the other analyzed photos.

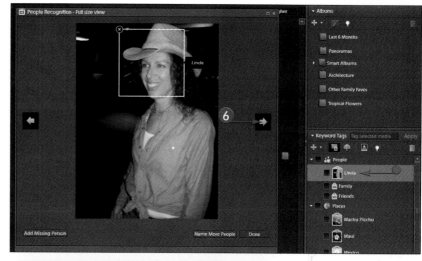

⑦ Repeat steps **4** and **5** for each recognized face.

● When adding tags to faces, Photoshop Elements lists previous tags that you have used. You can optionally click a previous tag to label a face.

⑧ When you finish adding tags, click **Done**.

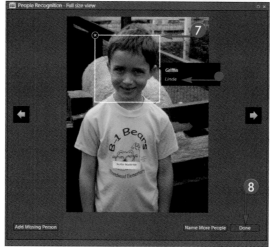

TIP

How can I automatically find visually similar photos?

① In the Organizer, click to select a photo.

② Click **Find**.

③ Click **By Visual Similarity with Selected Photo(s) and Video(s)**.

Photoshop Elements displays similar photos in the Organizer.

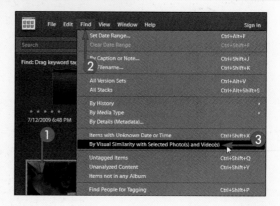

Map a Photo

You can place your Organizer photos on a geographic map to specify where they were taken. The mapping feature in Photoshop Elements uses navigable-map technology from Yahoo, allowing you to pan and zoom and then place your photos with precision.

You need an active Internet connection for the mapping feature to work in Photoshop Elements.

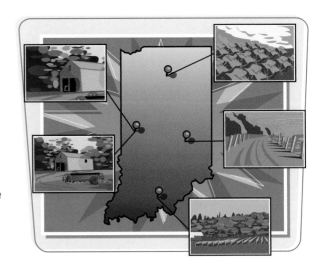

Map a Photo

① Right-click on a photo in the Organizer.

② Click **Place on Map**.

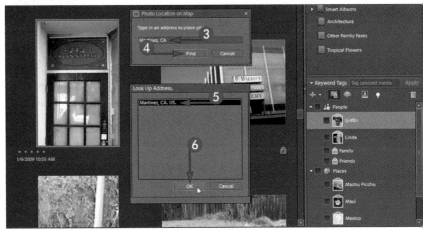

The Photo Location on Map dialog box opens.

③ Type a location for your photo.

In addition to specific addresses, cities, and states, you can type famous locations, such as the Golden Gate Bridge or the Eiffel Tower.

④ Click **Find**.

Photoshop Elements suggests one or more locations from its database.

⑤ Choose a location.

⑥ Click **OK**.

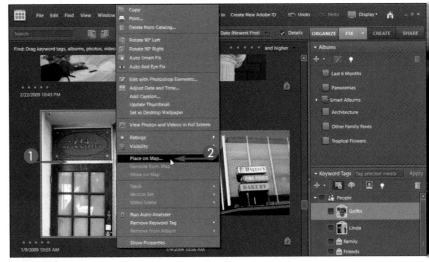

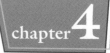

If a dialog box with tips about mapping photos opens, click **OK** to close it.

● Photoshop Elements displays a map with a red pushpin ( ) at the selected location.

● You can select the **Zoom In** tool ( ) and then click the map to zoom in.

● You can select the **Zoom Out** tool ( ) and then click the map to zoom out.

● You can select the **Hand** tool ( ) and then click and drag the map to scroll.

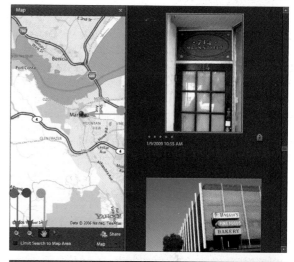

⑦ Zoom in to the location by using the map tools.

⑧ Click the **Move** tool ( ).

⑨ Click and drag the red pushpin ( ) to a more specific location.

⑩ To close the map, click .

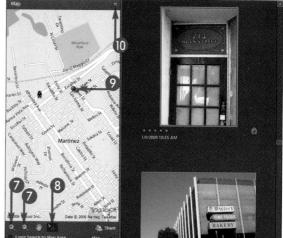

TIP

How else can I add photos to a map?
With the Map window open, you can click and drag thumbnails to place photos on a map.

① In the Organizer, click **Window**.

② Click **Show Map**.

If a dialog box about mapping opens, click **OK**.

The Map window opens.

③ Click and drag a thumbnail to the map.

Photoshop Elements maps the photo.

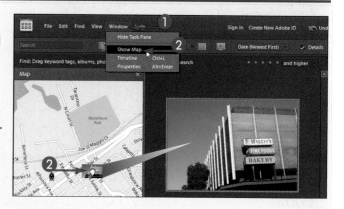

Apply Photo Fixes in Full Screen

You can optimize color, lighting, and other aspects of your photos in the Organizer's Full Screen view. This can be convenient when you want to make simple changes to your photos in the Organizer but do not want to switch to the Editor. You apply commands by using the Quick Edit panel.

For more on the Full Screen view, see Chapter 3. For more on opening the Editor, see Chapter 1.

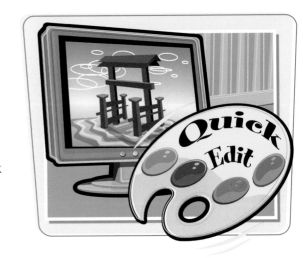

Apply Photo Fixes in Full Screen

① In the Organizer, click the photo you want to fix.

② Click 🖼.

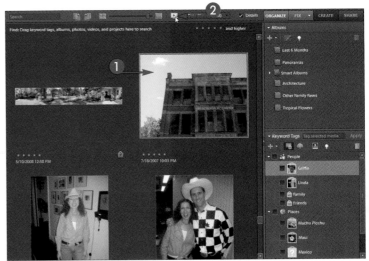

Photoshop Elements opens the photo in Full Screen.

● A Quick Edit panel is displayed.

● If the panel is hidden, you can click **Toggle Quick Edit Panel** (🖼) to open it.

③ Move the cursor over a button.

● A description of the edit command appears.

④ Click the button.

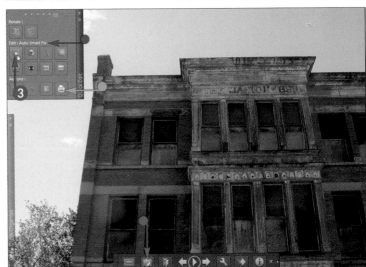

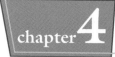

Photoshop Elements applies the edit.

5 Click ❌ or press Esc.

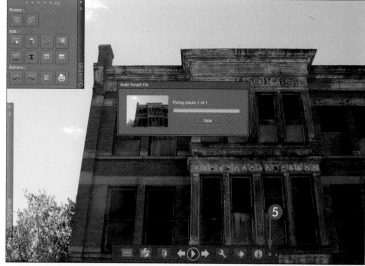

Photoshop Elements exits Full Screen view.

● The edited version of the photo is saved in a photo stack with the original version of the photo.

Note: For more on stacks, see the section "Stack Photos."

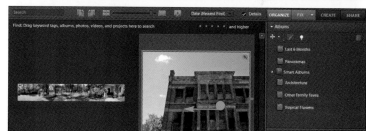

How do I add photos to albums or apply keyword tags while in Full Screen?
You can perform these actions by using the Quick Organize panel in Full Screen view.

1 If the Quick Organize panel is hidden, click **Toggle Quick Organize Panel** (🔆) to open it.

2 Click an album name.

Photoshop Elements adds the current photo to the album.

3 Click a keyword tag.

Photoshop Elements assigns the keyword tag to the current photo.

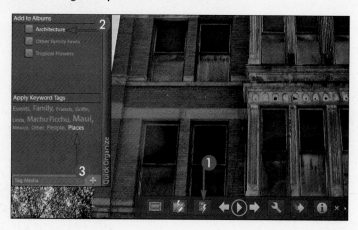

Stack Photos

In the Organizer, you can group similar photos into stacks. This can help you conserve space in the Organizer interface because stacks can be collapsed so that only the top photo on the stack appears. You can manually stack your photos or have Photoshop Elements suggest stacks based on photographic similarity.

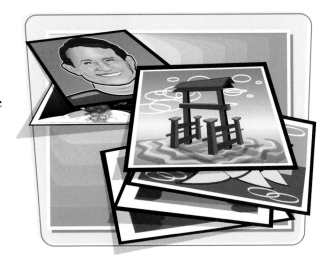

Stack Photos

Create a Stack

1 In the Organizer, **Ctrl** + click to select the photos you want to stack.

2 Right-click on one of the selected photos.

3 Click **Stack**.

4 Click **Stack Selected Photos**.

● You can click **Automatically Suggest Photo Stacks** to have Photoshop Elements suggest stacks based on photographic similarity.

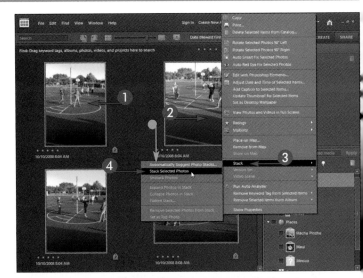

● Photoshop Elements creates a stack for the selected photos. The photo that you right-clicked on is placed on top of the stack and is displayed here.

5 Click to expand the stack (⏸).

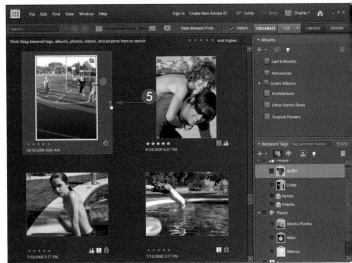

The stack expands to show its contents.

● You can click here to collapse the stack (◀).

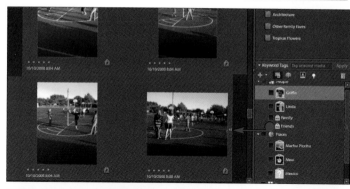

UNSTACK PHOTOS

① Right-click on a photo in a stack. If the stack is collapsed, right-click on the top photo.

② Click **Stack**.

③ Click **Unstack Photos**.

Photoshop Elements removes the stack and places photos in the Organizer separately.

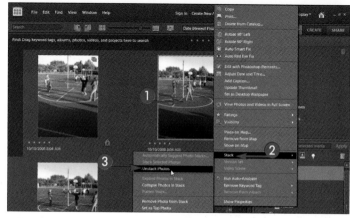

 TIP

How do I automatically stack photos as I import them?

You can have Photoshop Elements automatically group your photos into stacks by selecting an option in the Get Photos dialog box. The following steps show you how to do this when getting photos from a folder on your computer.

① Click **File**, click **Get Photos and Videos,** and click **From Files and Folders.**

② In the dialog box that opens, click the **Automatically Suggest Photo Stacks** check box (☐ changes to ☑).

When you import the photos, Photoshop Elements suggests groups of photos to be stacked based on their photographic similarity.

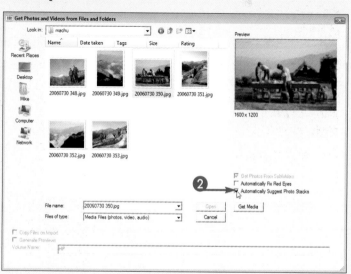

Image-Editing Basics

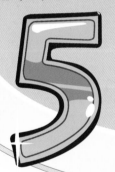

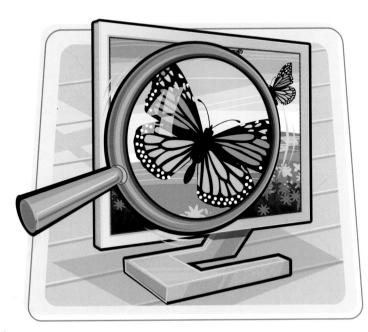

Are you ready to start working with images? This chapter shows you how to fine-tune your workspace to best arrange your open images. You also discover how to change the on-screen image size, set a print size, and change the print resolution.

Manage Open Images

Each image you open in Photoshop Elements appears in its own window. Tabs at the top of the windows enable you to switch between images. You can also use the Project Bin or Window menu to view different open images.

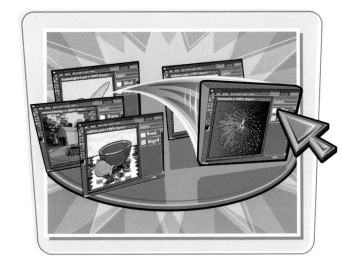

Using Tabs

1 In the Editor, open two or more images.

Note: For more on opening the Editor, see Chapter 1. See Chapter 2 for more on opening image files.

● The active or current image appears here.

● Each open image has its own tab, which displays its file name and magnification.

2 Click a tab for the image you want to view.

● The image appears as the active image. You can make changes to the active image by applying commands and effects.

Using the Project Bin

● By default, the Project Bin displays smaller versions, or *thumbnails*, of the images.

Note: See the tip on the next page for more on how to display other images in the Project Bin.

If the Project Bin is closed, you can click **Window** and then **Project Bin** to open it.

3 Double-click a thumbnail.

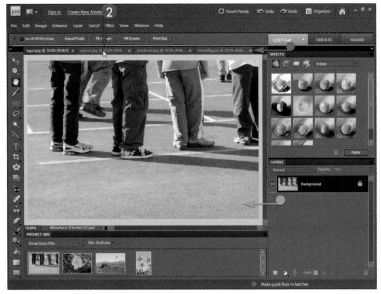

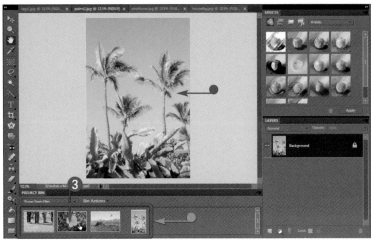

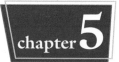

● The image appears as the active image.

Using the Window Menu

④ Click **Window**.

⑤ Click an image file name.

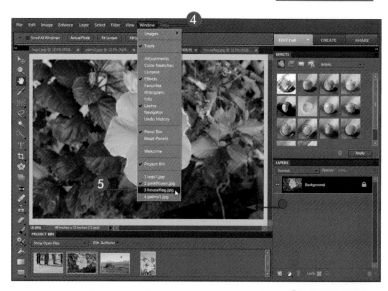

● The image appears as the active image.

● You can click to close an image.

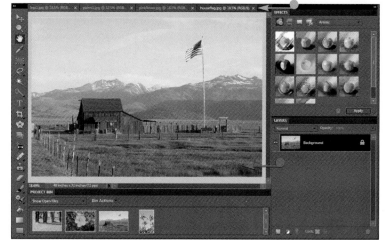

TIP

How do I display different images in the Project Bin?

In the Project Bin, you can display images from albums created in the Organizer.

① Click .

② Click an album name.

● You can click here to display all the images from the Organizer.

● Photoshop Elements displays the album images.

Note: See Chapter 3 for more on the Organizer and creating albums.

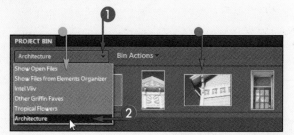

continued

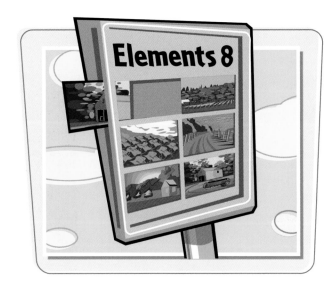

You can view multiple images at the same time by choosing a layout. New in Photoshop Elements 8, layouts allow you to display images as a grid, in vertical columns, or in horizontal rows.

Manage Open Images *(continued)*

Using Layouts

6 Click ▼.

Photoshop Elements displays a menu of layouts.

● The top row enables you to display images one at a time, as a grid, in vertical columns, or in horizontal rows.

7 Click a layout.

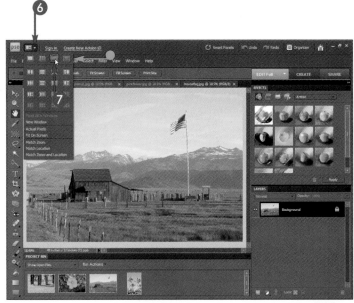

Photoshop Elements displays multiple windows — each with a different image.

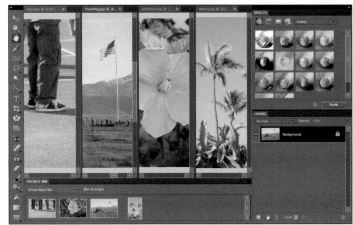

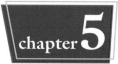

8 Click .

● The lower rows enable you to display a specific number of images at a time.

For example, selecting a 3 Up layout displays three windows, with an open image in each one.

9 Click a layout.

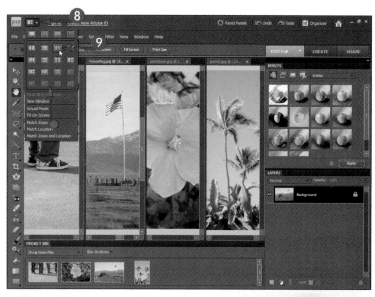

Photoshop Elements displays multiple windows at once — each with a different image.

● If you have more open images than windows, you can click tabs to switch between images.

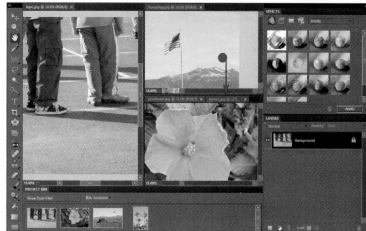

 TIPS

How can I magnify all my visible images at once?
When the Zoom tool (🔍) is selected, you can click the **Zoom All Windows** check box (▪ changes to ✔) in the Options bar to make the tool affect all windows. See the section "Magnify with the Zoom Tool" for more on changing magnification.

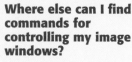

Where else can I find commands for controlling my image windows?
You can select various commands in the layout menu. If you are comparing several photos on-screen, you can click **Match Location** to view the same area in each open window. You can click **Match Zoom** to view each open window at the same zoom percentage.

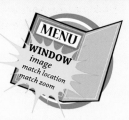

Magnify with the Zoom Tool

You can change the magnification of an image with the Zoom tool. This enables you to view small details in an image or view an image at full size.

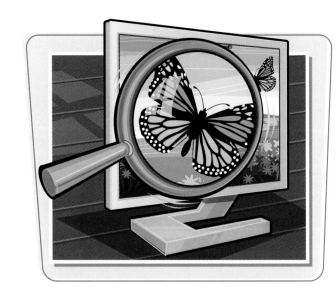

Magnify with the Zoom Tool

Increase Magnification

1 In the Editor, click the **Zoom** tool (🔍).

Note: For more on opening the Editor, see Chapter 1.

2 Click the image.

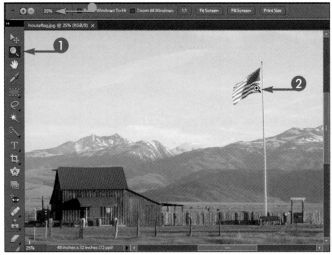

Photoshop Elements increases the magnification of the image.

The magnification appears in the image title bar and Options bar.

● You can select an exact magnification by typing a percentage value in the Options bar or in the lower-left corner of the image window.

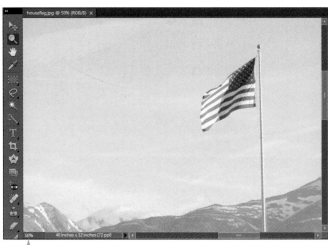

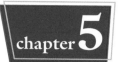

Decrease Magnification

1 Click the **Zoom Out** button (⊖).

2 Click the image.

Photoshop Elements decreases the magnification of the image.

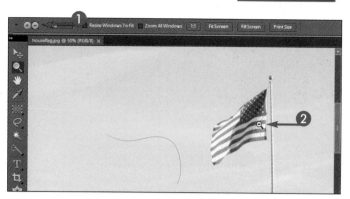

Magnify a Detail

1 Click the **Zoom In** button (⊕).

2 Click and drag with the **Zoom** tool (🔍) to select the detail.

The area appears enlarged on-screen.

The more you zoom in, the larger the pixels appear and the less you see of the image's content.

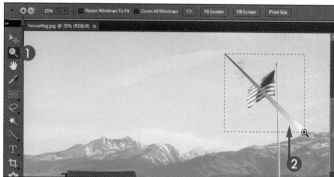

TIP

How do I quickly return an image to 100% magnification?

The following are seven ways to return the image to 100% magnification:

1 Double-click the **Zoom** tool (🔍).

2 Click **1:1** on the Options bar.

3 Click **View** and then **Actual Pixels** from the menu.

4 Type **100%** in the Options bar field.

5 Type **100%** in the lower-left corner of the image window.

6 Right-click on the image and select **Actual Pixels** from the pop-up menu.

7 Press Alt + Ctrl + 0.

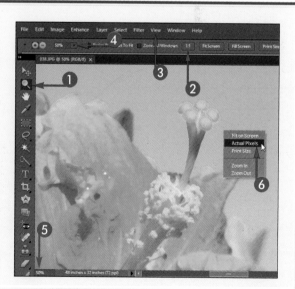

Adjust the Image View

You can move an image within the window by using the Hand tool or scrollbars. The Hand tool helps you navigate to an exact area in the image by dragging freely in two dimensions.

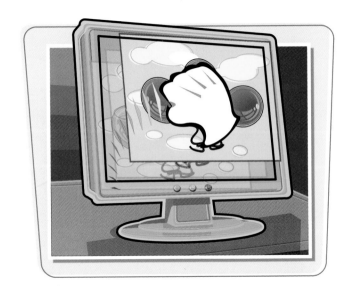

Using the Hand tool

1 In the Editor, click the **Hand** tool (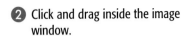).

Note: For more on opening the Editor, see Chapter 1.

Note: For the Hand tool ( ) to have an effect, the image must be larger than the image window. See the section "Magnify with the Zoom Tool" for more about enlarging an image by zooming.

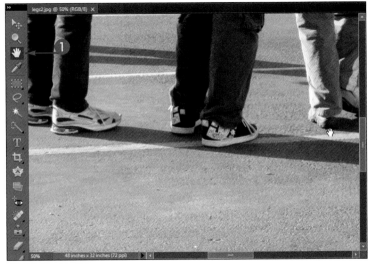

2 Click and drag inside the image window.

The view of the image shifts inside the window.

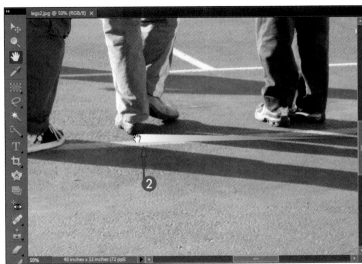

Using the Scrollbars

1 Click and hold one of the window's scrollbar buttons (▲, ▼, ◄, or ►).

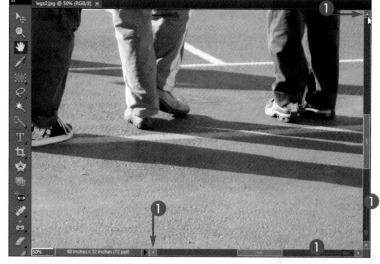

The image scrolls in the direction you select.

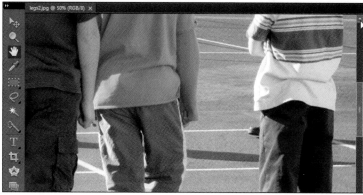

TIP

How can I quickly adjust the image window to see the entire image at its largest possible magnification on-screen?

The following are five ways to magnify the image to its largest possible size:

1 Double-click the **Hand** tool (✋).

2 Click **Fit Screen** on the Options bar.

3 Click **View** and then **Fit on Screen** from the menu.

4 Right-click on the image and choose **Fit on Screen** from the pop-up menu.

5 Press **Ctrl** + **0** .

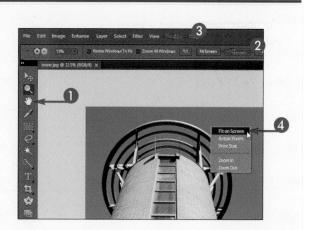

Change the Image Size

You can change the on-screen size of an image you are working with in Photoshop Elements to make it better fit the confines of your monitor. Shrinking an image can also lower its file size and make it easier to share via e-mail or on the Web.

When you change an image's on-screen size, you need to resample it. Resampling is the process of increasing or decreasing the number of pixels in an image.

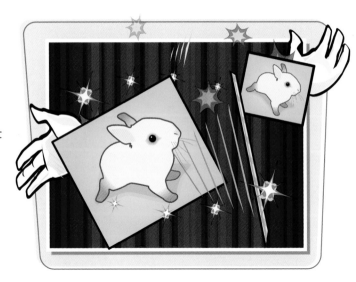

Change the Image Size

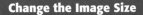

① In the Editor, click **Image**.

Note: *For more on opening the Editor, see Chapter 1.*

② Click **Resize**.

③ Click **Image Size**.

The Image Size dialog box opens, listing the width and height of the image in pixels.

You can also press Alt + Ctrl + I to open the Image Size dialog box.

● To resize by a certain percentage, click here and change the units to **percent**.

④ Click the **Resample Image** check box (changes to ✓).

Note: *Of the options in the Resample Image menu, Bicubic Smoother is often better for enlarging, while Bicubic Sharper is better for shrinking.*

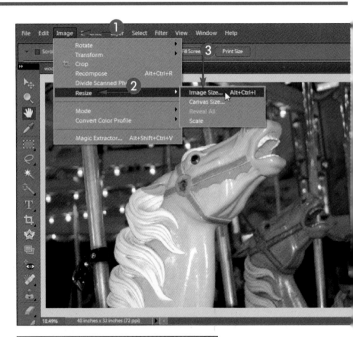

⑤ Type a size or percentage for a dimension.

● You can click the **Constrain Proportions** check box (■ changes to ☑) to cause the other dimension to change proportionally.

⑥ Click **OK**.

● You can restore the original dialog box settings without exiting the dialog box by pressing and holding **Alt** and then clicking **Cancel**, which changes to Reset.

Photoshop Elements resizes the image.

In this example, the image decreases to 50% of the original size.

Note: *Changing the number of pixels in an image can add blur. To sharpen a resized image, see Chapter 9.*

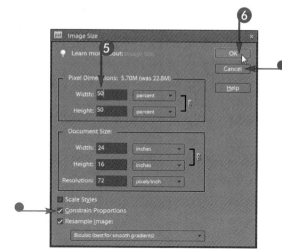

 TIP

How do I change the size of an image as I am saving it for the Web?

You can change the pixel dimensions of your image in the Save For Web dialog box. The saved image will have the new size. See Chapter 17 for more on saving images for the Web.

① Click **File** and then click **Save For Web**.

The Save For Web dialog box opens.

② Type a new value in the **Width** or **Height** field to change the dimensions of your image.

● You can also change the size of your image by a percentage.

③ Click **Apply** to resize the image.

④ Click **OK** to save the image.

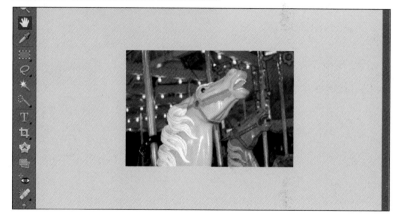

Change the Image Print Size

You can change the printed size of an image to determine how it appears on paper. Print size is also called *document size* in Photoshop Elements.

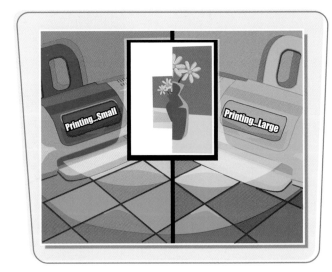

1 In the Editor, click **Image**.

Note: *For more on opening the Editor, see Chapter 1.*

2 Click **Resize**.

3 Click **Image Size**.

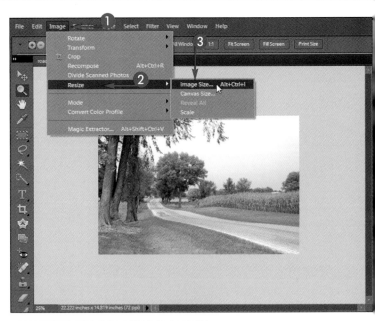

The Image Size dialog box opens, listing the current width and height of the printed image.

● You can click here to change the unit of measurement.

● If you click the **Resample Image** check box, Photoshop Elements adjusts the number of pixels in the image to resize. Otherwise, it adjusts the resolution.

Note: *For more on resolution, see the section "Change the Image Resolution."*

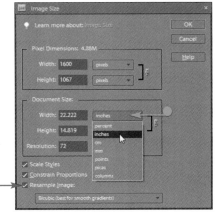

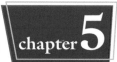

④ Type a size or percentage for a dimension.

● You can click the **Constrain Proportions** check box (■ changes to ✓) to cause the other dimension to change proportionally.

⑤ Click **OK**.

● You can restore the original dialog box settings by pressing and holding **Alt** and then clicking **Cancel**, which changes to Reset.

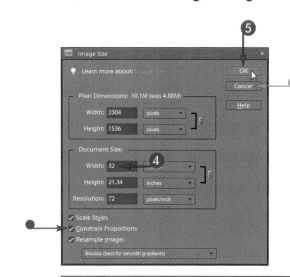

Photoshop Elements resizes the image.

Note: Changing the size of an image, especially enlarging, can add blur. To sharpen a resized image, see Chapter 9.

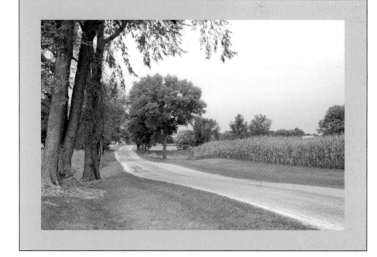

How do I preview an image's printed size?

① Click **File**.

② Click **Print**.

● The Print Preview dialog box shows how the image will print on the page.

● To select other dimensions, click here to choose a print size.

③ Click **Print** to print the image.

Note: For more on printing, see Chapter 17.

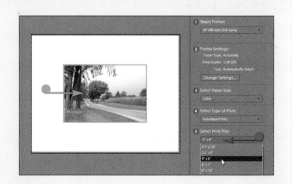

Change the Image Resolution

You can change the print resolution of an image to increase or decrease the print quality. The resolution, combined with the number of pixels in an image, determines the size of a printed image. The greater the resolution, the better the image appears on the printed page — up to a limit, which varies with the type of printer you use and the paper on which you are printing.

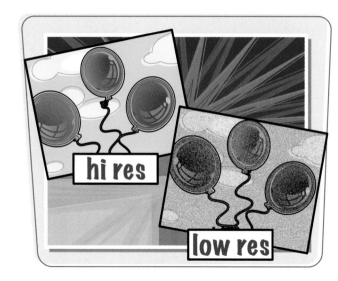

hi res

low res

Change the Image Resolution

① In the Editor, click **Image**.

Note: For more on opening the Editor, see Chapter 1.

② Click **Resize**.

③ Click **Image Size**.

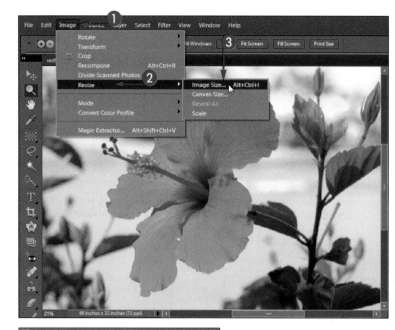

The Image Size dialog box opens, listing the current resolution of the image.

● You can click here to change the resolution units.

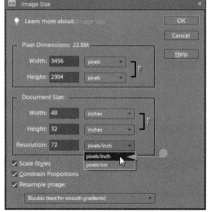

④ Type a new resolution.

● You can deselect the **Resample Image** check box (☑ changes to ■) to keep the number of pixels in your image fixed and change the printed dimensions. The print quality will change.

⑤ Click **OK**.

● You can restore the original dialog box settings by pressing and holding **Alt** and clicking **Cancel**, which changes to Reset.

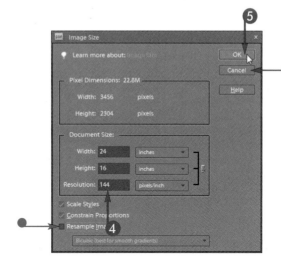

Photoshop Elements adjusts the image resolution.

If you deselected the Resample Image check box, the number of pixels stays the same, as does the on-screen image size. Increasing the resolution makes the print size smaller, and decreasing the resolution makes it bigger.

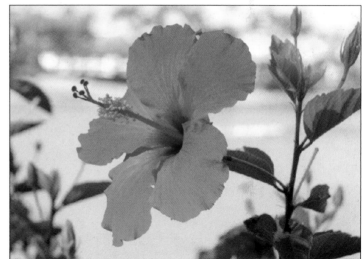

 TIPS

What is the relationship between resolution, on-screen size, and print size?

To determine the printed size of a Photoshop Elements image, you can divide the on-screen size by the resolution. If you have an image with an on-screen width of 480 pixels and a resolution of 120 pixels per inch, the printed width is 4 inches.

What resolution should I use for images that I intend to print?

The appropriate resolution depends on a variety of factors, including the type of printer and paper you are using. However, for most standard inkjet printers, a resolution of 300 pixels per inch should be sufficient to produce good-quality prints on photo-quality paper. A resolution of 150 pixels per inch is sufficient for regular copier paper. Printing at lower resolutions may cause elements in your image to appear jagged.

Change the Image Canvas Size

You can alter the canvas size of an image to change its rectangular shape or add space around its borders. The canvas is the area on which an image sits. Changing the canvas size is one way to crop an image or add *matting*, which is blank space, around an image.

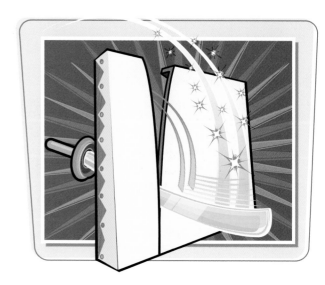

Change the Image Canvas Size

① In the Editor, click **Image**.

Note: *For more on opening the Editor, see Chapter 1.*

② Click **Resize**.

③ Click **Canvas Size**.

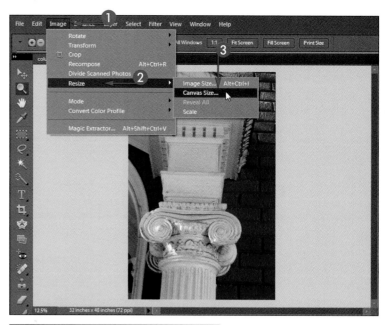

The Canvas Size dialog box opens, listing the current dimensions of the canvas.

● You can click here to change the unit of measurement.

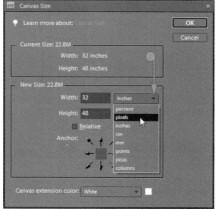

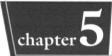

④ Type the new canvas dimensions.

● You can click an arrow (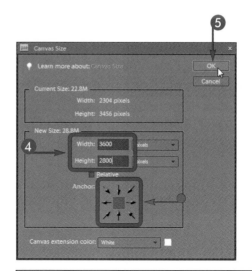) to determine in which directions Photoshop Elements changes the canvas size. Clicking the square in the middle of the arrows crops the image equally on opposite sides.

⑤ Click **OK**.

Note: If you decrease a dimension, Photoshop Elements displays a dialog box asking whether you want to proceed. Click **Proceed**.

Photoshop Elements changes the image's canvas size.

In this example, because the width is increased, Photoshop Elements creates new canvas space on the sides of the image.

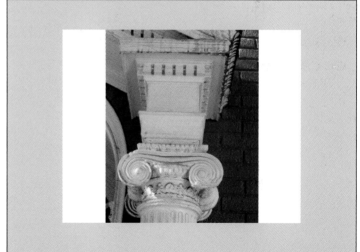

TIP

How do I specify the matte color around my canvas?

① In the Canvas Size dialog box, click here to specify the matte color.

● You can click here or select **Other** to select a custom color.

● The color appears when you enlarge a dimension of your image.

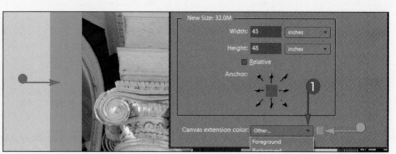

Crop an Image

You can use the Crop tool to quickly remove unneeded space on the top, bottom, and sides of an image. Cropping is a great way to edit out unwanted background elements or reposition a subject in your photo.

You can also crop an image by changing its canvas size. See the section "Change the Image Canvas Size" for more on setting a new canvas size. Another way is by selecting an area with a selection tool, clicking Image, and then clicking Crop. See Chapter 6 for more on making selections.

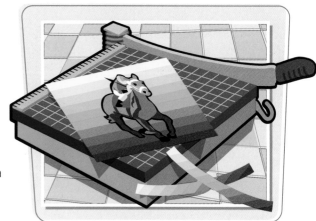

Crop an Image

1 In the Editor, click the **Crop** tool (⬚).

Note: *For more on opening the Editor, see Chapter 1.*

2 Click and drag to select the area of the image you want to keep.

Another way to crop an image is by changing its canvas size; you do this by clicking **Image**, **Resize**, and then **Canvas Size** and you can then type new dimensions for the image.

● You can set specific dimensions for a crop by using the Width and Height boxes in the Options bar.

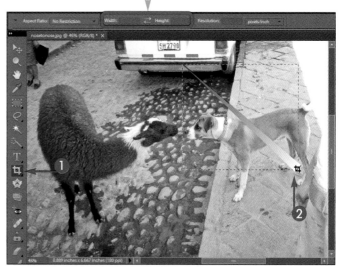

3 Click and drag the side and corner handles (□) to adjust the size of the cropping boundary.

You can click and drag inside the cropping boundary to move it without adjusting its size.

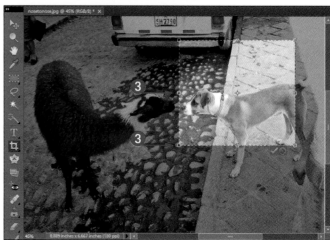

4 Click or press Enter to accept the crop.

You can also double-click inside the crop area to crop the photo.

● To exit the cropping process, you can click ⊘ or press Esc to reject.

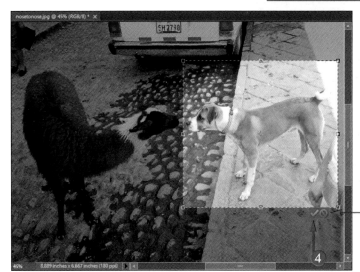

Photoshop Elements crops the image, deleting the pixels outside the cropping boundary.

Note: You can also crop images in the Quick Fix window. See the section "Quick Fix a Photo" to learn more on this window.

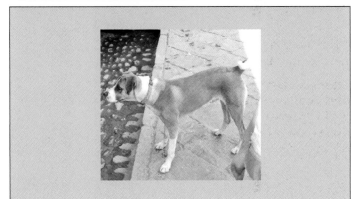

TIP

How do I crop my image into an interesting shape?

You can use the Cookie Cutter tool to crop your image into nonrectangular shapes.

1 Click the **Cookie Cutter** tool (⬟).

2 Click ⬛ and then click a shape for the crop.

● You can click here to access additional shapes.

3 Adjust the cropping boundary and then perform the crop similar to using the regular Crop tool.

Photoshop Elements crops the image as a shape.

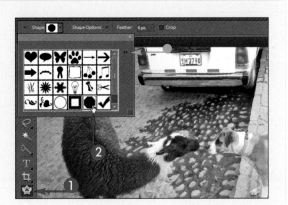

Rotate an Image

You can use the rotate actions on an image to turn it within the image canvas. If you import or scan a horizontal image vertically, you can rotate it so that it appears in the correct orientation.

You can also flip a photo to change the direction of the subject matter. Flipping it horizontally, for example, creates a mirror image of the photo.

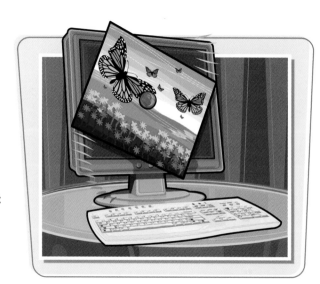

Rotate an Image

Rotate 90 Degrees

1 In the Editor, click **Image**.

Note: For more on opening the Editor, see Chapter 1.

2 Click **Rotate**.

3 Click **90° Left** or **90° Right** to rotate an image.

● To change subject direction, click **Flip Horizontal** or **Flip Vertical**.

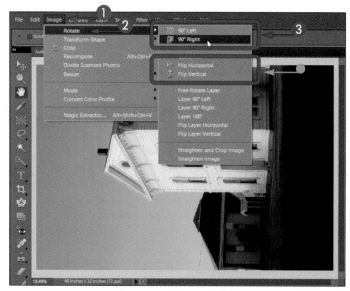

Photoshop Elements flips the image.

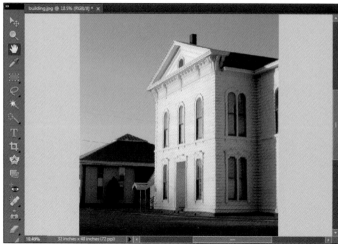

Rotate Precisely

1. Click **Image**.

2. Click **Rotate**.

3. Click **Custom**.

   The Rotate Canvas dialog box opens.

4. Type an angle from -359.99 to 359.99.

5. Click a direction to rotate.

6. Click **OK**.

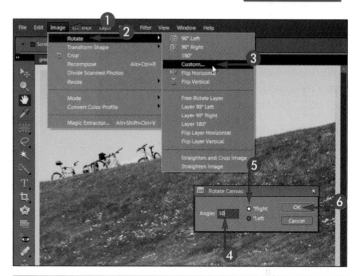

Photoshop Elements rotates the image to your exact specifications.

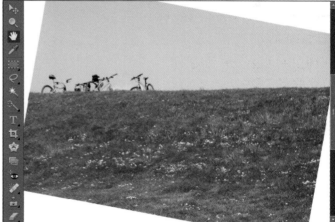

How can I automatically straighten a crooked image?

The Straighten Image command is useful for fixing photos that have been scanned crookedly.

1. Click **Image**.

2. Click **Rotate**.

3. Click **Straighten Image**.

   ● You can click **Straighten and Crop Image** to crop any space that is left after straightening.

   Photoshop Elements straightens the image.

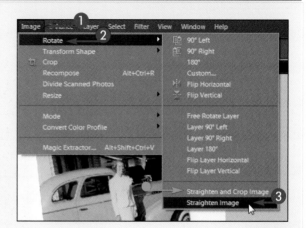

Undo Changes to an Image

You can undo commands by using the Undo History panel. This enables you to correct mistakes or change your mind about operations you have performed on your image.

The Undo History panel lists recently executed commands, with the most recent command at the bottom.

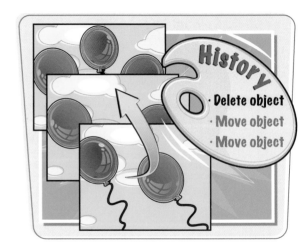

Undo Changes to an Image

1 In the Editor, click **Window**.

Note: For more on opening the Editor, see Chapter 1.

2 Click **Undo History**.

The Undo History panel opens.

3 Click the **History** slider (▣) and then drag it upward.

● Alternatively, you can click a previous command in the Undo History panel.

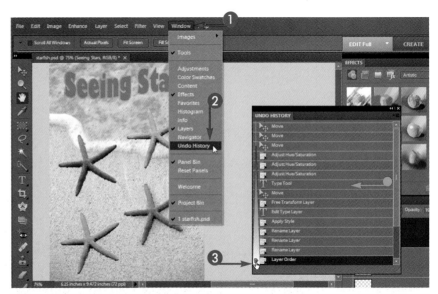

● Photoshop Elements undoes the previous commands.

● You can click and drag the slider down to redo the commands.

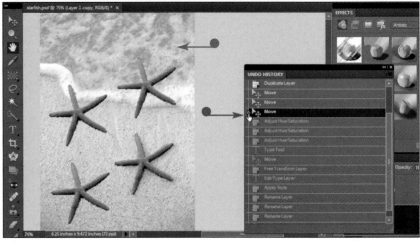

Revert an Image

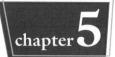

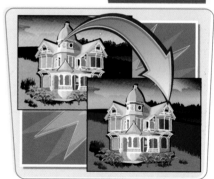

You can revert an image to the previously saved state.
This enables you to start your image editing over.

Revert an Image

① In the Editor, click **Edit**.

Note: For more on opening the Editor, see Chapter 1.

② Click **Revert**.

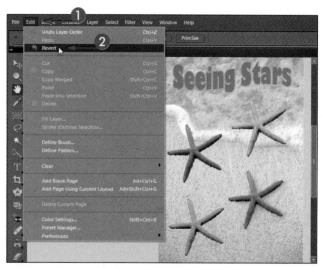

Photoshop Elements reverts the image to its previously saved state.

● To return to the unreverted state, click **Edit** and then **Undo Revert**.

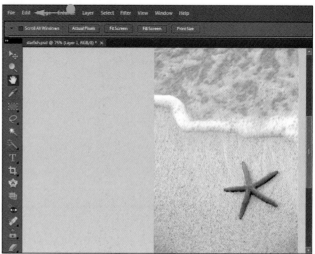

Selection Techniques

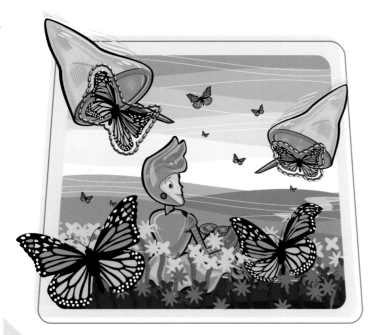

Do you want to move, color, or transform parts of your image independently from the rest of the image? The first step is to make a selection. This chapter shows you how to use the Photoshop Elements selection tools to isolate portions of your images for editing.

Select an Area with a Marquee

You can select parts of an image for editing by using a marquee. You can then make changes to the selected area by using other Photoshop Elements commands.

Two marquee tools are available: The Rectangular Marquee enables you to select rectangular shapes, including squares, and the Elliptical Marquee enables you to select elliptical shapes, including circles.

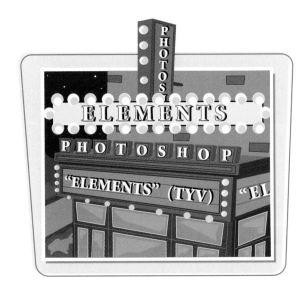

Select with the Rectangular Marquee

1 In the Editor, click the **Rectangular Marquee** tool (⬚).

Note: *For more on opening the Editor, see Chapter 1.*

2 Click and drag diagonally inside the image window.

You can press and hold Shift while you click and drag to create a square selection.

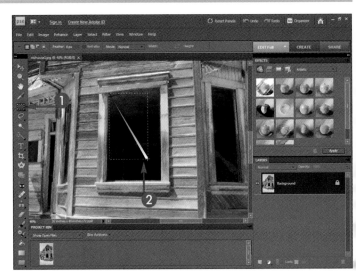

● Photoshop Elements selects a rectangular portion of your image.

You can reposition selections by pressing the keyboard arrow keys: ⬆, ⬇, ⬅, and ➡.

● You can deselect a selection by clicking **Select** and then **Deselect** or by clicking outside the selection area.

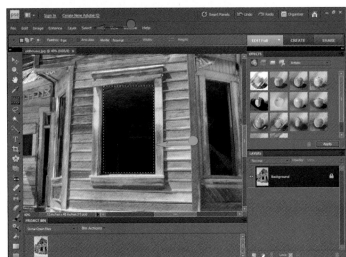

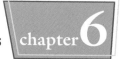

Select with the Elliptical Marquee

① Right-click on the **Rectangular Marquee** tool (▦).

② Click the **Elliptical Marquee** tool (▦).

③ Click and drag diagonally inside the image window.

You can press and hold Shift while you click and drag to create a circular selection or you can press and hold Shift and Alt to draw the circle directly out from the center.

● Photoshop Elements selects an elliptical portion of your image.

You can reposition selections by pressing the keyboard arrow keys: ⬆, ⬇, ⬅, and ➡.

You can deselect a selection by clicking **Select** and then **Deselect** or by clicking outside the selection area.

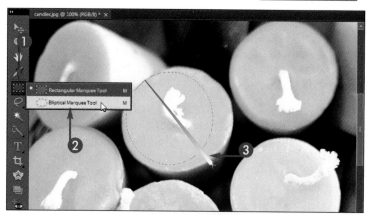

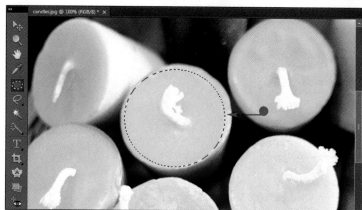

TIP

How do I customize the marquee tools?

You can customize the marquee tools (▦ and ▦) by using the boxes and menus in the Options bar. Marquee options appear only when you click a marquee tool.

Feather

Typing a Feather value softens your selection edge — Photoshop Elements partially selects pixels near the edge by building a transition between the selection and the surrounding pixels. Use a feathered selection to help you blend selections that you move, cut, or copy.

Mode

The Mode list enables you to define a marquee tool by a fixed size or aspect ratio.

Width and Height

You can also type an exact width and height for a fixed-size selection or a ratio for a fixed-aspect-ratio selection by entering values in the Width and Height boxes. These boxes are editable when you select a fixed-size or fixed-aspect-ratio marquee.

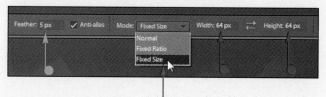

Select an Area with a Lasso

You can create oddly shaped selections with the lasso tools. You can then make changes to the selected area by using other Photoshop Elements commands. You can use three types of lasso tools: the regular Lasso, the Polygonal Lasso, and the Magnetic Lasso.

You can use the regular Lasso tool to create freehand selections. The Polygonal Lasso tool lets you easily create a selection composed of many straight lines. The Magnetic Lasso tool automatically applies a selection border to edges as you drag.

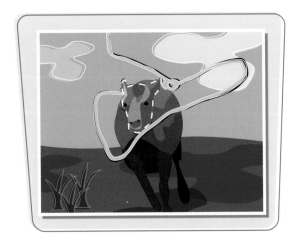

Select with the Regular Lasso

1 In the Editor, click the **Lasso** tool (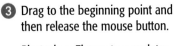).

Note: For more on opening the Editor, see Chapter 1.

2 Click and drag with your mouse pointer (🔲) to make a selection.

● To accurately trace a complicated edge, you can magnify that part of the image with the Zoom tool (🔍).

Note: See Chapter 5 for more on the Zoom tool.

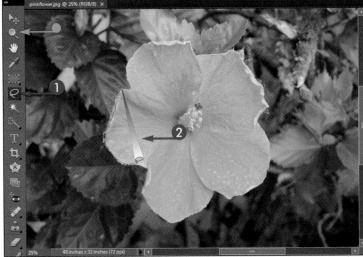

3 Drag to the beginning point and then release the mouse button.

Photoshop Elements completes the selection.

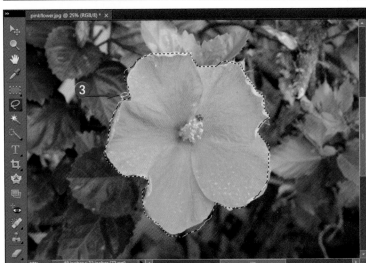

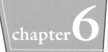
Select with the Polygonal Lasso

1 Right-click on the **Lasso** tool (⟋).

2 Click the **Polygonal Lasso** tool (▨).

3 Click multiple times along the border of the area you want to select.

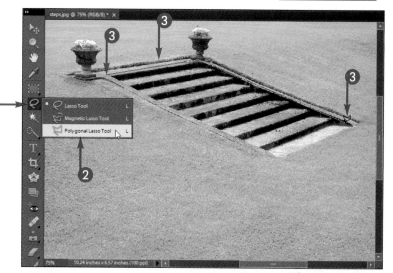

4 To complete the selection, click the starting point.

You can also double-click anywhere in the image. Photoshop Elements adds a final straight line that connects to the starting point.

Photoshop Elements completes the selection.

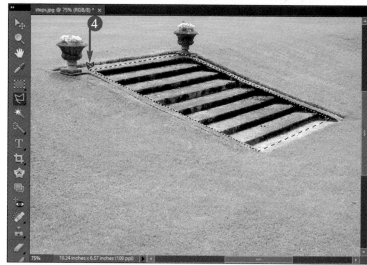

TIPS

How do I select all the pixels in my image?

For a single-layer image, you can use the Select All command to select everything in your image. Click **Select** and then click **All**. You can also press **Ctrl** + **A** on the keyboard. You can select all the pixels to perform an action on the entire image, such as copying the image. For multilayer images, Select All selects all the pixels in the currently selected layer.

What if my selection is not as precise as I want it to be?

You can deselect your selection by clicking **Select** and then **Deselect**. You can try to fix your selection; see the section "Add to or Subtract from a Selection." Or you can try switching to the Magnetic Lasso tool (▨); see the section "Select with the Magnetic Lasso."

continued 115

You can quickly and easily select elements of your image that have well-defined edges by using the Magnetic Lasso tool. The Magnetic Lasso works best when the element you are trying to select contrasts sharply with its background.

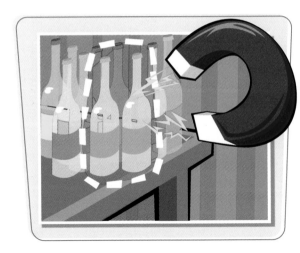

Select with the Magnetic Lasso

1 In the Editor, right-click on the **Lasso** tool (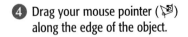).

Note: *For more on opening the Editor, see Chapter 1.*

2 Click the **Magnetic Lasso** tool ( ).

3 Click the edge of the object you want to select.

This creates a beginning anchor point, which is a fixed point on the lasso path.

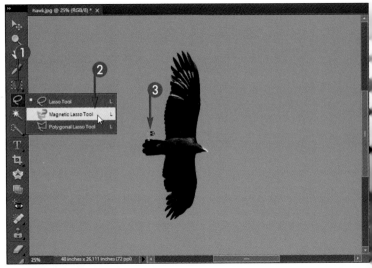

4 Drag your mouse pointer ( ) along the edge of the object.

The path snaps to the edge of the element as you drag.

To help guide the lasso, you can click to add anchor points as you go along the path.

You can press Del to remove the most recently added anchor point. This allows you to restructure a lasso path that is incorrect.

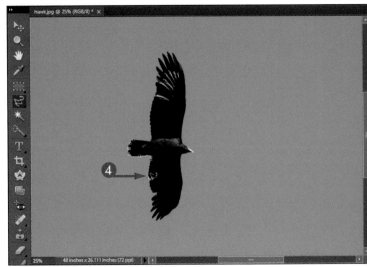

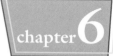

⑤ Click the beginning anchor point to finish your selection.

Alternatively, you can double-click anywhere in the image and Photoshop Elements completes the selection for you.

The path is complete, and the object is selected.

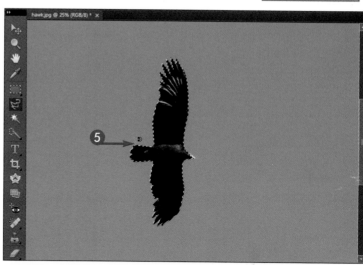

● This example shows that the Magnetic Lasso is less useful for selecting areas where you find little contrast between the image and its background.

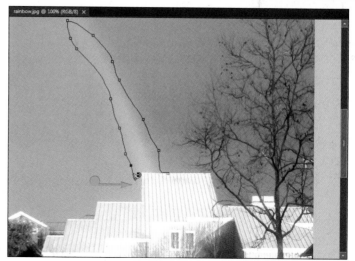

TIP

How can I adjust the precision of the Magnetic Lasso tool?
You can use the Options bar to adjust the Magnetic Lasso tool's precision:

Width

The number of nearby pixels the lasso considers when creating a selection.

Edge Contrast

How much contrast is required for the lasso to consider something an edge.

Frequency

How often anchor points appear.

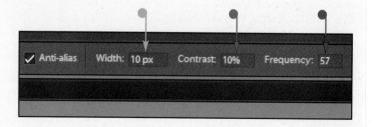

Select an Area with the Magic Wand

You can select groups of similarly colored pixels with the Magic Wand tool. You may find this useful if you want to remove an object from a background.

By specifying an appropriate tolerance value, you can control how similar a pixel needs to be for Photoshop Elements to select it.

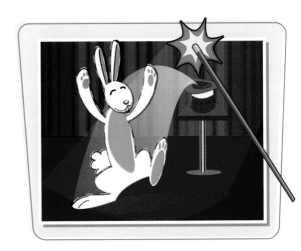

① In the Editor, click the **Magic Wand** tool (✴).

Note: For more on opening the Editor, see Chapter 1.

The mouse pointer (⬉) changes to a magic wand (✴).

② Type a number from 0 to 255 in the Tolerance field.

To select a narrow range of colors, type a small number; to select a wide range of colors, type a large number.

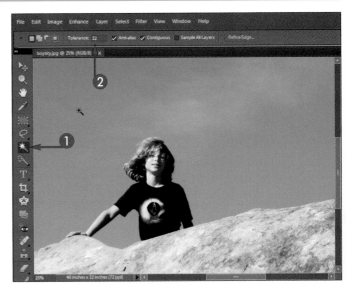

③ Click the area you want to select inside the image.

● Photoshop Elements selects the pixel you clicked plus any similarly colored pixels near it.

● To select all the similar pixels in the image, not just the contiguous pixels, deselect the **Contiguous** check box (✓ changes to ▇). See the Tip for more.

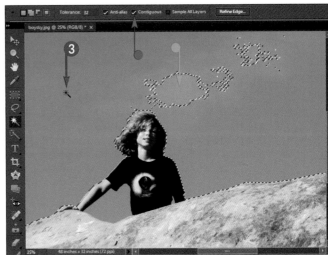

● This example shows a higher-tolerance value, resulting in a greater number of similarly colored pixels selected in the image.

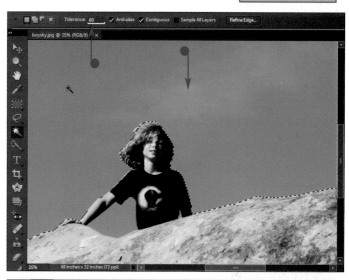

④ To add to your selection, press **Shift** and then click elsewhere in the image.

Photoshop Elements adds to your selection.

● You can also click one of three selection buttons in the Options bar to grow or decrease the selection.

Note: For more on adding to or subtracting from a selection, see Chapter 7.

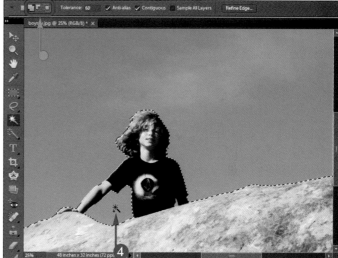

 TIP

How can I ensure that the Magic Wand tool selects all the instances of a color in an image?

You can deselect **Contiguous** (☑ changes to ■) on the Options bar so the Magic Wand tool selects similar colors, even when they are not contiguous with the pixel you click with the tool. This can be useful when objects intersect the solid-color areas of your image. You can also select **All Layers** (■ changes to ☑) to select similar colors in all layers in the image, not just in the currently selected layer.

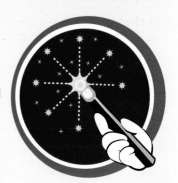

Select an Area with the Quick Selection Tool

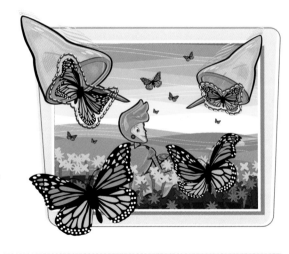

You can paint selections onto your images by using the Quick Selection tool. The tool automatically expands the area you paint over to include similar colors and textures. This tool offers a quick way to select objects that have solid colors and well-defined edges.

You can adjust the brush size of the tool to fine-tune your selections.

Select an Area with the Quick Selection Tool

① In the Editor, click the **Quick Selection** tool (■).

Note: For more on opening the Editor, see Chapter 1.

② Click here to open the Brush menu.

The Brush menu opens.

In the Brush menu, you can specify the tool's size and other characteristics. Decreasing the tool's hardness causes it to partially select pixels at the perimeter.

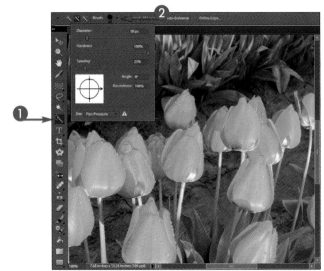

③ Click and drag inside the object you want to select.

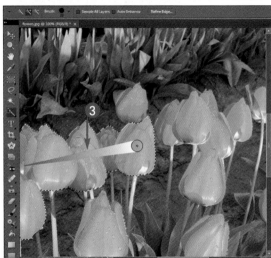

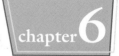

● Photoshop selects parts of the object based on its coloring and the contrast of its edges.

● After you make a selection, the Add to Selection button () becomes active.

④ Click and drag to select more of the object.

Note: *You can select an object and apply color and tonal adjustments at the same time with the Smart Brush. See Chapter 12 for more.*

● Photoshop adds to the selection.

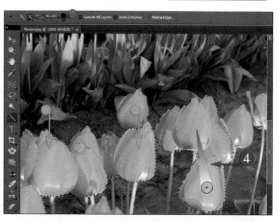

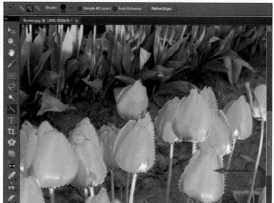

How can I adjust the selection made with the Quick Selection tool?

① In the Options bar, click **Refine Edge**. The Refine Edge dialog opens.

● You can increase **Smooth** to lessen the sharpness of any corners in your selection.

● You can increase **Feather** to make the edges of your selection partially transparent.

● You can use **Contract/Expand** to decrease or increase the selection slightly.

● You can click here to define your selection with a custom overlay color.

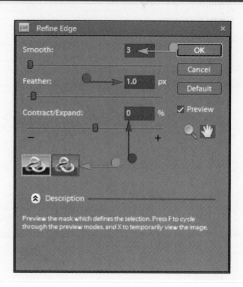

Select an Area with the Selection Brush

You can select oddly shaped areas in your image by painting with the Selection Brush. By customizing the size and hardness of the brush, you can accurately trace edges that are curved or not well-defined.

The Selection Brush differs from the Quick Selection tool in that it only selects the area you paint over and does not automatically select similar pixels.

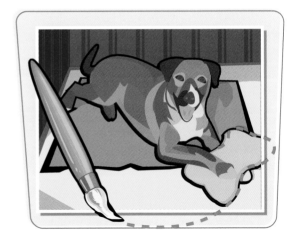

Select an Area with the Selection Brush

Select with the Selection Brush

1 Right-click on the **Quick Selection** tool (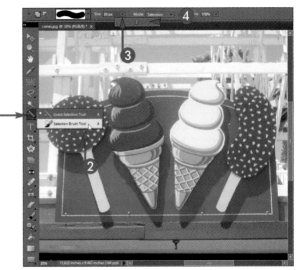).

2 In the Editor, click the **Selection Brush** tool ().

Note: For more on opening the Editor, see Chapter 1.

3 Click here.

A slider () appears.

4 Click and drag the slider to specify a size.

You can also type a size.

5 Type a hardness from 0% to 100%.

A smaller value produces a softer selection edge.

6 Click here and then click **Selection**.

7 Click and drag to paint a selection.

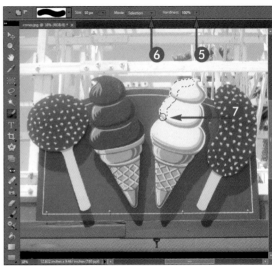

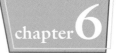

8 Click and drag multiple times to paint a selection over the area you want to select.

Photoshop Elements creates a selection.

You can change the brush settings as you paint to select different types of edges in your object.

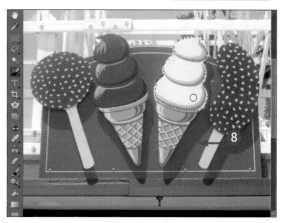

Deselect with the Selection Brush

1 Click the **Selection Brush** tool ().

2 Click the Subtract from Selection button (🔲).

3 Click and drag where you want to remove the selection area.

Photoshop Elements removes the selection.

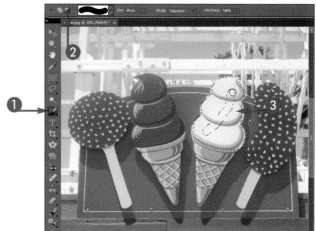

TIP

How do I paint a mask with the Selection Brush?

The Selection Brush's Mask option enables you to define the area that is not selected by using a partially transparent color. One advantage of using a mask is that it enables you to see the soft edges created by a soft selection brush.

1 Click the **Mode** drop-down arrow (▾) in the Options bar and then click **Mask**.

2 Click and drag to define the mask.

By default, the masked area appears as a see-through red color called a rubylith.

To turn a painted mask into a selection, click the **Mode** drop-down arrow (▾) in the Options bar and then click **Selection**.

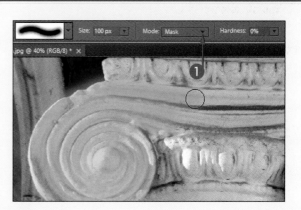

Save and Load a Selection

You can save a selected area in your image to reuse later. This can be useful if you anticipate future edits to the same part of your image. You can load the saved selection instead of having to reselect it.

See the previous sections in this chapter on choosing the appropriate tool for selecting areas in your image.

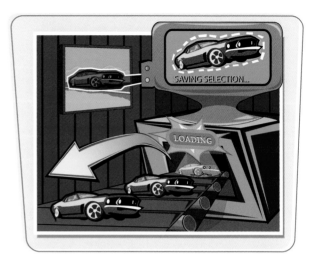

Save and Load a Selection

Save a Selection

1 In the Editor, make a selection by using one of the selection tools.

Note: For more on opening the Editor, see Chapter 1.

2 Click **Select**.

3 Click **Save Selection**.

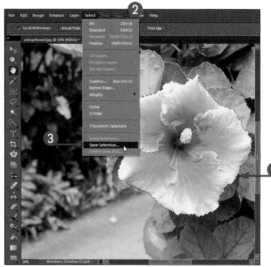

The Save Selection dialog opens.

4 Make sure New is chosen in the Selection field.

New is the default setting.

5 Type a name for the selection.

6 Click **OK**.

Photoshop Elements saves the selection.

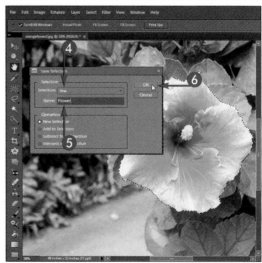

Load a Selection

① Click **Select**.

② Click **Load Selection**.

Note: See the section "Save a Selection" to learn how to save your selection.

The Load Selection dialog opens.

③ Click here and then choose the saved selection you want to load.

④ Click **OK**.

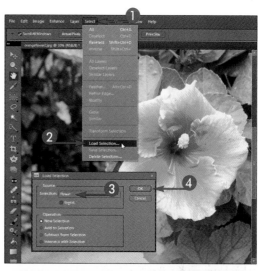

● The selection appears in the image.

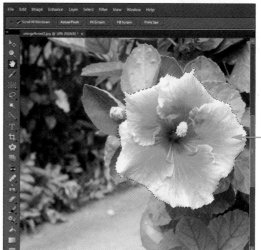

How can I modify a saved selection?

You can modify a saved selection by making a new selection in your image window, completing steps **2** and **3** of "Save a Selection" to open the Save Selection dialog and then choosing the selection you want to modify from the Selection menu. The Operation radio buttons enable you to replace, add to, subtract from, or intersect with your selection. Choosing **Intersect with Selection** (●) keeps any area where the new selection and the saved selection overlap. Click **OK** to modify your saved selection.

Invert a Selection

You can invert a selection to deselect what is currently selected and select everything else. This is useful when you want to select the background around an object.

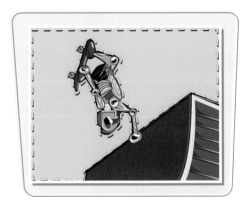

Invert a Selection

① In the Editor, make a selection by using one of the selection tools.

Note: For more on the various selection tools, see the previous sections in this chapter. For more on opening the Editor, see Chapter 1.

② Click **Select**.

③ Click **Inverse**.

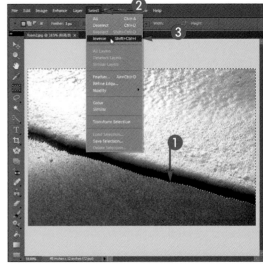

● Photoshop Elements inverts the selection.

Note: You can also press **Shift** + **Ctrl** + **I** *to invert a selection.*

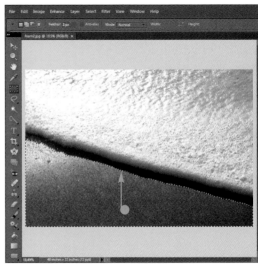

Deselect a Selection

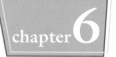
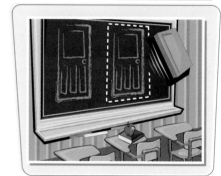

You can deselect a selection when you are done manipulating what is inside it or if you make a mistake and want to try selecting again.

Deselect a Selection

1 In the Editor, make a selection by using one of the selection tools.

Note: *For more on the various selection tools, see the previous sections in this chapter. For more on opening the Editor, see Chapter 1.*

In this example, a small penguin is selected.

2 Click **Select**.

3 Click **Deselect**.

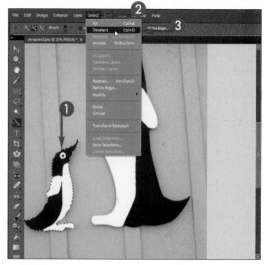

Photoshop Elements deselects the selection.

Note: *You can also press* Ctrl + D *to deselect a selection.*

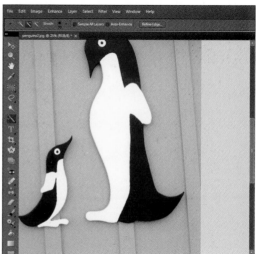

CHAPTER
7

Manipulating Selections

Making a selection in Photoshop Elements isolates a specific area of your image. This chapter shows you how to move, stretch, erase, and manipulate your selection in a variety of ways.

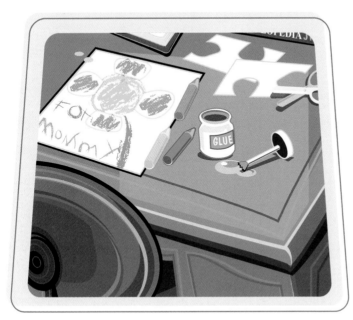

Add to or Subtract from a Selection

You can add to or subtract from your selection by using various selection tool options.

See Chapter 6 to learn how to choose the appropriate tool for selecting elements in your photo.

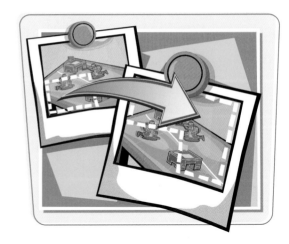

Add to or Subtract from a Selection

Add to Your Selection

1 In the Editor, make a selection by using one of the selection tools.

Note: For more on opening the Editor, see Chapter 1.

2 Click a selection tool.

This example uses the Magnetic Lasso tool (⬛).

3 Click the **Add to Selection** button (⬛).

4 Select the area you want to add.

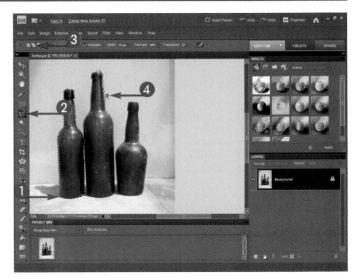

5 Complete the selection. In this example, the Magnetic Lasso is used, and the starting point is clicked to complete the selection.

Photoshop Elements adds to the selection.

You can enlarge the selection further by repeating steps **2** to **5**.

You can also add to a selection by pressing Shift as you select an area.

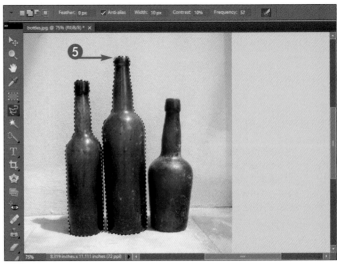

Subtract from Your Selection

① Make a selection by using one of the selection tools.

② Click a selection tool.

This example uses the Rectangular Marquee tool (▦).

③ Click the **Subtract from Selection** button (▣).

④ Select the area you want to subtract.

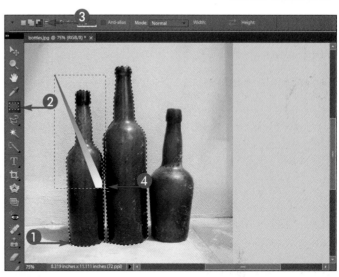

● Photoshop Elements deselects, or subtracts, the selected area.

You can subtract other parts of the selection by repeating steps **2** to **4**.

You can also subtract from a selection by pressing Alt as you select an area.

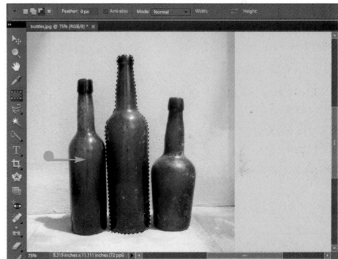

How do I add to or subtract from a selection by using the Quick Selection tool?

The Quick Selection tool (▨) features buttons for adding to or subtracting from a selection. In the Options bar, you can click the **Add to Quick Selection** button (▨) to add to a selection and the **Subtract from Quick Selection** button (▨) to subtract from a selection.

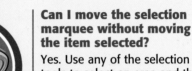

Can I move the selection marquee without moving the item selected?

Yes. Use any of the selection tools to select an area and then press an arrow key — ↑, ↓, ←, → — to move the selection in 1-pixel increments. Press and hold Shift while pressing an arrow key to move the selection in 10-pixel increments. This technique is handy when you need to slightly nudge the marquee across your image.

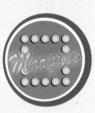

Move a Selection

You can rearrange elements of your image by moving selections with the Move tool. You can move elements of your image either in the default Background layer or in other layers you create for your image.

If you move elements in the Background layer, Photoshop Elements fills the original location with the current background color. If you move elements in another layer, Photoshop Elements makes the original location transparent, revealing any underlying layers. See Chapter 8 for more on layers.

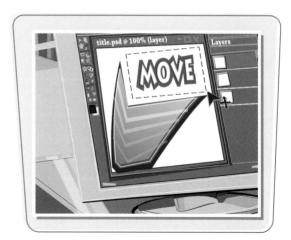

Move a Selection

Move a Selection in the Background

1 In the Editor, display the Layers panel.

Note: For more on opening the Editor or opening panels, see Chapter 1.

2 Click the Background layer.

A newly imported image has only a Background layer.

Note: See Chapter 8 for more on using layers.

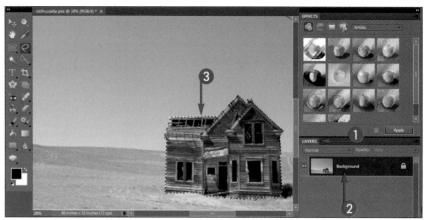

3 Make a selection with a selection tool.

Note: For more on selecting elements, see Chapter 6.

4 Click the **Move** tool (⊕).

5 Click inside the selection and then drag.

● Photoshop Elements fills the original location of the selection with the current background color.

● In this example, white is the background color.

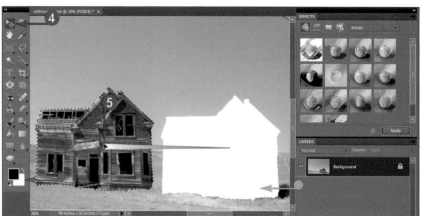

Move a Selection in a Layer

1 Click a layer in the Layers panel.

Note: See Chapter 8 for more on layers.

2 Make a selection with a selection tool.

Note: See Chapter 6 for more on making selections.

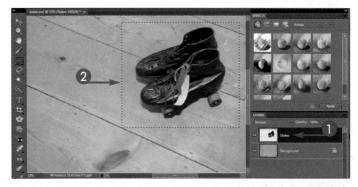

3 Click the **Move** tool ().

4 Click inside the selection and then drag.

Photoshop Elements moves the selection and fills the original location of the selection with transparent pixels.

Note: Unlike the Background — the opaque default layer in Photoshop Elements — other layers can include transparent pixels.

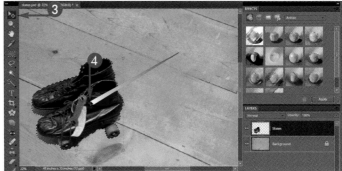

TIPS

How do I move a selection in a straight line?

Press and hold Shift while you drag with the **Move** tool (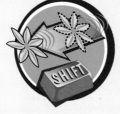). Doing so constrains the movement of your selection horizontally, vertically, or diagonally, depending on the direction you drag.

How do I move several layers at a time?

You can link the layers you want to move, select one of the linked layers, and then move them all with the Move tool. For more, see Chapter 8. You can also Ctrl + click to select multiple layers in the Layers panel. Using the Move tool moves the selected layers.

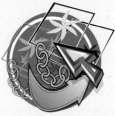

Copy and Paste a Selection

You can copy a selection and make a duplicate of it somewhere else in the image. You may use this technique to retouch an element in your photo by placing good content over bad.

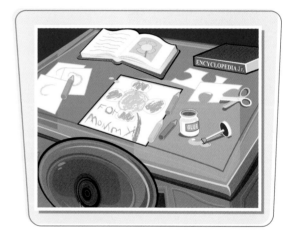

1. In the Editor, make a selection with a selection tool.

Note: *For more on opening the Editor, see Chapter 1. See Chapter 6 for more on using selection tools.*

2. Click the **Move** tool ().

● You can also click **Copy** and **Paste** in the Edit menu to copy and paste selections.

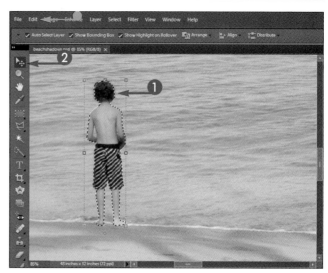

3. Press Alt while you click and drag the selection.

4. Release the mouse button to drop the selection into place.

   Photoshop Elements creates a duplicate of the selection and then places it in the new location.

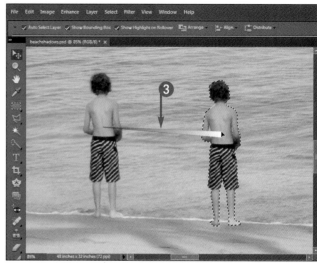

Delete a Selection

You can delete a selection to remove unwanted elements from an image.

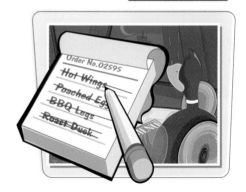

Delete a Selection

1 In the Editor, make a selection with a selection tool.

Note: *For more on opening the Editor, see Chapter 1. See Chapter 6 for more on using selection tools.*

2 Press **Del**.

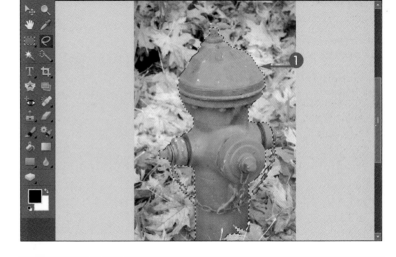

● Photoshop Elements deletes the selection.

● If you are working in the Background layer, the original location fills with the background color — in this example, it is white.

If you are working in a layer other than the Background layer, deleting a selection turns the selected pixels transparent and layers below it show through.

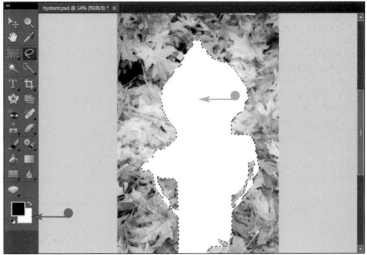

135

Rotate a Selection

You can rotate a selection to tilt an element or turn it upside down in your image. You may rotate an element to create a better composition or to correct the appearance of an element.

When you rotate a selection in the Background layer, Photoshop Elements replaces the exposed areas that the rotation creates with the current background color. If you rotate a selection in another layer, the underlying layers appear in the exposed areas. See Chapter 8 for more on layers.

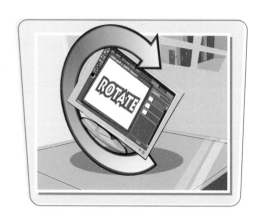

Rotate a Selection

1. In the Editor, make a selection with a selection tool.

   In this example, content in a layer is selected.

Note: See Chapter 6 for more on using selection tools. See Chapter 8 for more on layers.

2. Click **Image**.

3. Click **Rotate**.

4. Click **Free Rotate Selection**.

   You can click other commands under the Rotate menu to rotate your selection in a more constrained way.

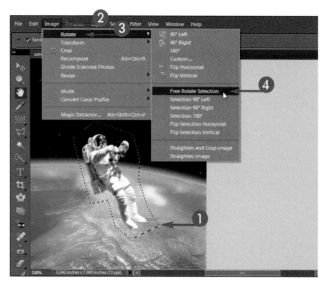

5. Click and drag outside the selection.

● You can precisely rotate your selection by typing a value in the degrees field on the Options bar.

   The selection rotates.

6. Click ✅ or press Enter to commit the rotation.

● You can click ⛔ or press Esc to cancel.

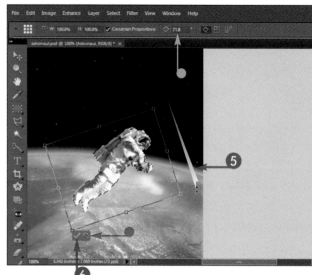

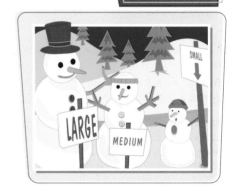

You can scale a selection to make it larger or smaller. Scaling enables you to adjust or emphasize parts of your image.

When you scale a selection in the Background layer, Photoshop Elements replaces the exposed areas, which scaling to a smaller size creates, with the current background color. If you scale a selection in another layer, the underlying layers appear in the exposed areas. See Chapter 8 for more on layers.

Scale a Selection

1 In the Editor, make a selection with a selection tool.

In this example, content in a layer is selected.

Note: See Chapter 6 for more on using selection tools. See Chapter 8 for more on layers.

2 Click **Image**.

3 Click **Resize**.

4 Click **Scale**.

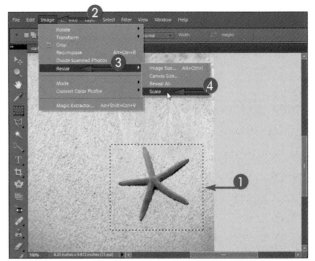

A box with handles on the sides and corners surrounds the selection.

5 Click and drag a handle to scale the selection.

Drag a corner handle to scale both the horizontal and vertical axes.

● You can precisely scale your selection by typing percentage values in the W and H fields on the Options bar.

● With Constrain Proportions selected, the height and width change proportionally.

6 Click ☑ or press Enter to apply the scale effect.

● You can click ☒ or press Esc to cancel.

Photoshop Elements scales the selection.

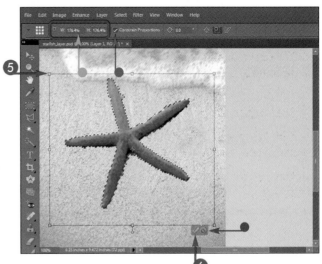

Skew or Distort a Selection

You can transform a selection by using the Skew or Distort commands. This enables you to stretch elements in your image into interesting shapes.

When you skew or distort a selection in the Background layer, Photoshop Elements replaces the exposed areas, which the skewing or distorting creates, with the current background color. If you skew or distort a selection in another layer, the underlying layers appear in the exposed areas. See Chapter 8 for more on layers.

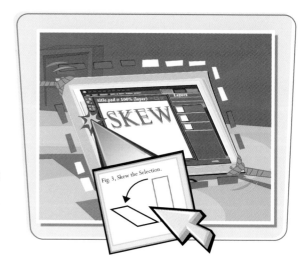

Fig. 3, Skew the Selection.

Skew or Distort a Selection

Skew a Selection

1 In the Editor, make a selection with a selection tool.

Note: For more on opening the Editor, see Chapter 1. See Chapter 6 for more on using selection tools.

2 Click **Image**.

3 Click **Transform**.

4 Click **Skew**.

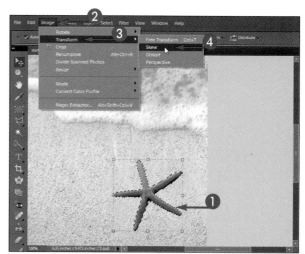

A rectangular box with handles on the sides and corners surrounds the selection.

5 Click and drag a handle.

Photoshop Elements skews the selection.

Because the Skew command works along a single axis, you can drag either horizontally or vertically.

Note: You can precisely skew your selection by typing percentage values in the W and H fields on the Options bar.

6 Click ✔ or press Enter to apply the skewing.

● You can click ⊘ or press Esc to cancel.

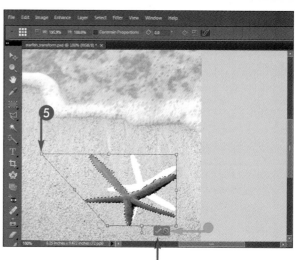

Distort a Selection

1 Make a selection with a selection tool.

Note: See Chapter 6 for more on using selection tools.

2 Click **Image**.

3 Click **Transform**.

4 Click **Distort**.

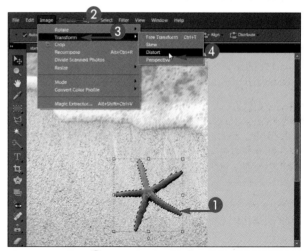

A rectangular box with handles on the sides and corners surrounds the selection.

5 Click and drag a handle.

Photoshop Elements distorts the selection.

The Distort command works independently of the selection's axes; you can drag a handle both vertically and horizontally.

Note: You can precisely distort your selection by typing percentage values in the W and H fields on the Options bar.

6 Click ✔ or press Enter to apply the distortion.

● You can click ⊘ or press Esc to cancel.

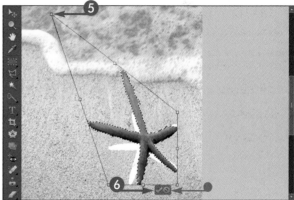

TIP

Can I perform several transforming effects at once on a selection?

1 Click **Image**.

2 Click **Transform**.

3 Click **Free Transform**.

You can also press Ctrl + T to apply the Free Transform command.

4 Click and drag a handle on the box that surrounds the selection to transform it.

● You can switch between transformation operations by clicking these buttons.

5 Click ✔ or press Enter to apply the effect.

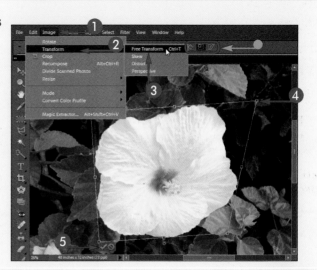

Feather the Border of a Selection

You can feather a selection's border to create soft edges. Feathering enables you to control the sharpness of the edges in a selection. You can use this technique with other layers to create a blending effect between the selected area and any underlying layers.

To create a soft edge around an object, you must first select the object, feather the selection border, and then delete the part of the image that surrounds your selection.

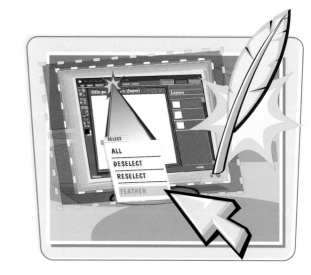

Feather the Border of a Selection

Feather a Selection

1 In the Editor, make a selection with a selection tool.

Note: *For more on opening the Editor, see Chapter 1. See Chapter 6 for more on using selection tools.*

2 Click **Select**.

3 Click **Feather**.

You can also press Alt + Ctrl + D to apply the Feather command.

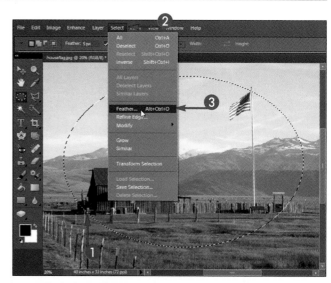

The Feather Selection dialog box opens.

4 Type a pixel value between 0.2 and 250 to determine the softness of the edge.

5 Click **OK**.

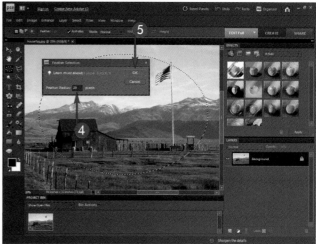

Delete the Surrounding Background

① Click **Select**.

② Click **Inverse**.

You can also press Shift + Ctrl + I to apply the Inverse command.

The selection inverts but remains feathered.

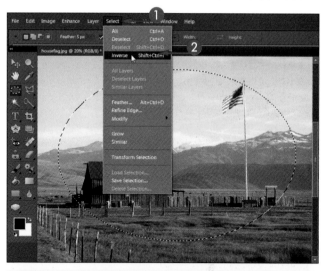

③ Press Del.

● If you are working with the Background layer, the deleted area is filled with the current background color.

If you are working with a layer other than the Background layer, the deleted area becomes transparent and the layers below show through.

You can now see the effect of the feathering.

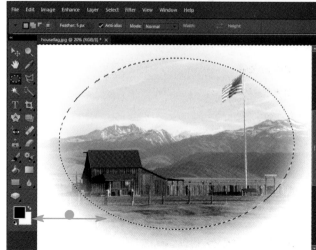

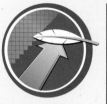

TIPS

How do I feather my selection into a colored background?

You can add a solid-color fill layer behind your photo and then blend the feathered selection into the new layer. The layer containing the selection appears on top of the solid-color fill layer, and the feathering technique creates a softened blend between the two layers. For more on creating a fill layer, see Chapter 8.

What happens if I feather a selection and then apply a command to it?

Photoshop Elements applies the command only partially to pixels near the edge of the selection. For example, if you are removing color from a selection by using the Hue/Saturation command, color at the feathered edge of the selection is only partially removed. For more on the Hue/Saturation command, see Chapter 10.

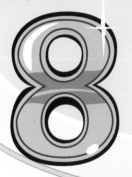
Layer Basics

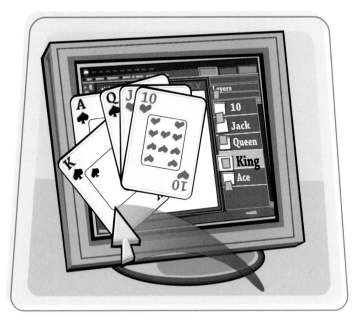

You can separate the elements in your image so you can move and transform them independently of one another. You can accomplish this by placing them in different layers.

What Are Layers?

A Photoshop Elements image can consist of multiple layers, with each layer containing different objects in the image.

When you open a digital camera photo or a newly scanned image in Photoshop Elements, it exists as a single layer known as the Background layer. You can add new layers on top of the Background layer as you work.

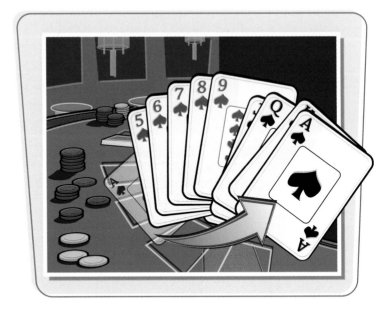

Layer Independence

Layered Photoshop Elements files act like several images combined into one. Each layer of an image has its own set of pixels that you can move and transform independently of the pixels in other layers.

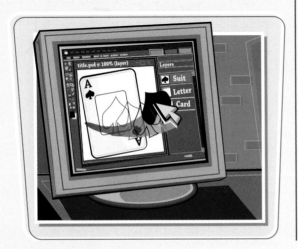

Apply Commands to Layers

Most Photoshop commands affect only the layer that you select. For example, if you click and drag by using the Move tool ( ), the selected layer moves, but the other layers stay in place. If you apply a color adjustment, only colors in the selected layer change.

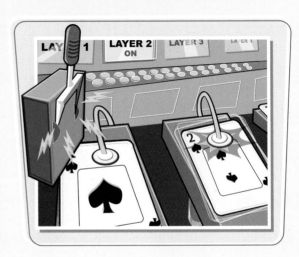

Manipulate Layers

You can combine, duplicate, and hide layers in an image and also shuffle their order. You can also link particular layers so they move in unison or you can blend content from different layers in creative ways. You manage all this in the Layers panel.

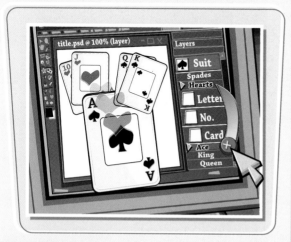

Transparency

Layers can have transparent areas, where the elements in the layers below can show through. When you perform a cut or erase command on a layer, the affected pixels become transparent. You can also make a layer partially transparent by decreasing its opacity.

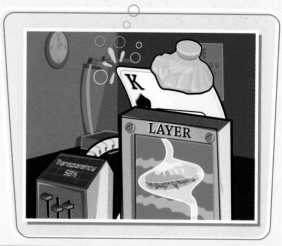

Adjustment Layers

Adjustment layers are special layers that contain information about color or tonal adjustments. An adjustment layer affects the pixels in all the layers below it. You can increase or decrease an adjustment layer's intensity to get precisely the effect you want.

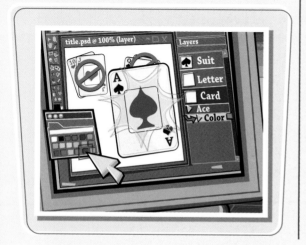

Save Layered Files

You can save multilayered images only in the Photoshop, PDF, and TIFF file formats. To save a layered image in another file format — for example, PICT, BMP, GIF, or JPEG — you must combine the image's layers into a single layer, a process known as flattening. For more on saving files, see Chapter 17.

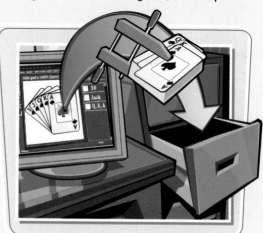

Create and Add to a Layer

To keep elements in your image independent of one another, you can create separate layers and add objects to them.

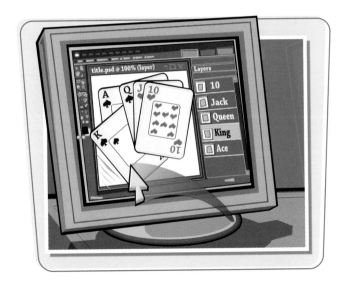

Create a Layer

① In the Editor, open the Layers panel.

Note: For more on opening the Editor or panels, see Chapter 1.

② Click the layer above which you want to add the new layer.

③ In the Layers panel, click the **Create a New Layer** icon (🔳).

Alternatively, you can click **Layer**, **New**, and then **Layer**.

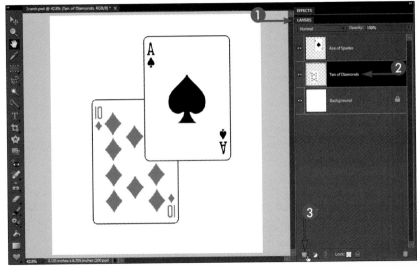

● Photoshop creates a new, transparent layer.

Note: To change the name of a layer, see the section "Rename a Layer."

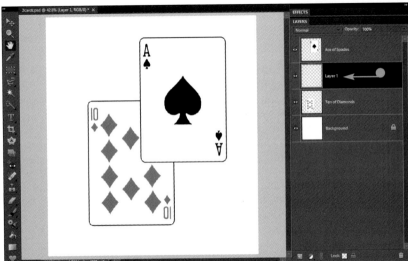

Copy and Paste Into a Layer

Note: This example shows how to add content to the new layer by copying and pasting from another image file.

1 Open another image.

2 Using a selection tool, select the content you want to copy into the other image.

Note: See Chapter 1 for more on opening an image. See Chapter 6 for more on the selection tools.

3 Click **Edit**.

4 Click **Copy**.

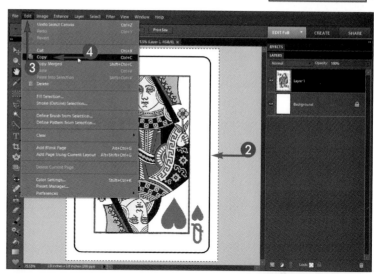

5 Click the tab for the image window where you created the new layer.

Note: See Chapter 1 for more on using tabs to select open images.

6 Click the new layer in the Layers panel.

7 Click **Edit**.

8 Click **Paste**.

● The selected content from the other image appears in the new layer.

Note: You can also click and drag selections between image windows by using the Move tool to add content to a new layer. See Chapter 5 to manage image windows, and see Chapter 7 for more on the Move tool.

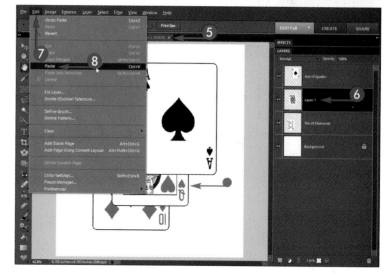

 TIPS

What is the Background layer?

The Background layer is the default bottom layer. It appears when you create a new image that has a nontransparent background color or when you import an image from a scanner or digital camera. You can create new layers on top of a Background layer but not below it. Unlike other layers, a Background layer cannot contain transparent pixels.

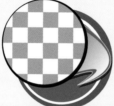

How do I turn the Background layer into a regular layer?

If you have the Background layer selected, you can click **Layer**, **New**, and then **Background from Layer** to turn it into a regular layer. The converted layer can be edited just like any other layer.

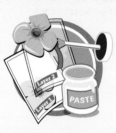

Hide a Layer

You can hide a layer to temporarily remove elements in that layer from view.

Hidden layers do not appear when you print or when you use the Save for Web command.

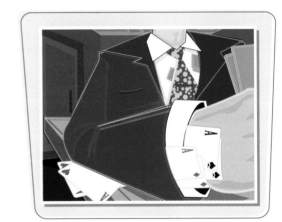

Hide a Layer

1 In the Editor, open the Layers panel.

Note: For more on opening the Editor or panels, see Chapter 1.

2 Click a layer.

3 Click the **Eye** icon ( ) for the layer.

The icon disappears.

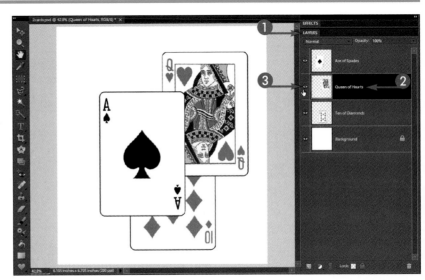

Photoshop hides the layer.

To show one layer and hide all the others, you can press Alt and then click the **Eye** icon ( ) for the layer you want to show.

Note: You can also delete a layer. See the section "Delete a Layer" for more.

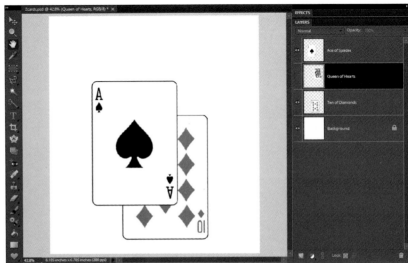

Move a Layer

You can use the Move tool to reposition the elements in one layer without moving those in others.

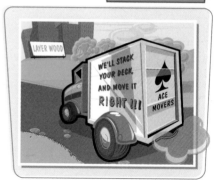

Move a Layer

① In the Editor, open the Layers panel.

Note: For more on opening the Editor or panels, see Chapter 1.

② Click a layer.

③ Click the **Move** tool ( ).

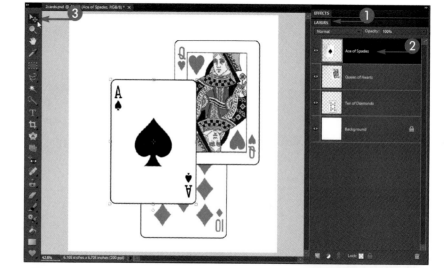

④ Click and drag inside the window.

Content in the selected layer moves.

Content in the other layers does not move.

Note: To move several layers at the same time, see the section "Link Layers."

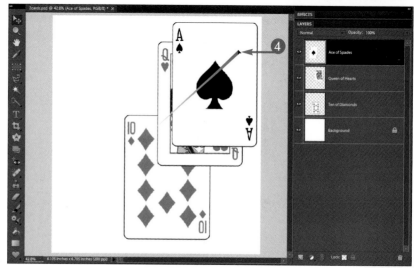

Duplicate a Layer

By duplicating a layer, you can manipulate elements in an image while keeping a copy of their original state.

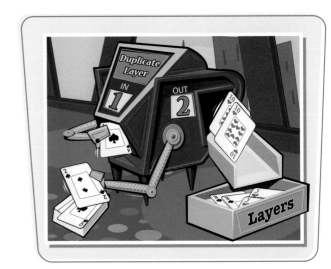

① In the Editor, open the Layers panel.

Note: *For more on opening the Editor or panels, see Chapter 1.*

② Click a layer.

③ Click and drag the layer to the **Create a New Layer** icon (▦).

Alternatively, you can click **Layer** and then **Duplicate Layer**; a dialog box opens, asking you to name the layer you want to duplicate.

You can also press Ctrl + J to duplicate a selected layer in the Layers panel.

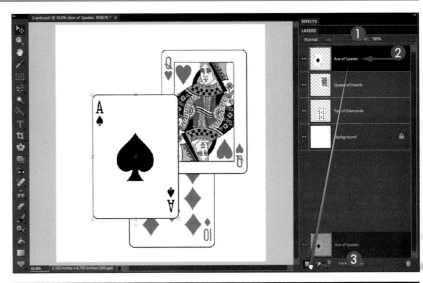

● Photoshop Elements duplicates the selected layer.

Note: *To rename the duplicate layer, see the section "Rename a Layer."*

● You can test that Photoshop Elements has duplicated the layer by selecting the new layer, clicking the **Move** tool (▸), and then clicking and dragging the layer.

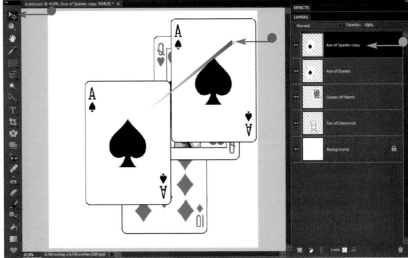

Delete a Layer

You can delete a layer when you no longer have a use for its contents.

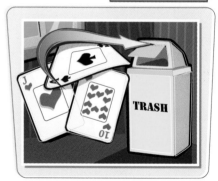

Delete a Layer

1 In the Editor, open the Layers panel.

Note: For more on opening the Editor or panels, see Chapter 1.

2 Click a layer.

3 Click and drag the layer to the **Trash** icon ( ).

Alternatively, you can click **Layer** and then **Delete Layer** or you can select a layer and then click the **Trash** icon ( ). In both cases, a confirmation dialog box opens.

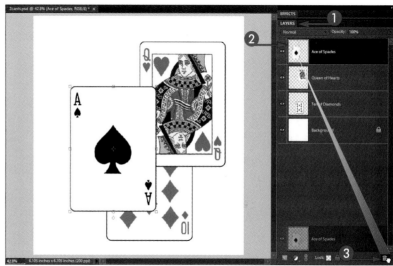

Photoshop Elements deletes the selected layer, and the content in the layer disappears from the image window.

Note: You can also hide a layer. See the section "Hide a Layer" for more.

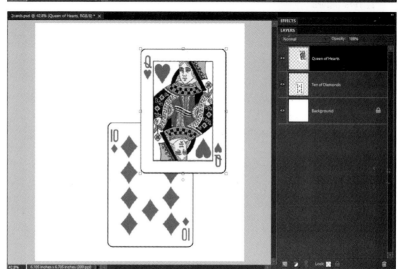

Reorder Layers

You can change the order of layers to move elements forward or backward in your image.

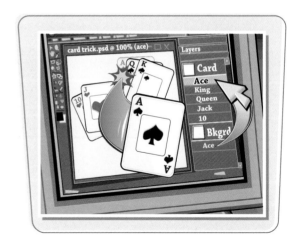

Reorder Layers

Using the Layers Panel

① In the Editor, open the Layers panel.

Note: For more on opening the Editor or panels, see Chapter 1.

② Click a layer.

③ Click and drag the layer to change its arrangement in the stack.

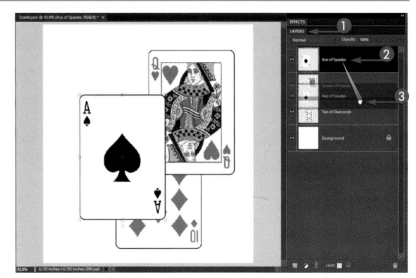

● The layer assumes its new position in the stack.

● In this example, the Ace of Spades layer moves down in the stack.

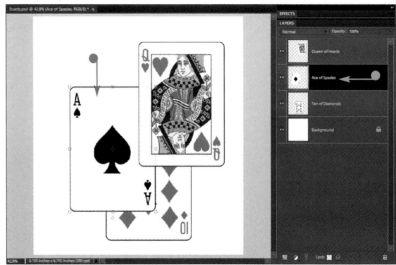

Using the Arrange Commands

1. Click a layer.

2. Click **Layer**.

3. Click **Arrange**.

4. Click the command for how you want to move the layer.

   You can choose Bring to Front, Bring Forward, Send Backward, Send to Back, or Reverse.

Note: *Reverse is only available if more than one layer is selected. You can* Ctrl *+ click in the Layers panel to select multiple layers.*

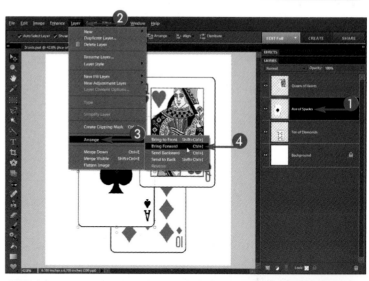

In this example, Bring Forward is chosen.

● The layer assumes its new position in the stack.

● In this example, the Ace of Spades layer moves to the top of the stack.

Note: *You cannot move a layer in back of the default Background layer.*

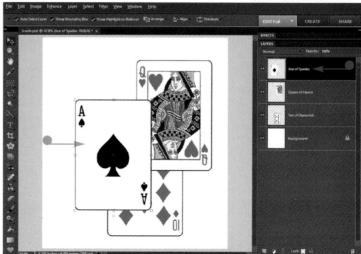

Are there shortcuts for changing the order of layers?

You can shift layers forward and backward in the stack by pressing the following shortcut keys:

Move ...	Shortcut
... forward one step	Ctrl +]
... backward one step	Ctrl + [
... to the very front	Shift + Ctrl +]
... to the very back	Shift + Ctrl + [

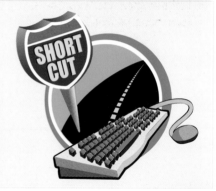

Change the Opacity of a Layer

You can adjust the opacity of a layer to let elements in the layers below show through. Opacity is the opposite of transparency — decreasing the opacity of a layer increases its transparency.

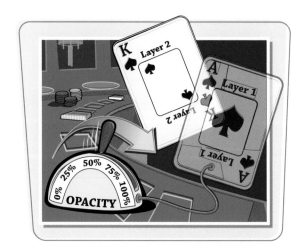

Change the Opacity of a Layer

1 In the Editor, open the Layers panel.

Note: *For more on opening the Editor or panels, see Chapter 1.*

2 Click the layer whose opacity you want to change.

Note: *You cannot change the opacity of the Background layer.*

● The default opacity is 100%, which is completely opaque.

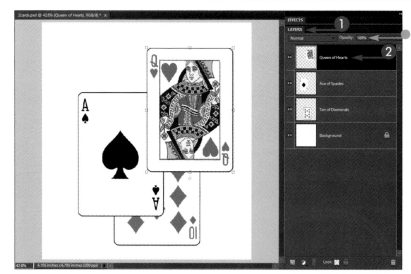

3 Type a new value in the Opacity field.

● You can also click here and then drag the selection slider (■).

A layer's opacity can range from 0% to 100%.

● The layer changes in opacity.

Changing the opacity of a layer also affects any layer styles applied to the layer. For more on layer styles, see Chapter 15.

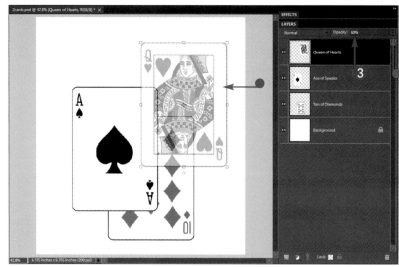

Link Layers

Linking causes different layers to move in unison when you move them with the Move tool. You may find linking useful when you want to keep elements of an image aligned with one another but do not want to merge their layers. Keeping layers unmerged lets you apply effects to each layer independently.

See the section "Merge Layers" for more on merging. For more on moving a layer, see the section "Move a Layer."

Link Layers

1. In the Editor, open the Layers panel.

Note: For more on opening the Editor or panels, see Chapter 1.

2. Click one of the layers you want to link.

3. Press **Ctrl** and then click one or more other layers that you want to link.

4. Click the **Link Layers** tool (⬚) in the Layers panel.

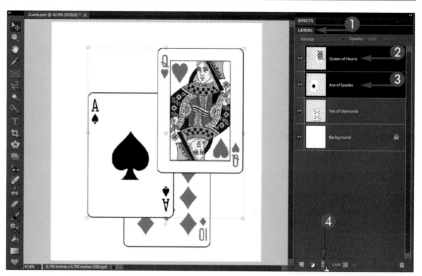

● A linking icon (⬚) appears next to each linked layer.

● To verify that Photoshop Elements has linked the layers, select one of the layers, click the **Move** tool (⬚), and then click and drag the layer.

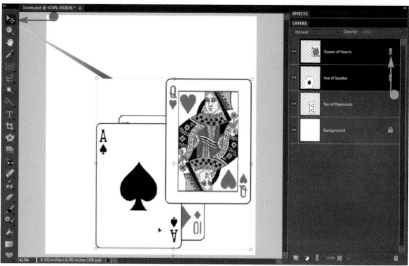

Merge Layers

Merging layers lets you permanently combine information from two or more separate layers. After merging layers, you can no longer move them independently of one another.

For more on moving a layer, see the section "Move a Layer."

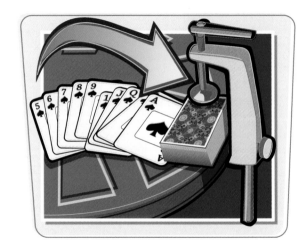

Merge Layers

1 In the Editor, open the Layers panel.

Note: For more on opening the Editor or panels, see Chapter 1.

2 Place the two layers you want to merge next to each other.

Note: See the section "Reorder Layers" to learn how to change the stacking order.

3 Click the topmost of the two layers.

4 Click **Layer**.

5 Click **Merge Down**.

You can merge all the layers together by clicking **Flatten Image** or just the visible layers by clicking **Merge Visible**.

You can also Ctrl + click to select multiple layers in the Layers panel and then click **Merge Selected** to merge them.

● The two layers merge.

Photoshop Elements keeps the name of the lower layer.

In this example, the Ace of Spades layer has merged with the Queen of Hearts layer.

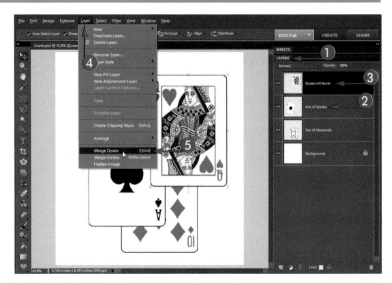

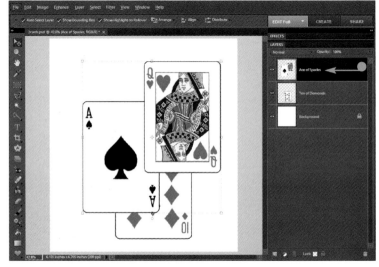

Rename a Layer

You can rename a layer to give it a name that describes its content.

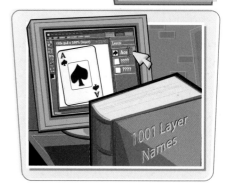

Rename a Layer

1 In the Editor, open the Layers panel.

Note: For more on opening the Editor or panels, see Chapter 1.

2 Click a layer.

3 Click **Layer**.

4 Click **Rename Layer**.

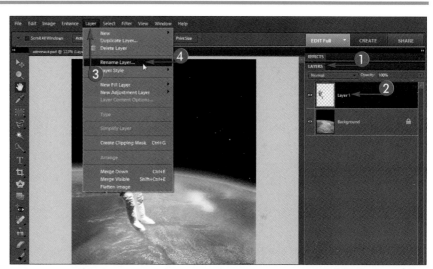

The Layer Properties dialog box opens.

5 Type a new name for the layer.

6 Click **OK**.

● The name of the layer changes in the Layers panel.

You can also double-click the name of the layer in the Layers panel to edit the name.

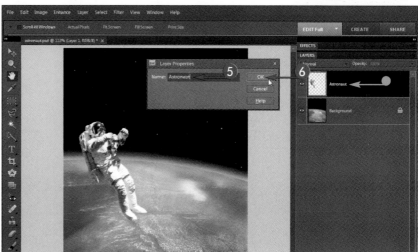

Create a Fill Layer

You can create a solid fill layer to place an opaque layer of color throughout your image. You can use fill layers behind layers containing objects to create all kinds of color effects in your photos.

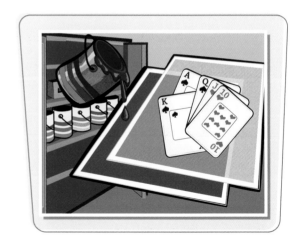

Create a Fill Layer

1. In the Editor, open the Layers panel.

Note: *For more on opening the Editor or panels, see Chapter 1.*

2. Click the layer you want to appear below the solid color layer.

3. Click **Layer**.

4. Click **New Fill Layer**.

5. Click **Solid Color**.

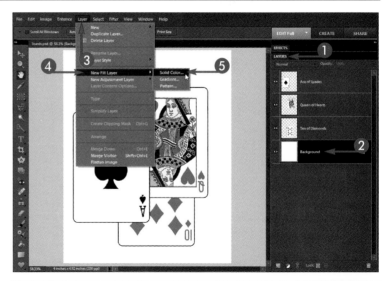

The New Layer dialog box opens.

6. Type a name for the layer or use the default name.

● You can specify a type of blend or opacity setting for the layer.

Note: *See the sections "Blend Layers" or "Change the Opacity of a Layer" for more.*

7. Click **OK**.

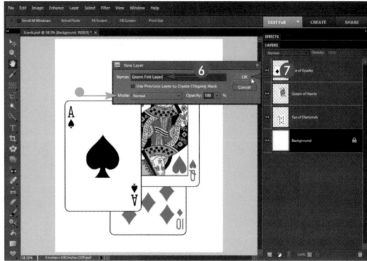

The Color Picker dialog box opens.

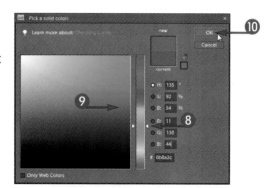

8 To change the range of colors that appears in the window, click and drag the slider ( ).

9 To select a fill color, click in the color window.

10 Click **OK**.

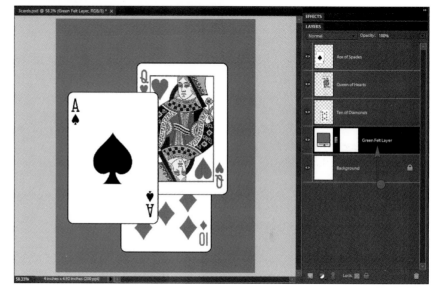

● Photoshop Elements creates a new layer filled with a solid color.

In this example, a solid green layer appears below the card layers.

How do I add solid color to just part of a layer?

To add color to a specific part of a layer, make a selection with a selection tool before creating the solid fill layer and then apply a color fill as outlined in the previous steps. Photoshop Elements adds color only inside the selection.

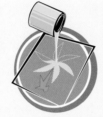

What other types of fill layers can I add?

In the New Fill Layer menu, you can create gradient fill layers, which apply bands of colors rather than a solid fill. Or you can create a pattern fill layer, which applies a repeating pattern as a fill instead of a solid color. You can select from a variety of preset gradient effects and patterns.

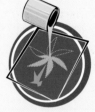

Create an Adjustment Layer

Adjustment layers let you store color and tonal changes in a layer instead of having them permanently applied to your image. The information in an adjustment layer is applied to the pixels in the layers below it.

You can use adjustment layers to test an editing technique without applying it to the original layer. Adjustment layers are especially handy for experimenting with colors, tones, and brightness settings.

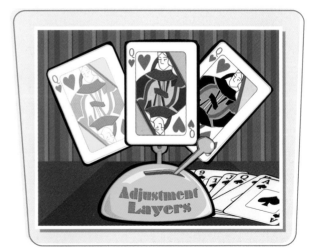

Create an Adjustment Layer

① In the Editor, open the Layers panel.

Note: *For more on opening the Editor or panels, see Chapter 1.*

② Click the layer you want to appear below the adjustment layer.

③ Click **Layer**.

④ Click **New Adjustment Layer**.

⑤ Click an adjustment command.

The New Layer dialog box opens.

⑥ Type a name for the adjustment layer or use the default name.

● You can specify a type of blend or opacity setting for the layer.

Note: *See the sections "Blend Layers" or "Change the Opacity of a Layer" for more.*

⑦ Click **OK**.

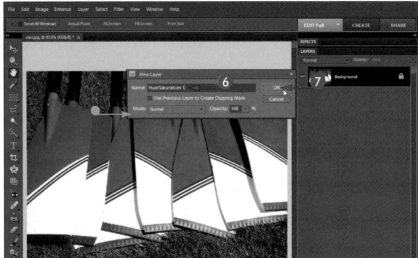

● Photoshop Elements adds an adjustment layer to the image.

The panel for the adjustment command appears.

Note: *Depending on the type of adjustment layer you create, different settings appear.*

In this example, an adjustment layer is created that changes the hue and saturation.

8 Click and drag the sliders (▇) or type values to adjust the settings.

You can see the adjustments take effect in the workspace.

● Photoshop Elements applies the effect to the layers that are below the adjustment layer.

You can double-click the adjustment layer to make changes to the settings.

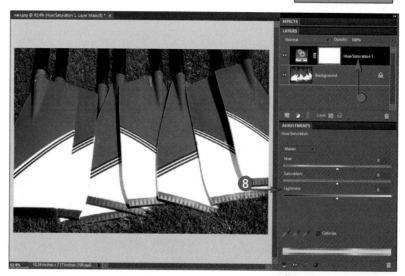

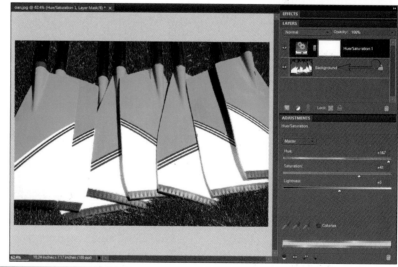

How do I apply an adjustment layer to only part of my image canvas?

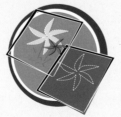

Make a selection with a selection tool before creating the adjustment layer. Photoshop Elements turns the selected area into an adjustment layer. You can experiment with edits to the adjustment layer; any changes you make to the selection affect the underlying layers. See Chapter 6 for more on the kinds of selections you can make with the selection tools in Photoshop Elements.

Is there a shortcut for creating an adjustment layer?

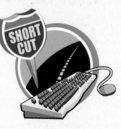

Yes. You can click the **Create Adjustment Layer** icon (◢) in the Layers panel and then click the type of adjustment layer you want to create.

Blend Layers

You can use the blending modes to specify how pixels in a layer should blend with the layers below. You can blend layers to create all kinds of visual effects in your photos.

In the following example, two photos are combined in one image file as two separate layers and then the layers are blended together. To copy a photo into a layer, see the section "Create and Add to a Layer."

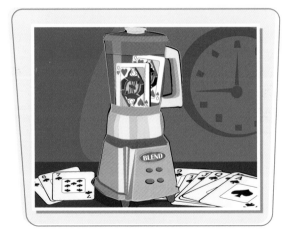

Blend a Regular Layer

① In the Editor, open the Layers panel.

Note: *For more on opening the Editor or panels, see Chapter 1.*

② Click the layer that you want to blend.

③ Click here to choose a blend mode.

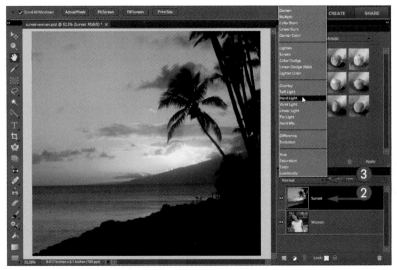

Photoshop Elements blends the selected layer with the layers below it.

This example blends a sunset image with the image of a woman by using the Hard Light mode.

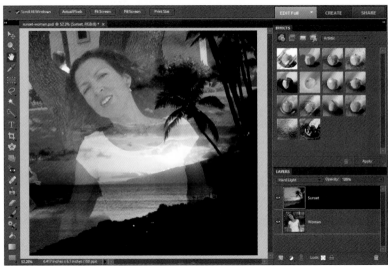

Blend an Adjustment Layer

1 Open the Layers panel.

Note: For more on opening panels, see Chapter 1.

2 Click an adjustment layer that you want to blend.

3 Click here to choose a blend mode.

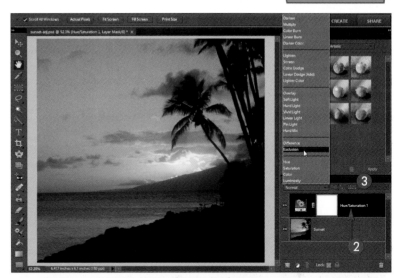

Photoshop Elements blends the selected layer with the layers below it.

This example shows the Exclusion mode applied to a Hue and Saturation adjustment layer, which creates a photonegative effect where the layers overlap.

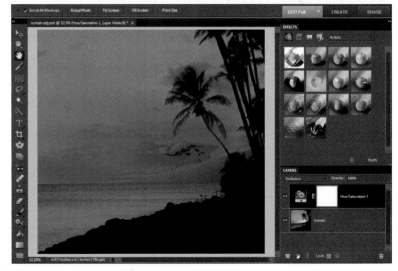

TIP

What effects do some of the different blending modes have?

Multiply: Darkens the colors where the selected layer overlaps layers below it.

Screen: The opposite of Multiply. It lightens colors where layers overlap.

Color: Takes the selected layer's colors and blends them with the details in the layers below it.

Luminosity: The opposite of Color. It takes the selected layer's details and mixes them with the colors below it.

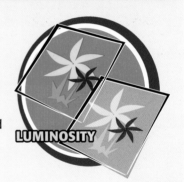

Retouching Photos

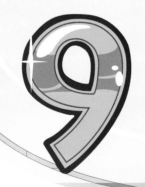

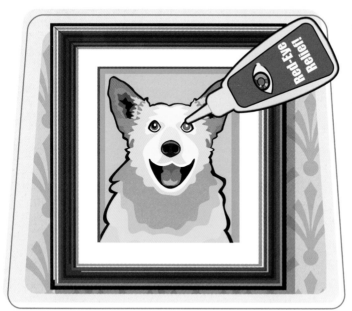

Do you need to fix a photo fast? This chapter offers you all kinds of techniques for retouching your digital photos, including correcting common color problems, making flaws disappear, and rearranging objects.

Retouch with Guided Edit

You can remove blemishes and unwanted objects by using the step-by-step instructions and adjustments in the Guided Edit view of Photoshop Elements.

You can retouch photos in Guided Edit by using the Spot Healing Brush or the Healing Brush. Both remove imperfections by copying from unblemished areas of your photo.

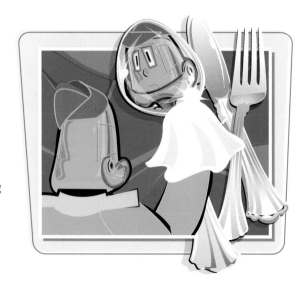

① In the Editor, click 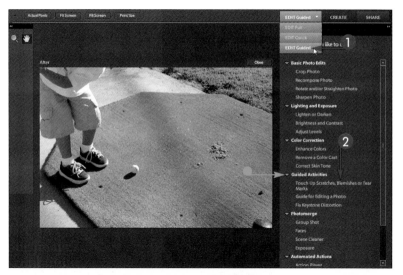 and then click **EDIT Guided**.

Note: For more on opening the Editor, see Chapter 1.

The Guided Edit view opens.

● Make sure the Guided Activities list is open. You can click the arrow (▶) to open it (▶ changes to ▼).

② Click **Touch Up Scratches, Blemishes or Tear Marks**.

③ Click the **Spot Healing Brush** (📷).

④ Click and drag the slider (🔲) to choose a brush size between 1 and 500.

Select a brush size that will cover the area you plan to touch up.

You can also type a value for the brush size.

⑤ Click an object in your image.

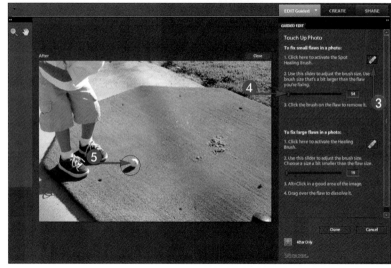

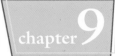

Photoshop Elements patches and blends the object with nearby pixels.

⑥ Click the **Healing Brush** ().

⑦ Click and drag the slider (▣) to choose a brush size between 1 and 2500.

Select a brush size that is slightly smaller than the area you plan to touch up.

You can also type a value for the brush size.

⑧ Press **Alt** and then click an unblemished area of your image that has a similar color and texture.

⑨ Click and drag across an object in your image.

Photoshop Elements covers the object with pixels from the unblemished area.

⑩ Click Done to return to the main Guided Edit view.

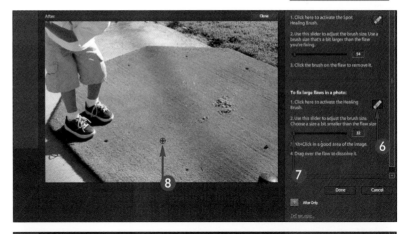

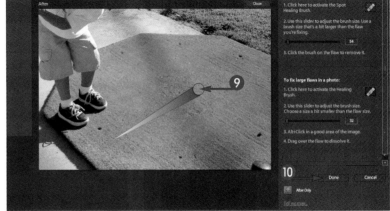

TIP

When retouching in Guided Edit, how can I accurately view the objects I want to remove?

Guided Edit offers you a Zoom tool and Hand tool for adjusting your image and locating objects.

① Click the **Zoom** tool (🔍).

② Click inside your image to zoom in.

③ Click the **Hand** tool (✋).

④ Click and drag to move your image horizontally and vertically.

Note: For more on the Zoom and Hand tools, see Chapter 5.

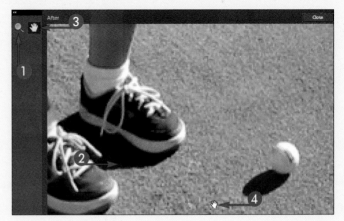

Quick Fix a Photo

You can use the Quick Fix view in Photoshop Elements to make fast corrections to your photos in one convenient window. You can adjust lighting, contrast, color, and focus as well as compare Before and After views of your adjustments.

The Quick Fix pane consists of a variety of panels. The General Fixes panel includes Red Eye Fix and Smart Fix, which automatically corrects lighting, color, and contrast. The Lighting panel fixes contrast and exposure problems; the Color panel fixes color problems; and the Sharpen panel sharpens photos.

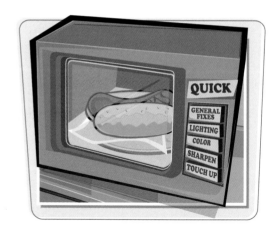

Quick Fix a Photo

1 In the Editor, click ☑ and then click **EDIT Quick**.

Note: For more on opening the Editor, see Chapter 1.

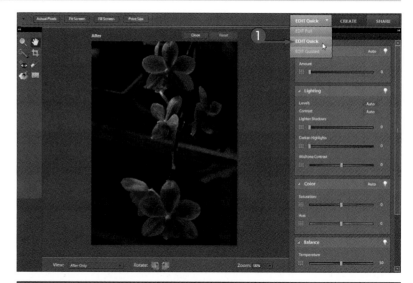

The Quick Fix pane opens.

● You can select objects, adjust colors, or crop the image with these tools.

2 Click here to choose a view mode.

The After Only view shows the results of your changes.

The Before Only view shows the original unedited photo.

The Before and After views show both the original image and the image with changes applied.

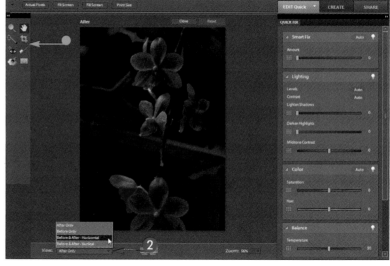

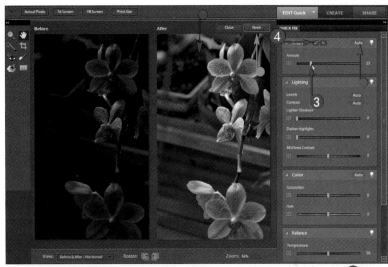

③ Click and drag the **Amount** slider ().

● You can also click **Auto** to have Photoshop Elements automatically adjust your image.

● Photoshop Elements makes immediate adjustments to the lighting, contrast, and colors.

● You can click **Reset** to return to the original settings.

④ Click or press Enter to accept.

● To make different types of adjustments automatically, click **Auto** for the type of correction you want to make.

● You can also click and drag a slider () to adjust a setting.

● In this example, the shadows in the image are lightened.

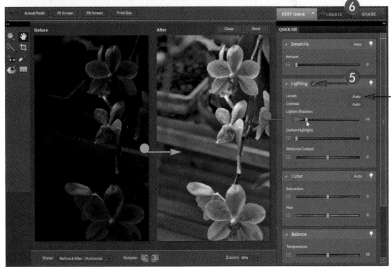

⑤ Click or press Enter to accept.

⑥ Click and then **EDIT Full**.

Photoshop Elements applies the changes and returns to the Full Edit interface.

Note: *If you do not like the result of a Quick Fix, you can click **Edit** and then click **Undo**.*

Must I always use the Quick Fix view to correct brightness, color, focus, and rotation problems?

No. You can make these corrections by using other tools in Photoshop Elements. The Enhance menu contains these same corrections, some of which open dialog boxes that enable you to fine-tune the adjustments.

What exactly does the Smart Fix feature do?

Smart Fix analyzes your image and attempts to correct lighting, contrast, and color based on preset algorithms. Depending on the condition of the photo, the changes may be quite pronounced or barely noticeable. You can click and drag the slider () in the Smart Fix panel to control the percentage amount of change made to the color, shadows, and highlights in the image.

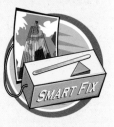

Improve Colors with Quick Fix

You can use the tools in the Quick Fix view to correct common color problems in your photos. The tools let you whiten teeth and boost the blue in a washed-out sky.

You can also access the Black and White – High Contrast tool, covered in the tip, and the Red Eye Removal tool in the Quick Fix view.

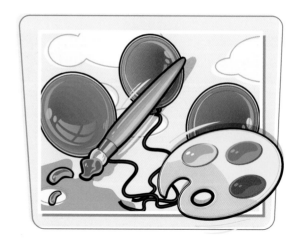

Improve Colors with Quick Fix

Add Blue to Skies

1 In the Editor, open a photo that includes a dull-colored sky.

Note: For more on the Editor, see Chapter 1. For more on opening a photo, see Chapter 2.

2 Click ☑ and then click **EDIT Quick**.

The Quick Fix view opens.

3 Click the **Make Dull Skies Blue** tool (▣).

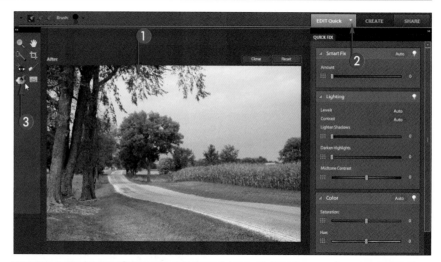

● You can click here to adjust the brush size.

4 Click and drag over the sky.

Photoshop Elements selects the sky and boosts the blue color.

● You can click **Reset** to revert the photo to its previous state.

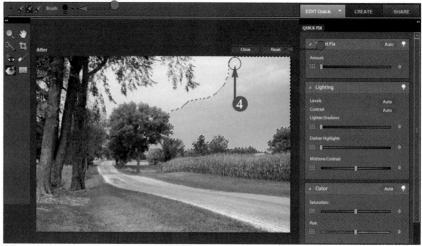

Whiten Teeth

① Open a photo that includes teeth.

② Click the **Whiten Teeth** tool ([ ]).

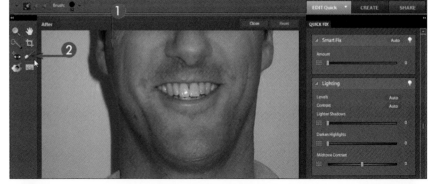

● You can click here to adjust the brush size.

③ Click and drag over teeth in the photo.

Photoshop Elements whitens the teeth, decreasing any colorcast they might have.

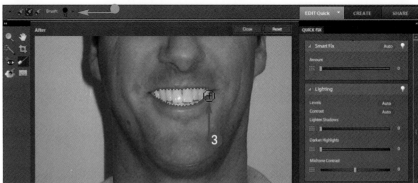

TIP

How can I easily turn an area of my photo to black and white?

One of the tools in the Touch Up panel selects objects and converts them to high-contrast black and white — all in one step.

① In the Touch Up panel, click the **Black And White – High Contrast** tool ([ ]).

② Click and drag across an object in your photo.

● You can click here to adjust the brush size to affect areas of the image more precisely.

Photoshop Elements selects the object and converts it to high-contrast black and white.

Note: For more on converting photos to black and white, see Chapter 11.

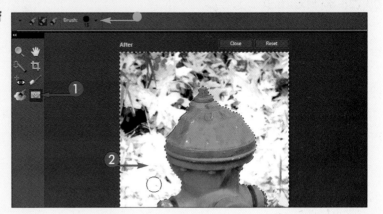

Remove Red-Eye

You can use the Red Eye Removal tool to remove the red-eye color that a camera flash can cause. Red-eye is a common problem in snapshots taken indoors with a flash. Light from the flash reflects off the back of the subject's eyes, creating the red-eye appearance. Using the Red Eye Removal tool, you can edit the eye to change its color without changing image details.

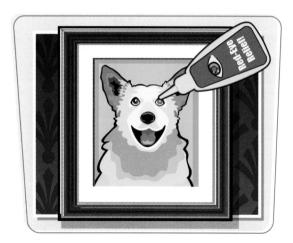

Remove Red-Eye

① In the Editor, click the **Red Eye Removal** tool ( ).

Note: For more on the Editor, see Chapter 1.

② Click here and then drag the slider ( ) to control the size of the area to correct.

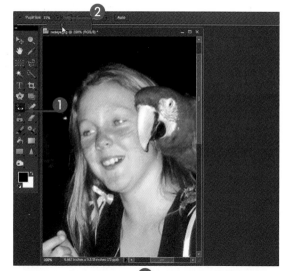

③ Click here and then drag the slider ( ) to the darkness setting you want.

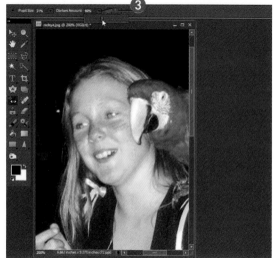

④ Click the eye you want to fix.

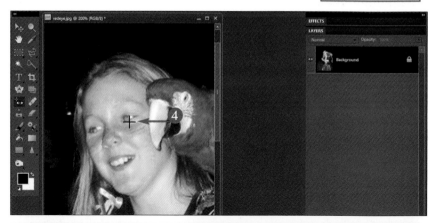

⑤ Release the mouse button.

● Photoshop Elements repairs the red-eye color.

If you need to change the settings, you can click **Undo** (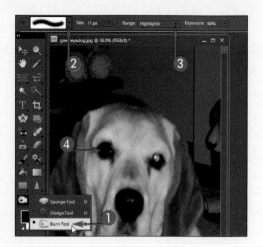) to undo the color change.

TIP

My pet photos have a green-eye problem. How do I fix this?

① Click the **Burn** tool (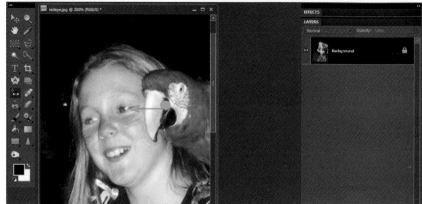).

② Set your brush style and size options.

③ Select **Highlights** in the Range menu.

④ Click the eye you want to darken.

Photoshop Elements darkens the eye. You can click as many times as needed to get the desired color.

Retouch with the Clone Stamp Tool

You can clean up small flaws or erase elements in your image with the Clone Stamp tool. The tool copies information from one area of an image to another. For example, you can use the Clone Stamp tool to remove unwanted blemishes of all kinds by cloning an area near the flaw and then stamping over the flaw.

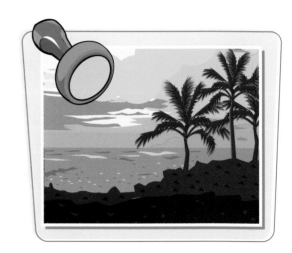

Retouch with the Clone Stamp Tool

1 In the Editor, click the **Clone Stamp** tool (■).

Note: For more on opening the Editor, see Chapter 1.

2 Click here to choose a brush size and type.

● You can also set an exact brush size here.

You can change the brush size while using the tool by pressing [and].

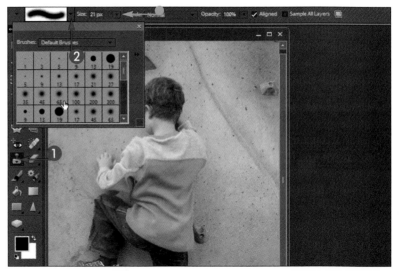

3 Click here to choose an opacity, which determines whether the tool covers an area completely or partially.

You can also type a value for the opacity.

4 Press and hold Alt and then click the area of the image from which you want to copy.

In this example, the Clone Stamp is used to remove a handhold from a climbing wall.

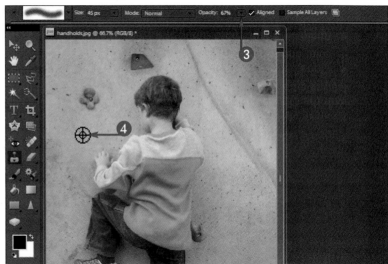

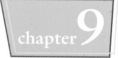

5 Click and drag on the area of the photo that you want to correct.

Photoshop Elements copies the cloned area to where you click and drag.

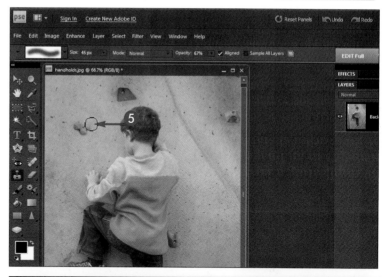

6 Continue clicking new areas to clone and dragging over the area as many times as needed to achieve the desired effect.

● You can click **Undo** () to undo the tool's effects.

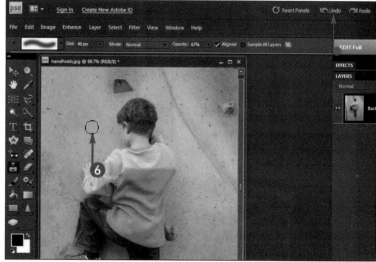

TIPS

How can I make the Clone Stamp's effects look seamless?

To erase elements from your image with the Clone Stamp without leaving a trace, try the following:

- Clone between areas of similar color and texture.

- Apply the stamp more subtly by lowering its opacity.

- Use a soft-edged brush shape.

What can I do with the Pattern Stamp?

You can use the Pattern Stamp, which shares space in the Toolbox with the Clone Stamp, to paint repeating patterns on your images. To find the Pattern Stamp tool, right-click on the **Clone Stamp** tool (🔲) and then click **Pattern Stamp** (🔲) from the menu that appears. Select a pattern, brush style, and brush size and then stamp the pattern on your photo.

Correct a Spot

You can use the Spot Healing Brush to quickly repair flaws in a photo. The tool works well on small spots or blemishes on both solid and textured backgrounds.

The tool's Proximity Match setting analyzes pixels surrounding the selected area and replaces the area with a patch of similar pixels. The Create Texture setting replaces the area with a blend of surrounding pixels.

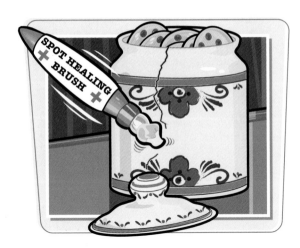

Correct a Spot

① In the Editor, click the **Spot Healing Brush** tool ( ).

Note: *For more on opening the Editor, see Chapter 1.*

② Click here to choose a brush size and type.

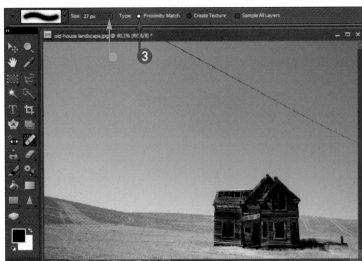

● You can also set an exact brush size here.

③ Click here to choose the type of healing effect you want to apply (● changes to ○).

Proximity Match applies pixels from around the selected area.

Create Texture applies a blend of pixels from the selected area.

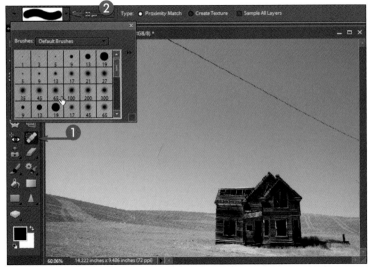

④ Click and drag over the spot you want to correct.

You may have to click and drag several times to get the effect you want.

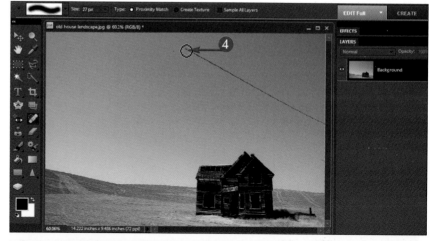

● Photoshop Elements replaces the selected area with pixels similar to those nearby.

You can click **Undo** () to undo the change.

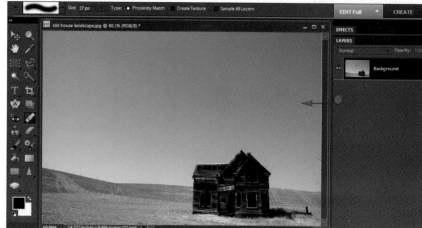

TIP

How do I correct larger areas of a photo?

Using the Healing Brush tool, follow these steps:

① Right-click on the **Spot Healing Brush** tool (⬜).

② Click the **Healing Brush** tool (⬜).

③ Adjust the tool's settings.

④ Press and hold Alt and then click the area you want to clone.

⑤ Drag over the problem area to blend the cloned pixels into the new area.

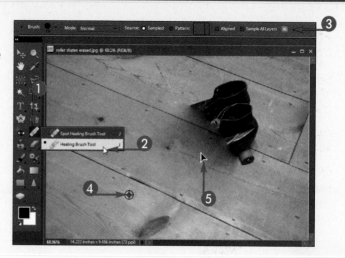

Sharpen an Image

You can use the Adjust Sharpness dialog box to sharpen an image suffering from focus problems. The tool lets you control the amount of sharpening you apply.

To apply the filter to just part of your image, you can select that part with a selection tool. To use the selection tools, see Chapter 6.

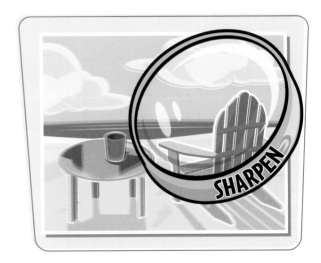

Sharpen an Image

1 In the Editor, select the layer to which you want to apply the enhancement.

Note: *For more on opening the Editor, see Chapter 1. For more on layers, see Chapter 8.*

In this example, the image has a single Background layer.

2 Click **Enhance**.

3 Click **Adjust Sharpness**.

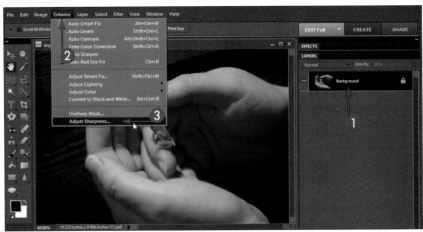

The Adjust Sharpness dialog box opens.

● A preview area displays the filter's effect.

● You can click the **Preview** check box to preview the effect in the main window (■ changes to ☑).

4 Click minus or plus (☐ or ☐) to zoom out or in.

5 Click and drag the sliders (■) to control the amount of sharpening you apply to the image.

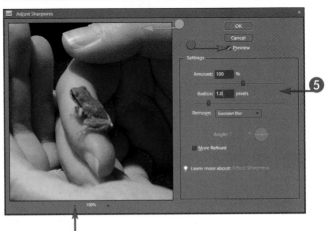

- **Amount** controls the overall amount of sharpening.

- You can confine sharpening to edges in the image by using a low radius setting or add sharpening across the entire image by using a high radius setting.

  You can also type values for the sharpening and radius settings.

- You can click here to remove a specific type of blur in the image. The default is Gaussian Blur.

6 Click **OK**.

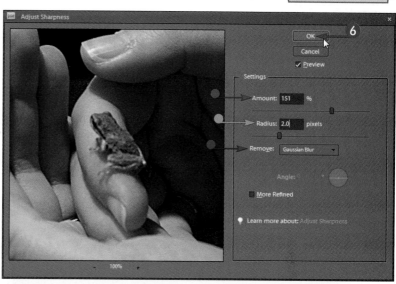

Photoshop Elements applies the enhancement.

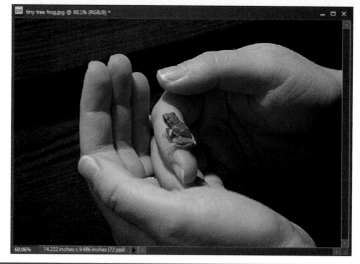

When should I apply sharpening?
Sharpening an image after you change its size can be a good idea because changing an image's size, especially enlarging, can add blurring. Adjusting sharpness can also help clarify scanned images. Although the tool cannot perform a miracle and make an unfocused image completely clear, it can sharpen slightly blurred images or blurring caused by applying other filters.

What does the Auto Sharpen button in the Quick Fix window do?
The Auto button on the Sharpen panel sharpens an image by a preset amount. If you use the Quick Fix window to retouch a photo, you can easily apply the Auto Sharpen command. However, you can fine-tune the sharpening effects to your liking when using the Adjust Sharpness dialog box.

Extract an Object from a Background

You can extract an object in your photo from its background by using the Magic Extractor tool. You define the object and background by brushing lines over them and then Photoshop Elements deletes the background automatically.

Using the Magic Extractor can be quicker than selecting the object with one of the Lasso tools, inverting the selection, and then deleting the background. For more on the Lasso tools, see Chapter 6.

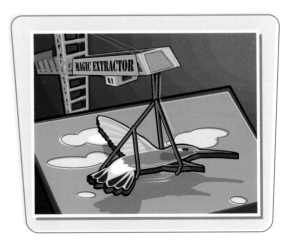

Extract an Object from a Background

① In the Editor, click **Image**.

Note: *For more on opening the Editor, see Chapter 1.*

② Click **Magic Extractor**.

You can also press Alt + Shift + Ctrl + V.

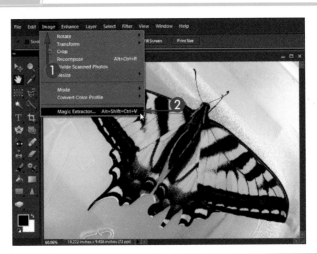

The Magic Extractor dialog box opens.

③ Click the **Foreground Brush** tool (✏).

④ Click here to specify the brush size you want.

⑤ Click and drag to apply brushstrokes to the object you want to keep.

The more of the object you cover, the greater the chance of a successful extraction.

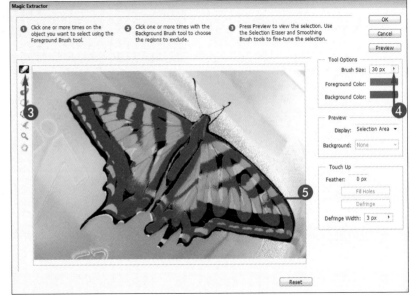

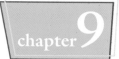
6 Click the **Background Brush**
tool ().

7 Click and drag to apply brush
lines on the background you want
to remove.

8 Click **Preview**.

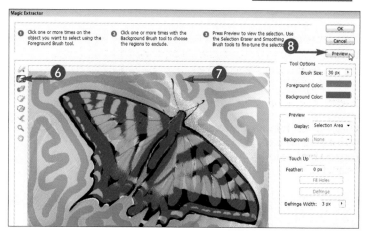

Photoshop Elements extracts the
object from the background and
displays a preview.

To repeat the process, click **Reset**.

9 Click **OK** to complete the
extraction and return to your
image.

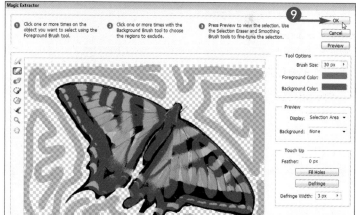

TIP

How can I clean up the edges of an object after extraction?

While still in the Magic Extractor dialog box, you
can remove unwanted pixels from the edges of
your object with the Remove from Selection
tool. Follow these steps:

1 Use the Magic Extractor tools and commands to
preview your extraction.

2 Use the **Zoom** (🔍) and **Hand** (✋) tools to
view the edges of the object.

3 Click the **Remove from Selection** (📷) tool.

4 Click and drag to clean up the edges of the
object.

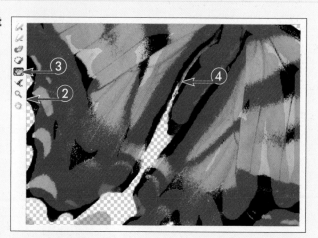

Merge Group Shots

You can take several photos of groups of people and then merge them so the good parts of the different versions are combined into a single optimized photo.

The Group Shot tool works best when the different photos have similar backgrounds. This allows Photoshop Elements to align the different photos and place the different parts in the correct places.

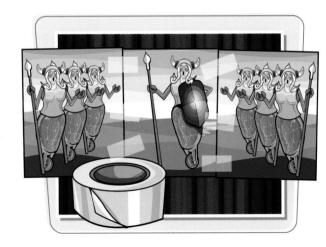

Merge Group Shots

1 In the Editor, open multiple versions of the same group photo.

Note: For more on opening the Editor, see Chapter 1.

2 Ctrl + click to select the photos in the Project Bin.

3 Click ▾ and then click **EDIT Guided**.

● Make sure the Photomerge panel is open. You can click the arrow (▶) to open it (▶ changes to ▼).

4 Click **Group Shot**.

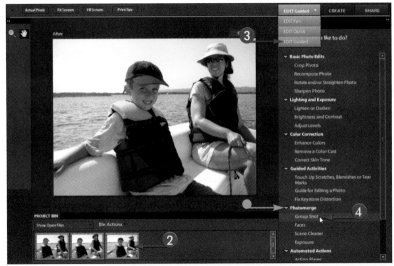

Photoshop Elements opens the photos in the Photomerge Group Shot tool.

5 In the Project Bin, click and drag the photo that you want to fix to the Final window.

6 Click to select the source photo you want to copy from.

● The photo to select from appears in the Source window.

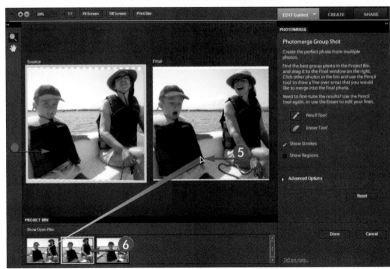

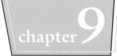

⑦ Click the **Pencil** tool (✏).

⑧ Click and drag to apply brushstrokes in the Source window to define the area you want replaced in the Final window.

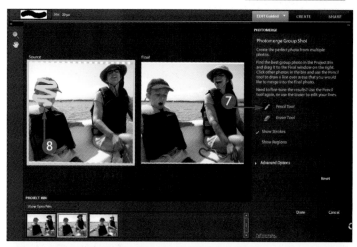

● Photoshop Elements takes the defined area and merges it into the similar area in the Final window.

You can click **Undo** (↩) to undo the change.

⑨ Repeat step **8** to replace different areas of the final photo.

You can select other photos in the Project Bin to replace more areas.

⑩ Click **Done** to exit the Photomerge Group Shot tool.

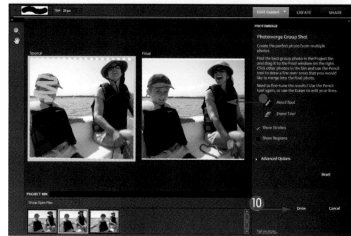

How can I view the areas that Photoshop Elements replaces in the Photomerge Group Shot window?

① Complete steps **1** to **8** above.

② Click the **Show Regions** check box (■ changes to ✓).

Photoshop Elements places coloring in the Final window to show which areas were merged from which photos.

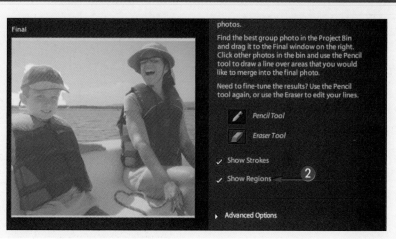

Combine Faces

The Faces tool enables you to put the eyes, nose, or mouth from one face onto another face. After you align the faces by using this tool, you can select the different features and then Photoshop Elements combines the faces automatically.

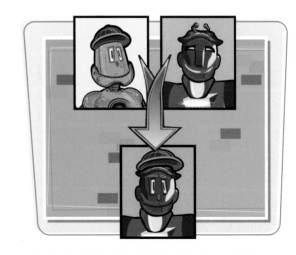

Combine Faces

1 In the Editor, open two or more face photos.

Note: For more on opening the Editor, see Chapter 1.

2 Ctrl + click to select the photos in the Project Bin.

3 Click and then click **EDIT Guided**.

● Make sure the Photomerge panel is open. You can click the arrow (▶) to open it (▶ changes to ▼).

4 Click **Faces**.

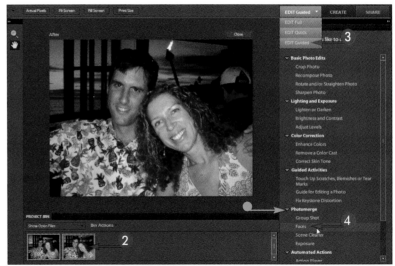

Photoshop Elements opens the photos in the Photomerge Faces tool.

5 Click and drag the photo you want to copy to into the Final window.

6 Click to select the photo you want to select from.

● The photo to select from appears in the Source window.

7 Click the **Alignment** tool (⊕).

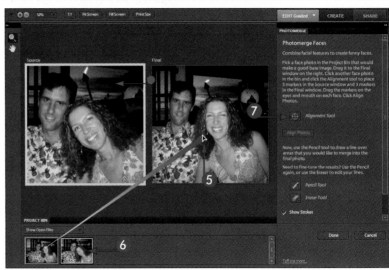

Numbered crosses (✛) appear on the Source photo.

8 Click and drag the crosses to features on the face you want to copy from.

9 Position the cursor over the Final window.

Numbered crosses (✛) appear on the Final photo.

10 Place the crosses on the same facial features as in step **8**.

11 Click **Align Photos**.

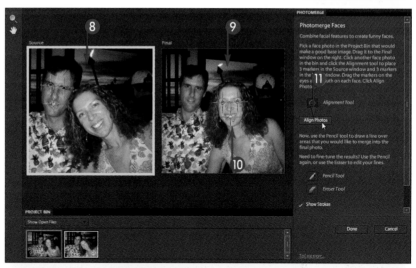

Photoshop Elements aligns the faces in the photos.

12 Click the **Pencil** tool (✏️).

13 Click and drag on the Source face to define a feature.

● Photoshop Elements places the feature on the Final face.

14 Repeat steps **8** and **9** to add more features.

15 Click **Done** to exit the Photomerge Faces tool.

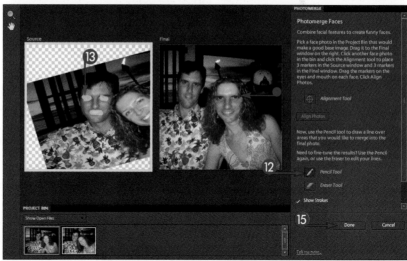

TIPS

How can I edit the facial features that Photoshop Elements merges in the Faces tool?

The Faces tool places the merged facial features in a separate layer above the original face. You can edit the added features by editing that layer in the Full Edit interface. For example, you can use the Eraser tool to remove extra skin around the eyes or mouth. To access the Full Edit interface, click the ▼ and then click **EDIT Full**.

How can I remove extraneous people or objects from a large scene?

If you have several versions of a scene shot from the same angle, you can use the Scene Cleaner tool to remove the people or objects from the scene. The tool allows you to select empty areas from one version of the scene and place them over the people or objects you want to remove in the other version of the scene. To access the Scene Cleaner, click **Scene Cleaner** in the Photomerge section of Guided Edit.

Recompose a Photo

You can recompose a photo to change its size while keeping important objects within it intact. Recomposition is an alternative to cropping for when you want to reduce an image's size without trimming or deleting certain subject matter. The Recompose tool is new to Photoshop Elements 8.

For more on using the Crop tool, see Chapter 5.

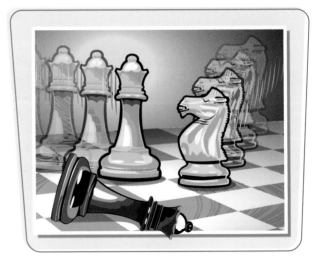

① In the Editor, right-click on the **Crop** tool ( ).

Note: *For more on opening the Editor, see Chapter 1.*

The Recompose tool shares space with the Crop tool in the Toolbox.

② Click the **Recompose** tool ( ).

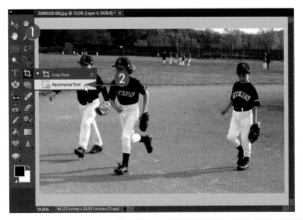

If a dialog box opens with tips about using the tool, click **OK**.

③ Click **Mark for Protection** ( ).

④ Click here to specify a brush size.

⑤ Click and drag over the objects you want to keep unchanged.

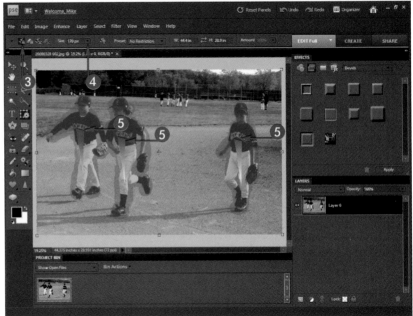

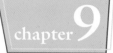
6 Click **Mark for Removal** (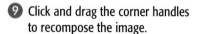).

7 Click here to specify a brush size.

8 Click and drag over the areas that can be deleted.

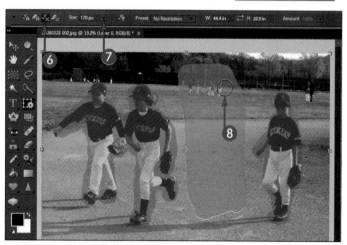

9 Click and drag the corner handles to recompose the image.

Photoshop Elements rearranges content in the image, keeping the protected objects intact.

10 Click ✔ or press Enter to commit the changes.

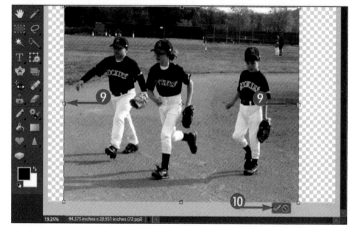

TIP

How do I edit my selections when using the Recompose tool?

1 With the Recompose tool selected, click **Erase Highlights Marked for Protection** (🔲).

2 Click and drag to erase protected coloring.

3 Click **Erase Highlights Marked for Removal** (🔲).

4 Click and drag to erase coloring marking deletable areas.

● You can click **Highlight Skin Tones** (🔲) to automatically detect skin tone colors and mark them for protection.

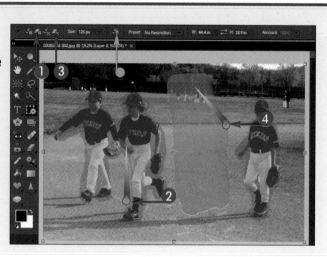

You can use the camera distortion tools in Photoshop Elements to fix keystone effects. This can occur when taking pictures with the camera tilted horizontally or vertically, which can cause rectangular objects — such as tall buildings — to appear trapezoidal.

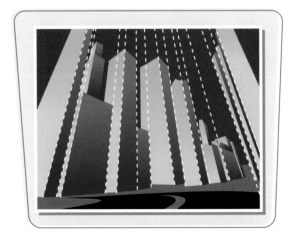

1 In the Editor, open a photo that has keystone distortion.

Note: *For more on opening the Editor, see Chapter 1.*

2 Click ▼ and then click **EDIT Guided**.

3 Click **Fix Keystone Distortion**.

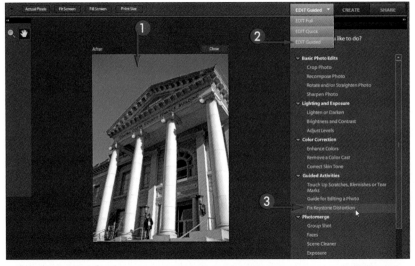

The Fix Keystone Distortion panel opens.

4 Click here to scroll to the bottom of the panel.

5 Click **Correct Camera Distortion**.

● You can click here to view Before and After versions of the image.

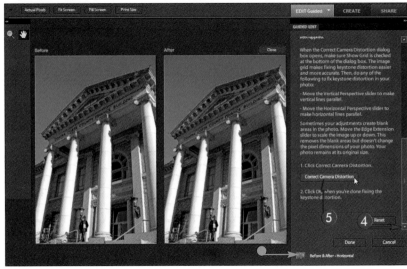

The Correct Camera Distortion window opens.

6 Click and drag the sliders (⊟) to correct the horizontal and vertical perspectives.

7 Click here to correct distortion that can be caused by fisheye lenses.

8 Click here to scale the photo.

You can also type values for the horizontal and vertical perspectives, the distortion, and the scale.

9 Click **OK**.

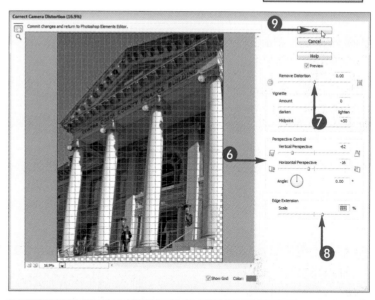

Photoshop Elements corrects the photo.

10 Click **Done** to exit the tool.

● You can click **Reset** to undo the correction.

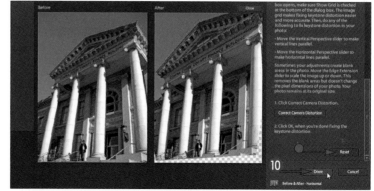

TIP

How can I use the Perspective command to correct buildings with keystone distortion?

1 Click **Image**.

2 Click **Transform**.

3 Click **Perspective**.

Handles appear on the edges and corners of the image.

4 Drag the top-corner handles outward to fix the distortion.

5 Click ✓ or press Enter to commit the changes.

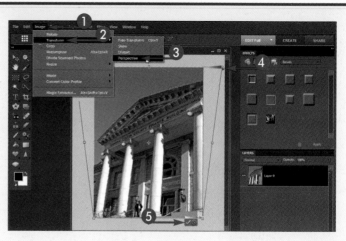

Enhancing Contrast and Exposure

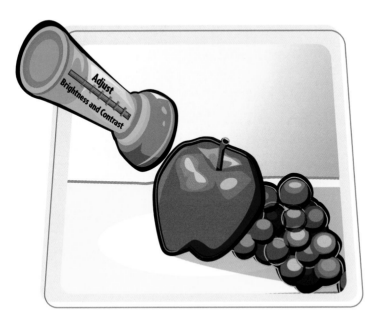

Does your photo suffer from shadows that are too dark or highlights that are too light? Or perhaps you have an old photo in which the entire image is faded? You can correct tone, contrast, exposure, and lighting problems by using several nifty tools in Photoshop Elements. This chapter shows you how.

Enhance Lighting with Guided Edit

You can fix simple lighting problems in your images by using the step-by-step instructions and adjustments in the Guided Edit interface in Photoshop Elements. This feature lets you compare before-and-after versions of an image as you change the lighting.

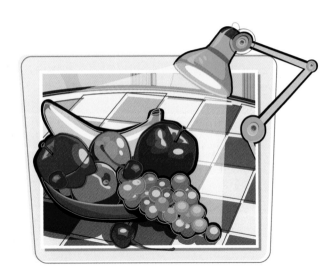

① In the Editor, click **EDIT Guided**.

Note: For more on opening the Editor, see Chapter 1.

The Guided Edit view opens.

● Make sure the Lighting and Exposure list is open. You can click here to open it (▶ changes to ▼).

② Click **Lighten or Darken**.

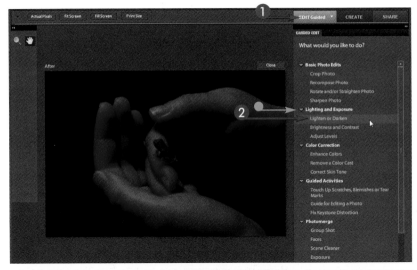

● You can click **Auto** to have Photoshop Elements automatically adjust the lighting in your image by using its built-in optimization routines.

③ Click the View button (▦) to open Before and After views of the image (▦ changes to ▦).

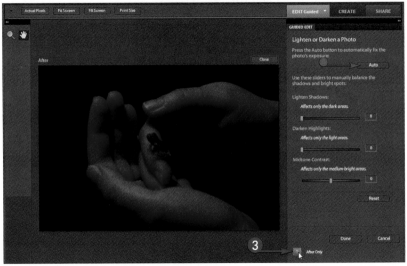

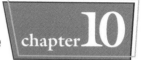

④ Click and drag the slider (■) to lighten shadows in the image.

⑤ Click and drag the slider to darken highlights in the image.

⑥ Click and drag the slider to increase or decrease the contrast in the image.

You can also type values for the shadows, highlights, and contrast.

⑦ Click **Done**.

Photoshop Elements enhances the lighting in the image.

● You can click ▣ and then **EDIT Full** to switch to the Full Edit view.

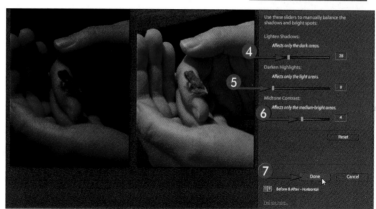

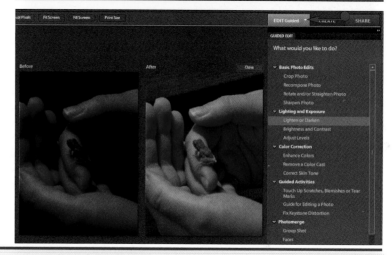

TIP

Is there a way to automatically adjust lighting and color in one step?
Yes. You can have Photoshop Elements automatically optimize the light and color at the same time with the Smart Fix feature. The feature can be a good first step in trying to fix exposure problems.

① Click **Enhance**.

② Click **Adjust Smart Fix**.

The Adjust Smart Fix dialog box opens.

③ Click and drag the slider (■) to control the strength of the adjustment.

④ Click **OK**.

Photoshop Elements applies the adjustment.

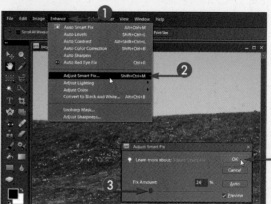

Adjust Levels

You can use the Levels dialog box to fine-tune shadows, highlights, and midtones in your image. Input sliders enable you to manipulate the tonal qualities and color balance of an image, and output sliders let you adjust contrast.

You can adjust levels in just a part of your image by making a selection or selecting a layer before executing the command. For more on making selections, see Chapter 6. For more on working with layers, see Chapter 8.

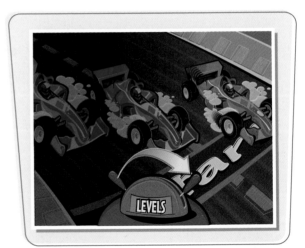

Adjust Levels

① In the Editor, click **Enhance**.

Note: For more on opening the Editor, see Chapter 1.

② Click **Adjust Lighting**.

③ Click **Levels**.

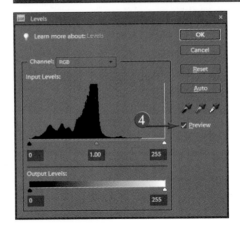

The Levels dialog box opens.

④ Make sure to click the **Preview** check box (■ changes to ☑).

The Preview option enables you to see your adjustments as you make them.

⑤ Click and drag this slider (◆) to darken shadows and increase contrast.

⑥ Click and drag this slider (◆) to adjust the midtones of the image.

⑦ Click and drag this slider (◆) to lighten the bright areas of the image and increase contrast.

You can also type values for the contrast and midtones.

● Photoshop Elements displays a preview of the adjustments in the workspace.

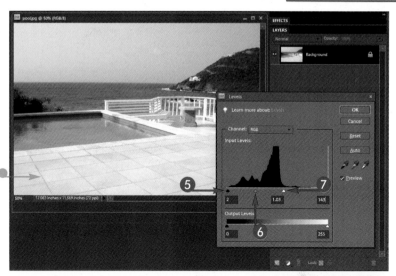

⑧ Click and drag this slider (◆) to the right to lighten the image.

⑨ Click and drag this slider (◆) to the left to darken the image.

⑩ Click **OK**.

Photoshop Elements applies the adjustments.

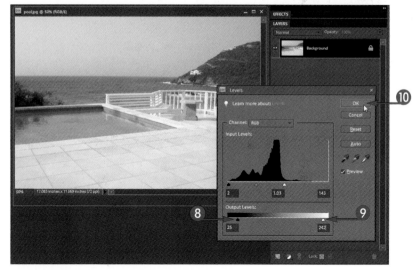

TIPS

How do I automatically adjust the brightness levels of an image?

Click **Enhance** and then **Auto Levels**. Photoshop Elements sets the lightest pixels to white and the darkest pixels to black and then redistributes the intermediate values proportionately throughout the rest of the image. You can use the Auto Levels command to make immediate corrections to shadows, midtones, and highlights.

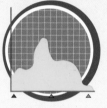

Can I tell Photoshop Elements which pixels to use as the darkest, midtone, and brightest levels in my image?

Yes. The Levels dialog box includes three Eyedropper tools, one each for the darkest (✎), midtone (✎), and lightest tones (✎). You can click the Eyedropper tool for the tone you want to set and then click the appropriate pixel(s) in your image.

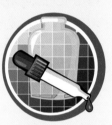

Adjust Shadows and Highlights

You can use the Shadows and Highlights feature to make quick adjustments to the dark and light areas of your image. The feature is less complicated than the Levels tool but also less flexible.

You can adjust shadows and highlights in just a part of your image by making a selection or selecting a layer before executing the command. For more on making selections, see Chapter 6. For more on working with layers, see Chapter 8.

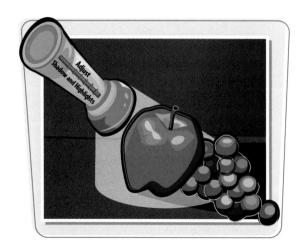

Adjust Shadows and Highlights

① In the Editor, click **Enhance**.

Note: For more on opening the Editor, see Chapter 1.

② Click **Adjust Lighting**.

③ Click **Shadows/Highlights**.

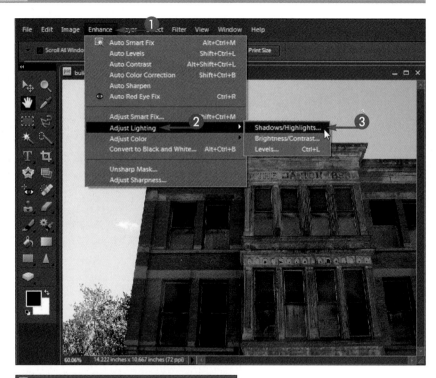

The Shadows/Highlights dialog box opens.

④ Make sure to click the **Preview** check box (■ changes to ✓).

The Preview option lets you view and verify your adjustments as you make them.

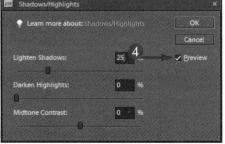

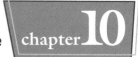

⑤ Click and drag the slider (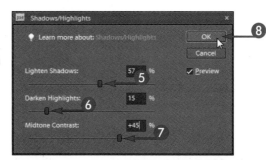) to lighten shadows in the image.

⑥ Click and drag the slider to darken highlights in the image.

⑦ Click and drag the slider to adjust midtone contrast in the image.

You can also type values for the shadows, highlights, and contrast.

⑧ Click **OK**.

Photoshop Elements applies the adjustments.

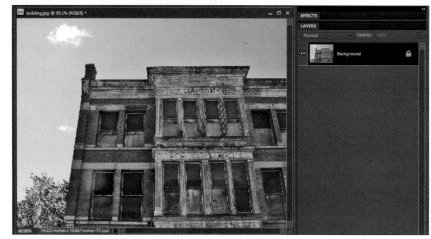

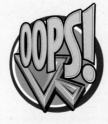

How do I cancel my adjustments without exiting the Shadows/Highlights dialog box?

If you press and hold Alt, Cancel changes to Reset. Click **Reset** to return the settings to their default values.

When I open the Shadows/Highlights dialog box, Photoshop Elements immediately adjusts my image. What is happening?

The Shadows/Highlights filter is set to automatically lighten shadows in your image by 25%. When you open the dialog box, you will see this applied. You can reduce the effect by dragging the **Lighten Shadows** slider (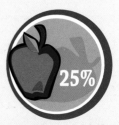) to the left.

Change Brightness and Contrast

You can use the Brightness/Contrast dialog box to adjust the brightness and contrast levels in a photo or a selected portion of a photo. *Brightness* refers to the intensity of the lighter pixels in an image, and *contrast* refers to the relative difference between dark and light areas in an image.

To make more complex adjustments to the tonal qualities in an image, use the Levels dialog box. See the section "Adjust Levels" for more. You can also use the Adjust Color Curves command, which is covered in Chapter 11.

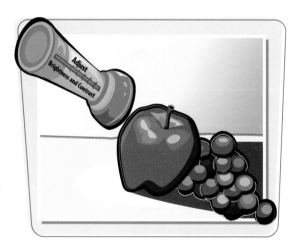

Change Brightness and Contrast

1 In the Editor, click **Enhance**.

Note: For more on opening the Editor, see Chapter 1.

2 Click **Adjust Lighting**.

3 Click **Brightness/Contrast**.

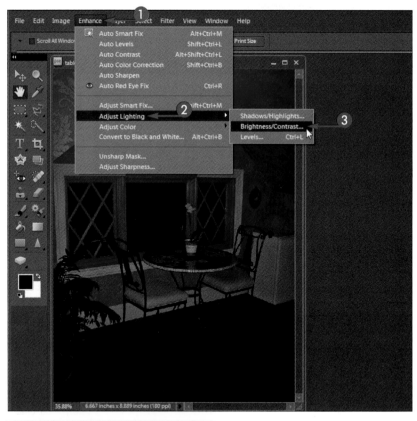

The Brightness/Contrast dialog box opens.

If you want to restrict changes to a selection or layer, select the layer or make the selection before executing the command.

● The Preview check box is selected by default.

4 Click and drag the **Brightness** slider (■) to adjust brightness.

Drag the slider to the right to lighten the image.

Drag the slider to the left to darken the image.

● You can also type a number from 1 to 150 to lighten the image or from -1 to -150 to darken the image.

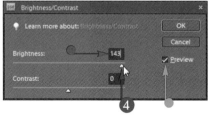

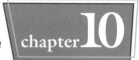

⑤ Click and drag the **Contrast** slider
(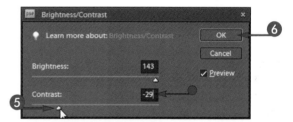) to adjust contrast.

Drag the slider to the right to
increase contrast.

Drag the slider to the left to
decrease contrast.

● You can also type a number from
1 to 100 to increase contrast or
from -1 to -50 to decrease
contrast.

⑥ Click **OK**.

Photoshop Elements applies the
adjustments to the image,
selection, or layer.

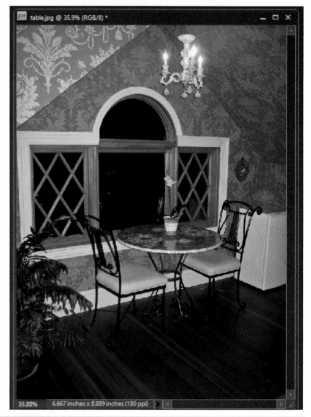

TIPS

How can I automatically adjust the contrast of an image?

You can click **Enhance** and then **Auto Contrast**. Photoshop Elements automatically converts light and dark pixels for you. The Auto Contrast feature converts the very lightest pixels in the image to white and the very darkest pixels to black. Unlike with the Brightness/Contrast dialog box, you cannot fine-tune the contrast settings with Auto Contrast.

Does Photoshop Elements offer a tool for evaluating tones in an image?

Yes. You can use the Histogram panel to evaluate tonal qualities in your images. Click **Window** and then **Histogram** to open the panel. The Histogram is a graphical representation of the light and dark pixels in an image plotted by intensity. The density of each color intensity is plotted, with the darker pixels plotted on the left and the lighter pixels plotted on the right.

Lighten Areas with the Dodge Tool

You can use the Dodge tool to quickly brighten a specific area of an image. *Dodge* is a photographic term that describes the diffusing of light when developing a film negative. For example, you can tweak a dark area of an image by brushing over the area with the Dodge tool.

You can fine-tune the effects of the Dodge tool by specifying what to correct — midtones, shadows, or highlights. You can also specify the strength of the lightening effect by selecting an exposure setting.

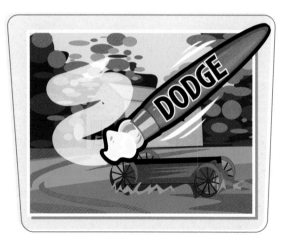

Lighten Areas with the Dodge Tool

1 In the Editor, right-click on the **Sponge** tool (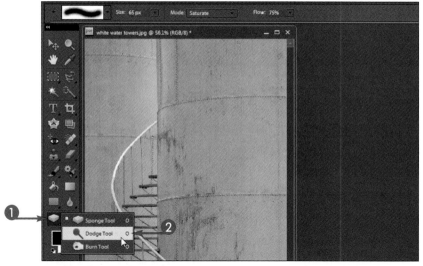).

Note: For more on opening the Editor, see Chapter 1.

The Dodge tool shares space with the Sponge and Burn tools in the Toolbox.

2 Click the **Dodge** tool (■).

Note: You can constrain the tool's effects by making a selection before applying. See Chapter 6 for more on making selections.

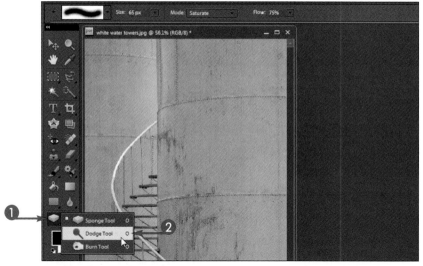

3 Click here to choose the brush you want to use.

● You can also select an exact brush size here.

You can change the brush size while using the tool by pressing ▯ and ▯.

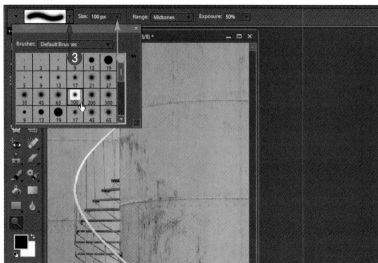

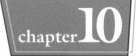

- You can click here to choose the range of tones you want to affect.

- You can click here to choose the tool's exposure, or strength.

4 Click and drag the mouse pointer (○) over the area you want to lighten.

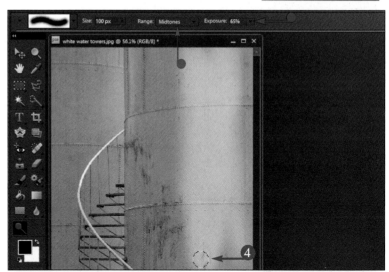

- Photoshop Elements lightens the area.

  If you continue to click or click and drag over an area, the area is lightened more with each application of the tool.

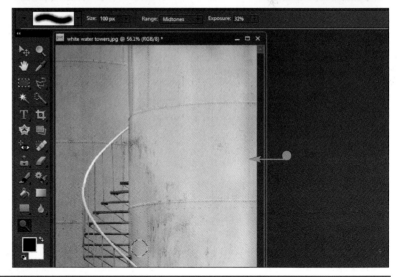

 TIPS

Is there a way to gradually brighten an area?

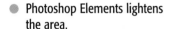

If you set the Exposure level to a low value, you can drag repeatedly over the area you want to correct to gradually brighten the area or you can click multiple times to gradually brighten just the area under the cursor.

How can I add extra highlights to the lighter area of an object?

You can apply the Dodge tool with the Range set to Highlights to brighten the lighter areas of an object in your image. Likewise, you can use the Burn tool (○) with the Range set to Shadows to add shadows to the shaded side of an object. For more on the Burn tool, see the section "Darken Areas with the Burn Tool."

Darken Areas with the Burn Tool

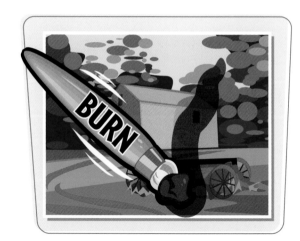

You can use the Burn tool to darken a specific area of an image. *Burn* is a photographic term that describes the focusing of light when developing a film negative. For example, you can tweak a bright area of an image by brushing over the area with the Burn tool.

You can fine-tune the effects of the Burn tool by specifying what to correct — midtones, shadows, or highlights. You can also specify the strength of the darkening effect by selecting an exposure setting.

Darken Areas with the Burn Tool

① In the Editor, right-click on the **Sponge** tool (🔲).

Note: *For more on opening the Editor, see Chapter 1.*

The Burn tool shares space with the Sponge and Dodge tools in the Toolbox.

② Click the **Burn** tool (🔲).

Note: *You can constrain the tool's effects by making a selection before applying. See Chapter 6 for more on making selections.*

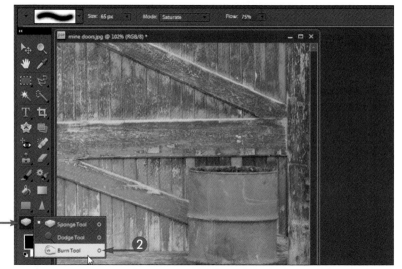

③ Click here to choose the brush you want to use.

● You can also select the range of colors you want to affect and the tool's exposure, or strength.

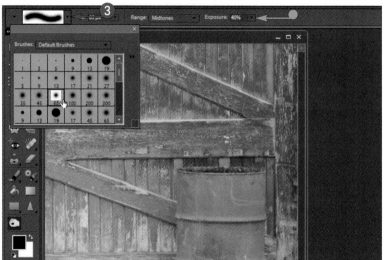

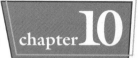

④ Click and drag the mouse pointer (○) over the area you want to darken.

Photoshop Elements darkens the area.

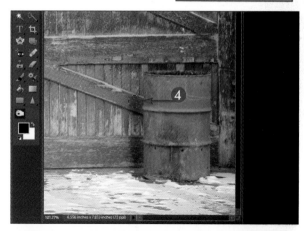

● If you continue to click areas or click and drag over an area, the area is darkened more with each application of the tool.

In this example, a shadow is cast against the ground and wall.

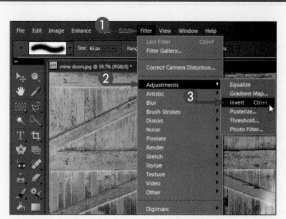

TIP

How do I invert the bright and dark colors in an image?

You can apply the Invert filter to make the image look like a film negative. Bright colors become dark — and vice versa. To apply the Invert filter:

❶ Click **Filter**.

❷ Click **Adjustments**.

❸ Click **Invert**.

You can also press Ctrl + I to apply the Invert command.

Photoshop Elements inverts the image.

For more on filters in Photoshop Elements, see Chapter 13.

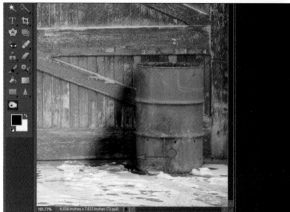

Add a Spotlight

You can use the Lighting Effects filter in Photoshop Elements to create the illusion of spotlights and directional lights in an image. Photoshop Elements offers 17 light styles that can help add ambiance to your images. After you assign a light style, you can control the direction of the light source and the focus of the beam.

Omni lights shine directly over an object. Spotlights create an elliptical beam of light. Directional lights shine light from one angle.

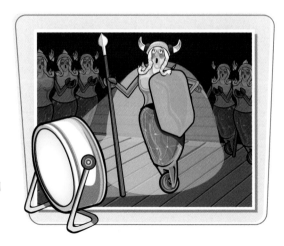

Add a Spotlight

① In the Editor, select the layer to which you want to apply the filter.

Note: For more on opening the Editor, see Chapter 1. For more on layers, see Chapter 8.

② Click **Filter**.

③ Click **Render**.

④ Click **Lighting Effects**.

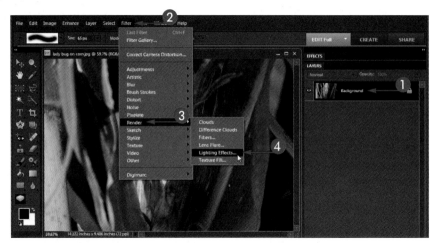

The Lighting Effects dialog box opens.

● Photoshop Elements displays a small preview of the effect.

⑤ Click here to choose a lighting style.

Note: Some light styles use multiple lights; you must position each light in the set and adjust the settings individually.

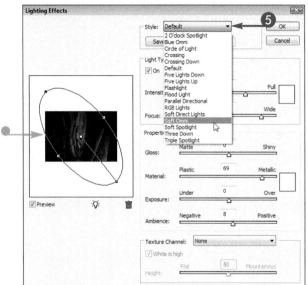

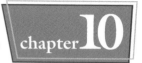

● Optionally, you can click here to choose a light type.

⑥ Adjust the position and shape of the lighting by clicking and dragging the handles in the preview window.

● You can click and drag the center point to change where the light is focused.

⑦ Click and drag the **Intensity** slider (⊡) to control the light intensity.

You can also type a value for the intensity.

⑧ Click **OK**.

Photoshop Elements applies the filter.

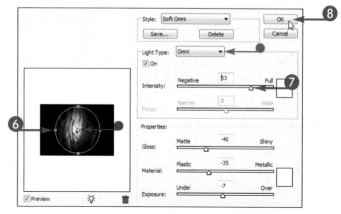

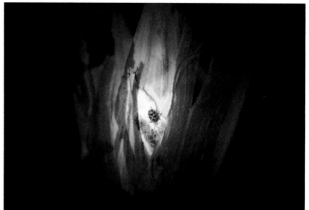

What is a lens flare, and how can I add it to an image?

Lens flare is the extra flash of light that sometimes appears in a photo when too much light enters the camera lens.

① Click **Filter**, click **Render**, and then click **Lens Flare**.

The Lens Flare dialog box opens.

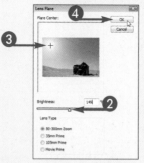

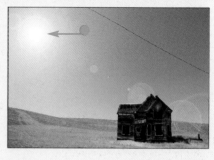

② Click and drag this slider (⊡) to control the brightness. You can also type a value for the brightness.

③ Drag the mouse pointer (✛) to position the lens flare in your image.

④ Click **OK**.

● Photoshop Elements adds the lens flare effect.

Fix Exposure

You can use the Photomerge Exposure tool to combine photos of the same scene taken with different exposure settings. You can choose areas with good lighting and contrast from one photo and then copy them to another photo where they are poorly lit.

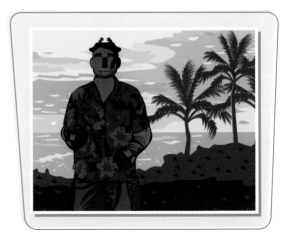

Fix Exposure

① In the Editor, open two or more photos of the same scene but with different exposures.

Note: For more on opening the Editor, see Chapter 1.

② In the Editor, click ▾ and then click **EDIT Guided**.

The Guided Edit view opens.

③ Ctrl + click to select the photos in the Project Bin.

④ Click **Exposure**.

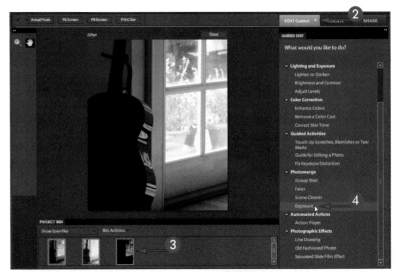

The Photomerge Exposure panel opens and automatically combines the photos to blend their exposures.

⑤ Click and drag this slider to adjust the details in the lighter areas of the composite.

⑥ Click and drag this slider to adjust the details in the darker areas of the composite.

⑦ Click and drag this slider to adjust the overall color intensity.

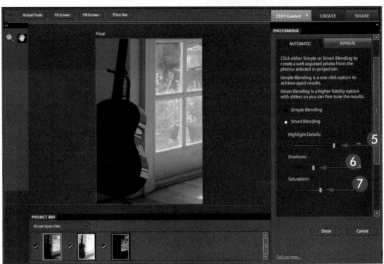

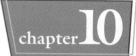

- Photoshop Elements applies the adjustments.

- You can click here to remove a photo from the composite.

⑧ Click **Done** to save the changes and then return to the Guided Edit view.

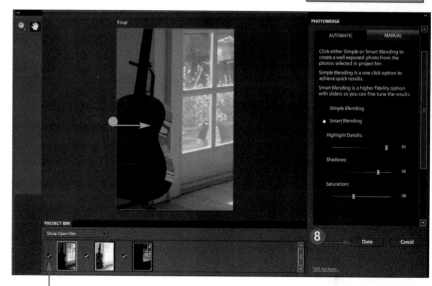

How can I manually combine the elements in my photos?

You can use the Manual mode in the Photomerge Exposure tool to control how areas in one photo are combined with another:

① Click **Manual**.

② Click and drag a photo to the Background window.

③ Click to select a photo with objects to combine with the background. This photo appears in the Foreground window.

④ Click the **Selection** tool ().

⑤ Click and drag over an object to select it.

- Photoshop merges the selected object with the background photo.

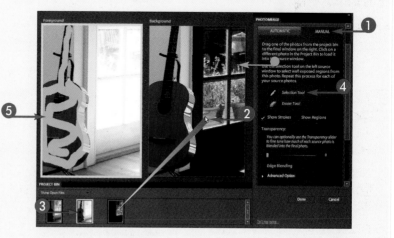

Using the Blur and Sharpen Tools

You can sharpen or blur specific areas of your image with the Blur and Sharpen tools. This allows you to emphasize or de-emphasize objects in a photo. You can use the Blur tool to make tiny specks and other small flaws less noticeable in your photos. You can use the Sharpen tool to increase the contrast of edges.

You can blur or sharpen the entire image by using one of the Blur or Sharpen filters located in the Photoshop Elements Filter menu. See Chapter 13 for more.

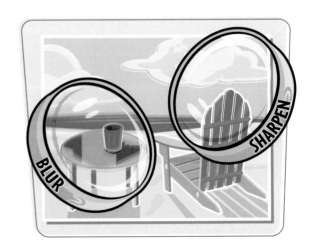

Using the Blur Tool

1 In the Editor, click the **Blur** tool (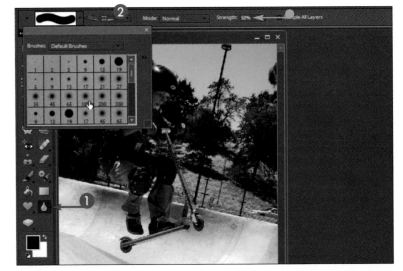).

Note: *For more on opening the Editor, see Chapter 1.*

The Blur tool shares space in the Toolbox with the Sharpen and Smudge tools.

2 Click here to choose the brush you want to use.

● To change the strength of the tool, type a value from 1% to 100%.

3 Click and drag the mouse pointer (○) to blur an area of the image.

Photoshop Elements blurs the area.

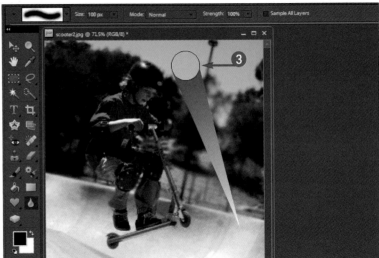

Using the Sharpen Tool

① Right-click on the **Blur** tool (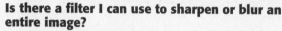).

② Click the **Sharpen** tool ().

The Sharpen tool shares space in the Toolbox with the Blur and Smudge tools.

③ Click here to choose the brush you want to use.

● To change the strength of the tool, type a value from 1% to 100%.

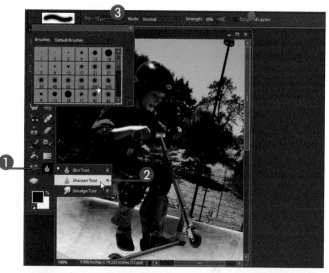

④ Click and drag the mouse pointer (○) to sharpen an area of the image.

Photoshop Elements sharpens the area.

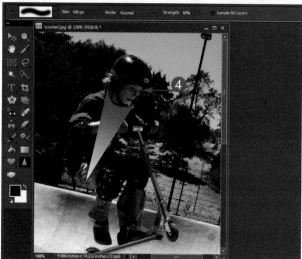

TIPS

What is the Smudge tool?

The Smudge tool () is another tool you can use to create interesting blur effects in your photos. It simulates dragging a finger through wet paint, shifting and smearing colors in your image. The Smudge tool shares space in the Toolbox with the Blur and Sharpen tools.

Is there a filter I can use to sharpen or blur an entire image?

Yes. Photoshop Elements includes a sharpening feature called Unsharp Mask that you can use to sharpen the appearance of pixels in a photo. For more on sharpening an image, see Chapter 9. You can also select from several blurring filters, including Gaussian Blur, to make your image appear blurry. For more on blurring an image, see Chapter 13.

Enhancing Colors

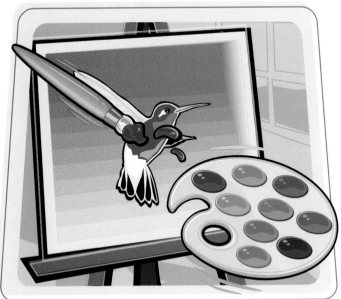

Do your photos suffer from faded colors or unattractive colorcasts? This chapter shows you how to use the tools in Photoshop Elements to correct color problems in your images by adding, removing, or shifting colors.

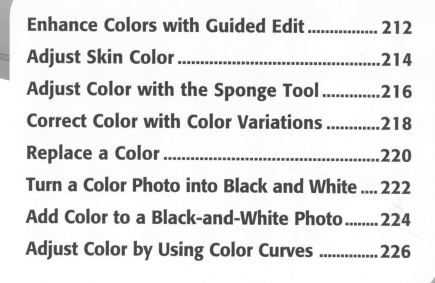

Enhance Colors with Guided Edit

You can enhance or shift the colors in your images by using the step-by-step instructions and adjustments in the Photoshop Elements Guided Edit interface. The interface lets you compare before-and-after versions of an image as you adjust the colors.

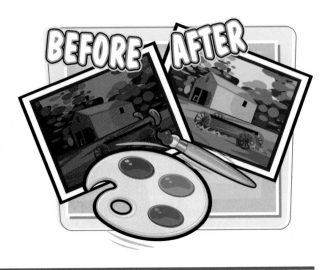

Enhance Colors with Guided Edit

1. In the Editor, click ▾ and then click **EDIT Guided**.

Note: For more on opening the Editor, see Chapter 1.

The Guided Edit interface opens.

● Make sure the Color Correction list is open. You can click the arrow (▶) to open it (▶ changes to ▼).

2. Click **Enhance Colors**.

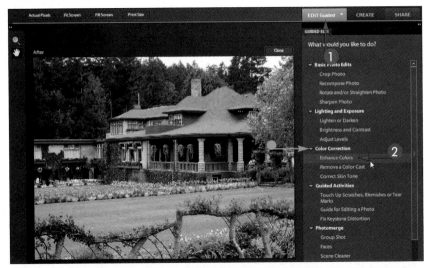

● You can click **Auto** to have Photoshop Elements automatically balance the colors and contrast by using its built-in optimization routines.

3. Click the view icon (▣) to open Before and After views of the image (▣ changes to ▥).

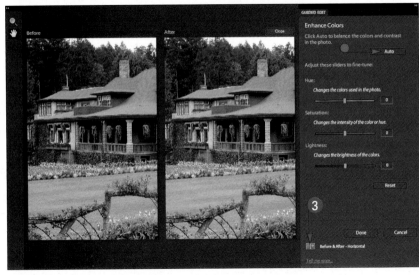

212

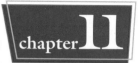

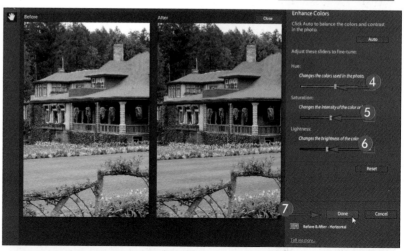

4 Click and drag the **Hue** slider (▣) to shift the colors in the image.

5 Click and drag the **Saturation** slider to change the color intensity in the image.

6 Click and drag the **Lightness** slider to change the lightness of the colors in the image.

You can also type values for the hue, saturation, and lightness.

7 Click **Done**.

Photoshop Elements adjusts the colors in the image.

● You can click here and then click **EDIT Full** to switch to the Full Edit interface.

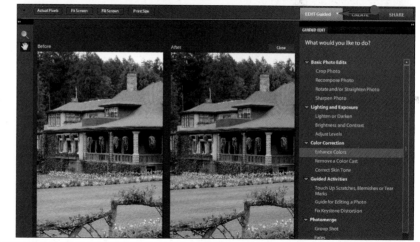

How can I limit my color adjustments to one type of color in my image?

The Hue/Saturation dialog box lets you make some of the same color adjustments as in Guided Edit. It also lets you limit the adjustments to a specific type of color:

1 Click **Enhance**, click **Adjust Color**, and then click **Adjust Hue/Saturation**.

2 In the Hue/Saturation dialog box, click here to choose a color type.

3 Click and drag the sliders (▣) to make adjustments.

4 Click **OK**.

Photoshop Elements adjusts the color.

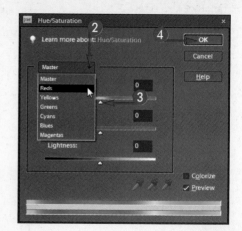

You can improve skin colors that may appear tinted or washed out in your images. After you sample an area of skin with the eyedropper, Photoshop Elements adjusts the skin color to make it look more natural. Photoshop Elements also adjusts other colors in the image based on the sampled skin.

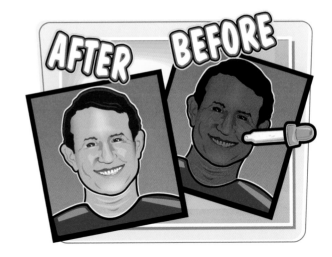

Adjust Skin Color

① In the Editor, click **Enhance**.

Note: For more on opening the Editor, see Chapter 1.

② Click **Adjust Color**.

③ Click **Adjust Color for Skin Tone**.

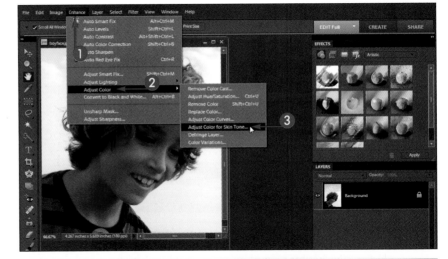

The Adjust Color for Skin Tone dialog box opens.

● The mouse pointer (🖑) changes to an eyedropper (🖊).

④ Click an area of skin in your image.

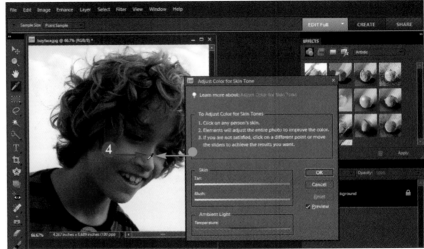

Photoshop Elements adjusts the skin tones and other colors in your image.

⑤ Click and drag the **Tan** slider (▣) to adjust the level of brown in the skin tones.

⑥ Click and drag the **Blush** slider (▣) to adjust the level of red in the skin tones.

⑦ Click and drag the **Temperature** slider (▣) to adjust the overall coloring of the skin tones.

⑧ Click **OK**.

Photoshop Elements makes adjustments to the skin in the image.

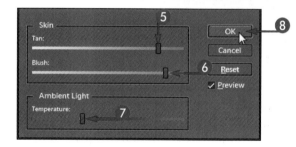

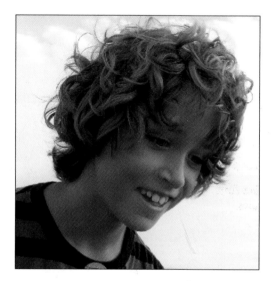

TIP

Can I have Photoshop Elements correct all the colors in my image automatically?

The Auto Color Correction command adjusts the photo based on the mix of highlights, midtones, and shadows in the image. It maps the darkest and lightest pixels based on a default set of values and neutralizes the midtones. Follow these steps to apply the command:

① Click the layer you want to adjust.

② Click **Enhance**.

③ Click **Auto Color Correction**.

Photoshop Elements adjusts the image colors.

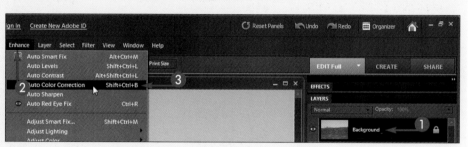

Adjust Color with the Sponge Tool

You can use the Sponge tool to make simple adjustments to the color saturation or color intensity of a specific area of an image. For example, you may want to make a person's clothing appear more colorful or tone down an element that is too colorful.

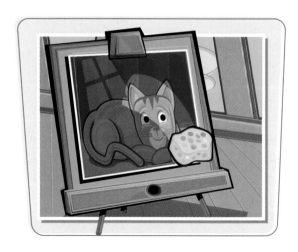

Adjust Color with the Sponge Tool

Decrease Saturation

1 In the Editor, click the **Sponge** tool (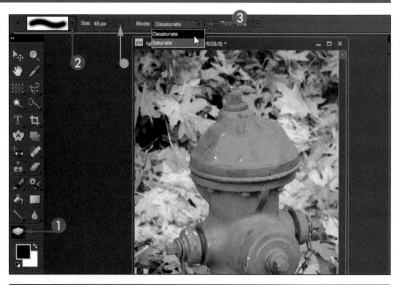).

Note: *For more on opening the Editor, see Chapter 1.*

The Sponge tool shares space with the Dodge and Burn tools in the Toolbox. You may need to click and hold the Dodge or Burn tool and then select the Sponge tool from the menu.

2 Click here to choose the brush style you want to use.

● You can also click here and then drag the slider (■) that appears to set a brush size.

3 Click here and then choose **Desaturate**.

4 Click and drag the mouse pointer (○) to decrease the saturation of an area of the image.

In this example, a section of the hydrant is desaturated.

To confine the effect to a particular area, you can make a selection prior to applying the tool. See Chapter 6 for more on making selections.

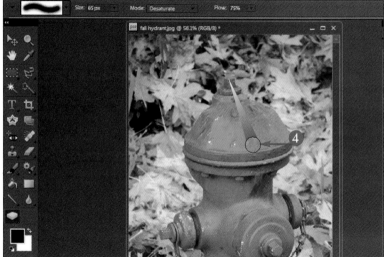

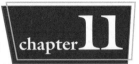

Increase Saturation

1 Perform steps **1** and **2** on the previous page.

2 Click here and then choose **Saturate**.

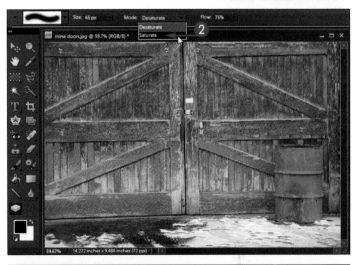

3 Click and drag the mouse pointer (○) to increase the saturation of an area of the image.

● You can adjust the strength of the Sponge tool by clicking here and moving the slider (▣) between 1% and 100%.

In this example, the colors of a barn door and a trash can are intensified.

To confine the effect to a particular area, you can make a selection prior to applying the tool. See Chapter 6 for more on making selections.

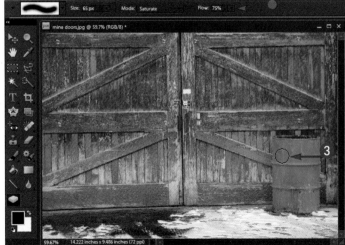

TIPS

What does the Flow setting do?

Clicking the **Flow** drop-down arrow (▾) in the Options bar displays a Flow slider (▣) that you can use to control the intensity of the saturation. You can set the Flow anywhere from 1% to 100% to determine how much the sponge saturates or desaturates the pixels in your image. Start with the 50% Flow setting and then experiment with increasing or decreasing the percentage to get the amount of control you want.

How do I find the right brush style and size?

The Brushes panel displays a variety of brush styles with soft, hard, and shaped edges. To blend your sponging effect into the surrounding pixels, select a soft-edge brush style. To make your sponging effect appear more distinct, use a hard-edge brush style. Shaped edges can help you produce textured effects. Clicking the **Size** drop-down arrow (▾) in the Options bar lets you modify the brush size. You can also press **[** or **]** while sponging to change your brush size. To check how your brush size compares to your image, move the Sponge tool over the image window without clicking.

Correct Color with Color Variations

You can use the Color Variations feature to quickly fix colorcasts and other color problems in a photo. Colorcasts result from unfavorable lighting conditions. For example, when you shoot a subject under fluorescent lights, your photograph may take on a greenish color. Age can also add casts to a photo.

If you make a selection before performing the Color Variations command, you affect only the selected pixels. Similarly, if you have a multilayered image, your adjustments affect only the selected layer. See Chapter 6 for more on making a selection, and see Chapter 8 for more on layers.

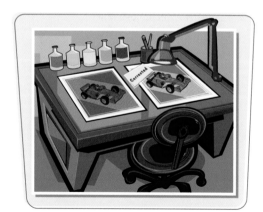

Correct Color with Color Variations

1 In the Editor, click **Enhance**.

Note: For more on opening the Editor, see Chapter 1.

2 Click **Adjust Color**.

3 Click **Color Variations**.

To apply color corrections to a particular layer, select the layer before opening the Color Variations dialog box.

Note: For more on layers, see Chapter 8.

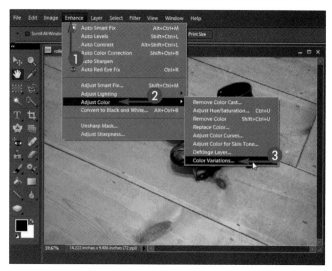

The Color Variations dialog box opens.

4 Choose a tonal range to apply effects to the different tones of your image (● changes to ○).

● Alternatively, you can click the **Saturation** radio button (● changes to ○).

5 Click and drag the slider (⬚) left to make small adjustments or right to make large adjustments.

6 To add or subtract a color, click one of the thumbnails.

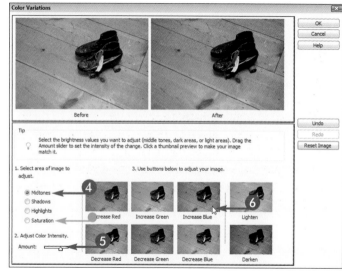

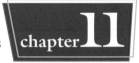

● The result of the adjustment appears in the After preview.

To increase the effect, click the thumbnail again.

● You can increase the brightness by clicking **Lighten**.

● You can decrease the brightness of the image by clicking **Darken**.

⑦ Continue adjusting other tonal ranges as needed.

⑧ Click **OK**.

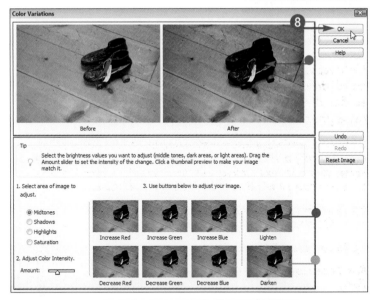

Photoshop Elements makes the color adjustments to the image.

In this example, the objects in the photo are overly yellow. The Color Variations dialog box enables you to adjust the color and bring out the shadowing.

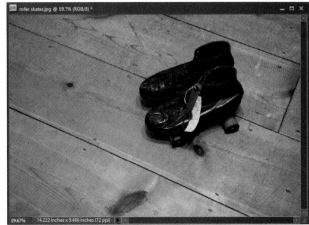

How can I undo color adjustments while using the Color Variations dialog box?

● If you have clicked a Decrease thumbnail image, you can click the corresponding **Increase** thumbnail image to undo the effect.

● If you have clicked an Increase thumbnail image, you can click the corresponding **Decrease** thumbnail image to undo the effect.

● Click **Undo** to cancel the last color adjustment.

● Click **Reset Image** to return the image to its original state — as it looked before you opened the dialog box.

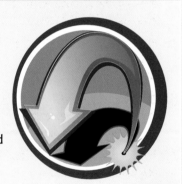

Replace a Color

The Replace Color command lets you change one or more colors in your image by using the hue, saturation, and lightness controls.

If you make a selection before executing the Replace Color command, only the selected pixels are affected. Similarly, if you have a multilayered image, your adjustments affect only the selected layer. See Chapter 6 for more on making a selection, and see Chapter 8 for more on layers.

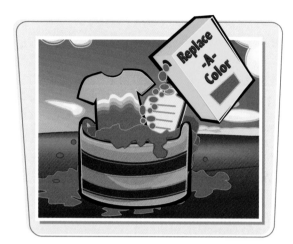

Replace a Color

1. In the Editor, click **Enhance**.

Note: For more on opening the Editor, see Chapter 1.

2. Click **Adjust Color**.

3. Click **Replace Color**.

   To apply color corrections to a particular layer, select the layer before opening the Replace Color dialog box.

Note: See Chapter 8 to read more on layers.

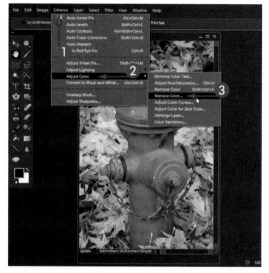

The Replace Color dialog box opens. The mouse pointer (⬚) changes to an eyedropper (✐).

4. Click in the image to select a color to replace.

● Photoshop Elements turns the selected color to white in the preview window.

5. Click and drag the **Fuzziness** slider (⬚) to control the degree of tolerance for related colors within the image or selection.

   Dragging to the right selects more color, and dragging to the left selects less color.

   You can also type a value for the fuzziness.

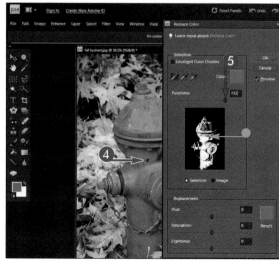

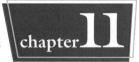

6 Click and drag the sliders () to change the colors inside the selected area.

You can also type values for the hue, saturation, and lightness.

Note: *For more on these controls, see the section "Enhance Colors with Guided Edit."*

7 Click **OK**.

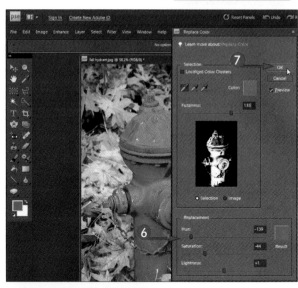

Photoshop Elements replaces the selected color.

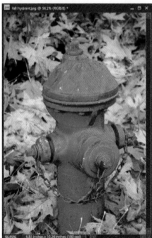

How can I replace more than one area of color?

You can press Shift and then click inside your image to add other colors to your selection. If you are viewing the Selection preview, the white area inside the preview box increases as you click. To deselect colors from your selection, press Alt and then click a color inside your image.

Can I replace a color in my image by using the painting tools?

Yes. For example, you can click the **Paint Bucket** tool (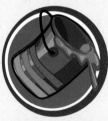), select a foreground color, and then replace a color in your image with the selected color. For more on using the painting tools in Photoshop Elements, see Chapter 12.

Turn a Color Photo into Black and White

You can turn a color photo into a black-and-white photo to create a dramatic effect or before publishing the photo in a noncolor newsletter or brochure. The conversion tool in Photoshop Elements enables you to adjust the contributions of the different colors to the effect.

You may want to copy the color image file before making the change and saving so the full-color original file remains intact. See Chapter 2 to read about how to save files.

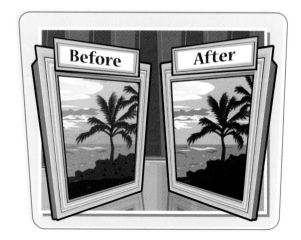

Before   After

Turn a Color Photo into Black and White

① In the Editor, click **Enhance**.

Note: For more on opening the Editor, see Chapter 1.

② Click **Convert to Black and White**.

To confine the conversion to a particular area, you can make a selection prior to applying the command. See Chapter 6 for more on making selections.

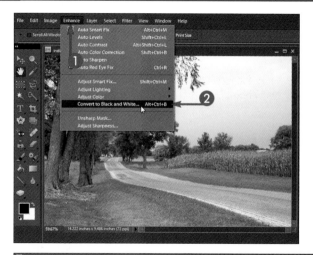

The Convert to Black and White dialog box opens.

③ Click a style.

● Photoshop Elements displays a preview of the black-and-white version.

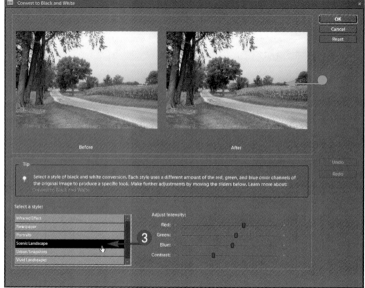

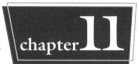

④ You can click and drag the sliders (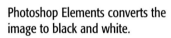) to adjust the contributions of the original colors to the final black-and-white version.

⑤ You can also click this slider to increase or decrease the contrast.

⑥ Click **OK**.

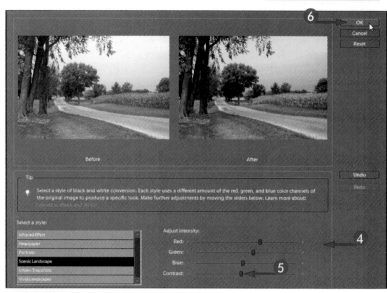

Photoshop Elements converts the image to black and white.

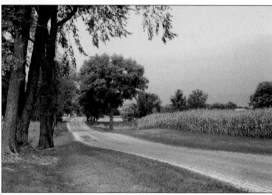

TIP

Can I remove color from just one color channel?

Yes. Working with channels allows you to choose which colors become black and white. You can leave your image in RGB color mode and desaturate the color channels by using the Hue/Saturation dialog box.

① Click **Enhance**, **Adjust Color**, and then **Adjust Hue/Saturation**.

② In the Hue/Saturation dialog box, click here and then choose a color channel.

③ Drag the **Saturation** slider (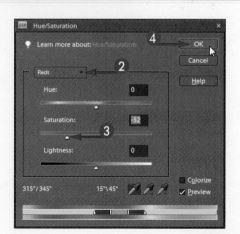) to the left.

You can also type a value for the saturation.

④ Click **OK** to desaturate the color channel.

Add Color to a Black-and-White Photo

You can enhance a black-and-white photo by adding color with the painting tools in Photoshop Elements. For example, you can add color to a baby's cheeks or to articles of clothing. To add color, you must first make sure your image's mode is RGB Color.

You can retain the original black-and-white version of your photo by making color changes on duplicate or adjustment layers. See Chapter 8 for more on layers.

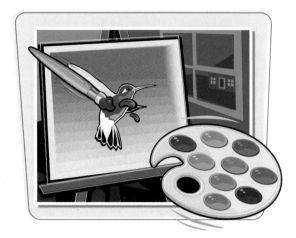

Add Color to a Black-and-White Photo

① In the Editor, click **Image**.

Note: For more on opening the Editor, see Chapter 1.

② Click **Mode**.

③ Click **RGB Color**.

If your image has multiple layers, you may need to flatten the layers before proceeding. In the prompt box that opens, click **Flatten** to continue.

④ Duplicate the Background layer.

⑤ Click the **Brush** tool (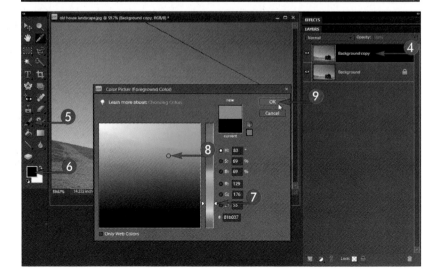).

⑥ Click the foreground color.

⑦ In the Color Picker dialog box, click a color range.

⑧ Click a color.

You can also type values for a color.

⑨ Click **OK**.

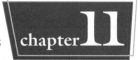

⑩ Click here to set the blending mode to Color. This enables you to retain the lighting details of the objects that you paint over.

To confine the effect to a particular area, you can make a selection prior to applying the tool. See Chapter 6 for more on making selections.

⑪ Click and drag to paint the color on the photo.

Photoshop Elements applies the color to the black-and-white image.

This example shows color added to a grassy area.

● You can click the visibility icon () to hide the layer with the color and revert the image to black and white.

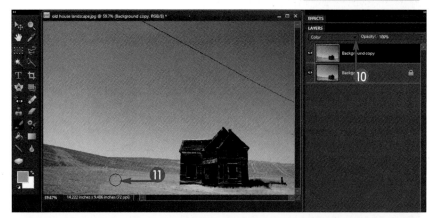

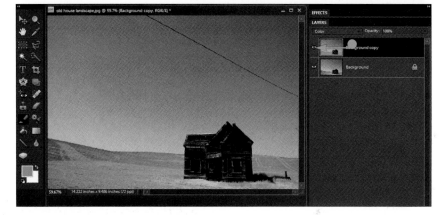

TIP

How do I tone down a layer color?

You can change the layer opacity in the Layers panel to make the color more transparent. Follow these steps:

① Click the layer containing the color you want to edit.

② Click here and then click and drag the slider (■) that appears.

● Photoshop Elements automatically adjusts the color as you drag.

Note: See Chapter 8 to read about working with layers.

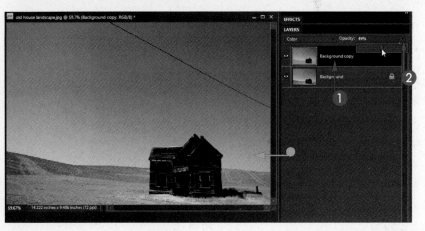

Adjust Color by Using Color Curves

You can manipulate the tones and contrast of your image with the Color Curves dialog box. In the dialog box, the colors in the image are represented by a sloping line graph. The top-right part of the line represents the highlights, the middle part the midtones, and the bottom-left part the shadows.

You can adjust curves in just a part of your image by making a selection or selecting a layer before executing the command. For more on making selections, see Chapter 6. For more on working with layers, see Chapter 8.

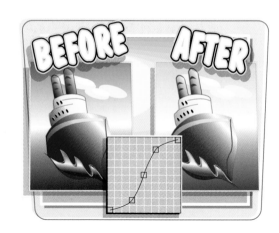

Adjust Colors by Using Color Curves

1 In the Editor, click **Enhance**.

Note: For more on opening the Editor, see Chapter 1.

2 Click **Adjust Color**.

3 Click **Adjust Color Curves**.

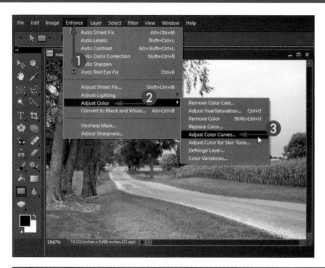

The Adjust Color Curves dialog box opens.

4 Click a style.

● Photoshop Elements displays a preview of the adjusted version.

● The curves graph changes depending on the style.

In this example, choosing the Increase Contrast style gives the graph a slight S shape.

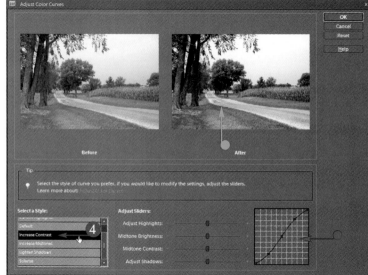

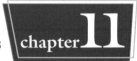

5 You can click and drag the sliders (■) to make more adjustments to the tones and contrast in the image.

6 Click **OK**.

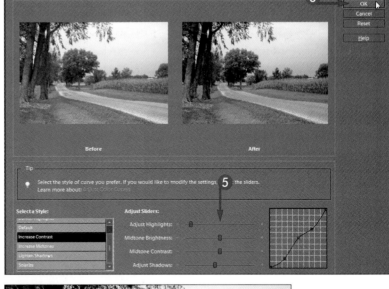

Photoshop Elements applies the adjustment to the image.

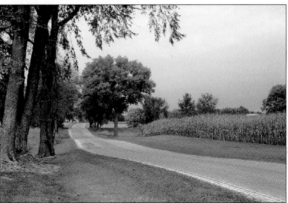

 TIP

How can I give the colors in my image an out-of-this-world appearance?

You can choose the Solarize style in the Color Curves dialog box.

1 Follow steps **1** to **3** in this task.

2 Click **Solarize** in the Select a Style menu.

3 Click **OK** to apply the effect.

Photoshop Elements also has a Solarize filter that generates a similar effect. See Chapter 13 for more on filters.

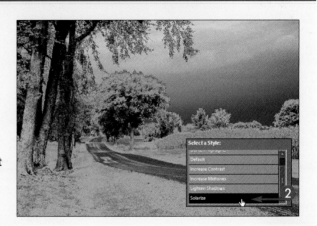

Painting and Drawing on Photos

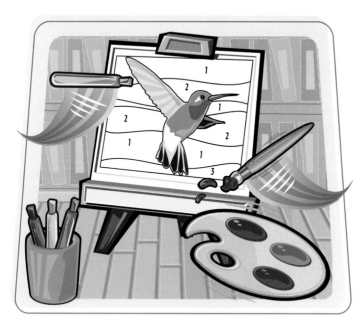

Want to add extra elements to your photos, such as lines, shapes, or solid areas of color? Photoshop Elements offers a variety of tools you can use to paint and draw on your images as well as add shapes and colors. This chapter introduces you to some of those tools and their many uses.

Set the Foreground and Background Colors

You can select colors to use with many of the painting and drawing tools in Photoshop Elements by setting the foreground and background colors. The Brush and Pencil tools apply the foreground color, and the Eraser tool applies the background color.

See the section "Add Color with the Brush Tool" for more on how to paint on a photo. See the section "Erase an Area" for more on using the Eraser.

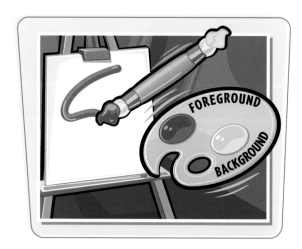

Set the Foreground and Background Colors

Set the Foreground Color

① In the Editor, click the **Foreground Color** box (■).

Note: *For more on opening the Editor, see Chapter 1.*

The Color Picker dialog box opens.

② Click and drag the color slider (▷ ◁) to select a color range.

③ Click a color.

You can click outside the dialog box in the image window to select a color from your photo.

You can also type values for a color.

④ Click **OK**.

● The selected color appears in the Foreground Color box.

● When you use a tool that applies the foreground color, Photoshop Elements paints or draws the foreground color on the photo.

This example uses the Brush tool.

Note: *For more on painting tools, see the section "Add Color with the Brush Tool."*

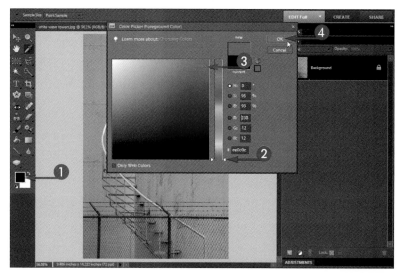

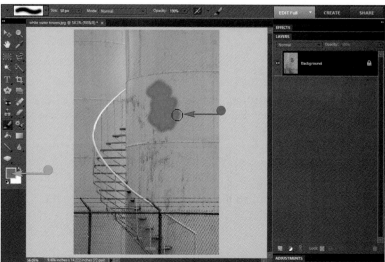

Set the Background Color

① Click the **Background Color** box (☐).

The Color Picker dialog box opens.

② Click and drag the color slider (◁▭▷) to select a color range.

③ Click a color.

You can click outside the dialog box in the image window to select a color from your photo.

You can also type values for a color.

④ Click **OK**.

● The selected color appears in the Background Color box.

● When you use a tool that applies the background color, such as the Eraser tool, Photoshop Elements applies the background color on the photo.

The Eraser tool applies color only in the Background layer; in other layers, the Eraser tool turns pixels transparent.

Note: See Chapter 8 for more on layers.

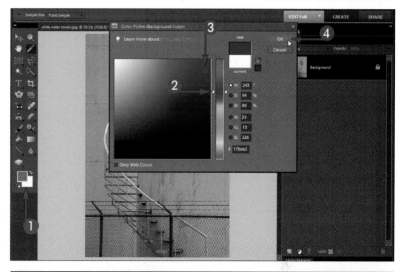

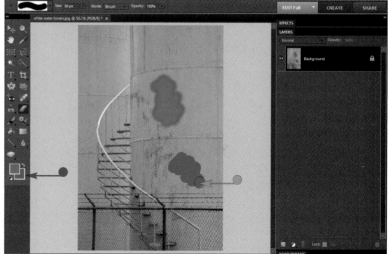

How do I reset the foreground and background colors?

Click the **Default** button (▣) to the lower left of the Foreground and Background icons or press D. Doing so resets the colors to black and white. You can also click the **Switch** icon (⤡) or press X to swap the foreground and background colors.

Does Photoshop Elements offer a set of common colors?

Yes. You can select a color to paint or draw on your photo from the Color Swatches panel, which includes a set of commonly used colors. To view the panel, click **Window** and then **Color Swatches**. You can click the color you want to use, and the Foreground Color box in the Toolbox reflects your choice. To set the Background Color, you can Ctrl +click a color in the panel.

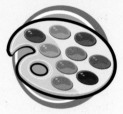

Add Color with the Brush Tool

You can use the Brush tool to add patches of solid color to your image. You can use the tool to cover unwanted elements or change the appearance of clothing or a backdrop. When applying the Brush tool, you can control the size of the brushstrokes by choosing a brush size. For realistic results, turn on the Airbrush feature to apply a softer line of color.

To limit where the brush applies color, create a selection before using the tool. For more, see Chapter 6.

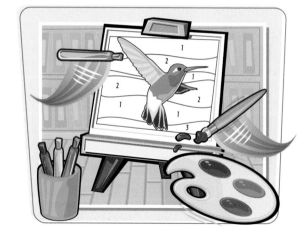

Add Color with the Brush Tool

① In the Editor, click the **Brush** tool (■).

Note: For more on opening the Editor, see Chapter 1.

② Click the **Foreground Color** box (■) to select a color with which to paint.

You can also press and hold Alt and then click inside your image to select a color.

③ Click **OK**.

Note: For more, see the section "Set the Foreground and Background Colors."

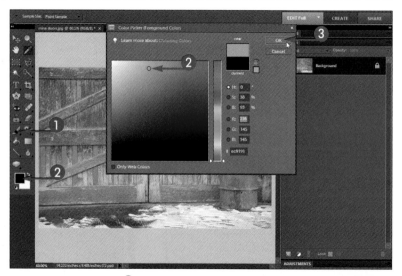

④ Click here and then choose a brush size and type.

● To set a brush size, you can also click here and adjust the slider that appears.

You can also type a brush size.

⑤ Press Enter to close the Brushes menu.

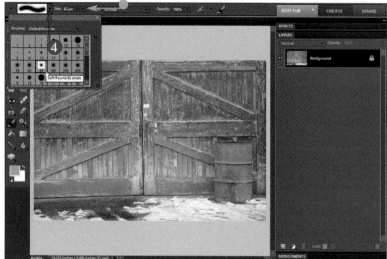

⑥ Click and drag the mouse pointer
(○) on the image.

Photoshop Elements applies color
to the image.

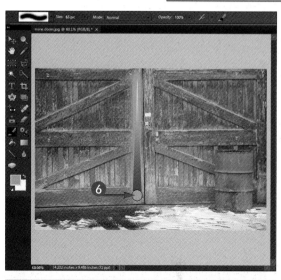

⑦ Click here to reduce the opacity of
the paint effect.

You can also type a value for the
opacity.

⑧ Click and drag the mouse pointer
(○) on the image.

Photoshop Elements applies
transparent color to the image.

To undo the most recent
brushstroke, you can click **Edit**
and then **Undo Brush Tool** or
click the **Undo** button ().

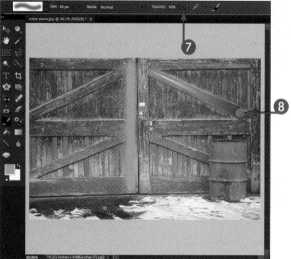

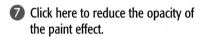

TIPS

How do I paint thin lines?
Use the Pencil tool (✏),
which is similar to the Brush
tool (🖌) except that it
paints hard-edged lines. Like
the Paintbrush, the Pencil
applies the foreground color.
See the section "Draw a Line"
for more on the Pencil tool.

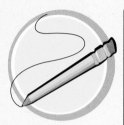

What can I do with the Impressionist Brush tool?
The Impressionist Brush (🖌)
creates artistic effects by
blending existing colors in an
image together. The
Impressionist Brush does not
add any foreground or
background color to your
image. You can select the tool from the menu that
appears when you right-click on the Brush tool (🖌).

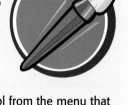

You can select from a variety of predefined brush styles in Photoshop Elements to apply color to your image in different ways. You can also create a custom brush style by specifying spacing, fade, and other characteristics for your brush.

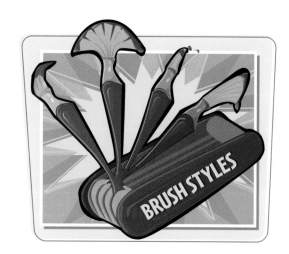

Select From a Predefined Set

1 In the Editor, click the **Brush** tool ( ).

Note: For more on opening the Editor, see Chapter 1.

2 Click the **Brush** .

3 Click here to choose a set of brushes.

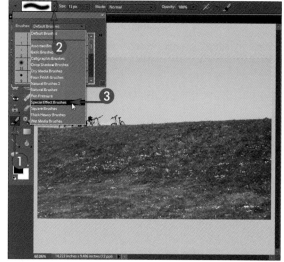

The set appears in the Brushes menu.

4 Click a brush style to select it.

The mouse pointer changes to the new brush shape.

● You can click here to adjust the brush size.

You can also type a brush size.

5 Click here to choose a color to apply with the brush. The actual color applied may vary depending on the brush type.

6 Click and drag the brush on the photo.

Photoshop Elements applies the brush to the area.

Note: To apply the brush, see the section "Add Color with the Brush Tool."

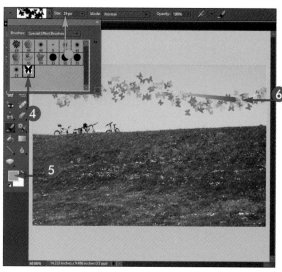

Customize a Brush

1. Click the **Show Options** button ().

   A panel of brush options appears.

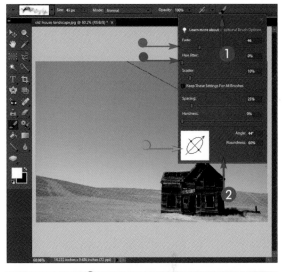

2. Click and drag the slider (□) or type values to define the new brush attributes.

● You can limit the length of your brushstrokes with the Fade slider.

● You can randomize the painted color with the Hue Jitter slider.

● You can change the shape of the brush tip by clicking and dragging here.

   You can also type values for the fade, the hue jitter, and the shape of the brush tip.

● The brush style appears in the Brushes menu.

3. Click and drag the brush on the photo.

   Photoshop Elements applies the customized brush to the area.

Note: For more on applying the brush, see the section "Add Color with the Brush Tool."

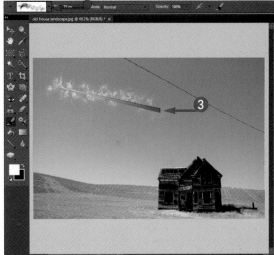

TIP

How can I make a brush apply dots instead of a line?

1. Click the **Show Options** button () to open brush settings in the Options bar.

2. Click and drag the slider (□) to increase the Spacing value to greater than 100%.

● When you click and drag a brush shape, you get dots or patches instead of a contiguous line.

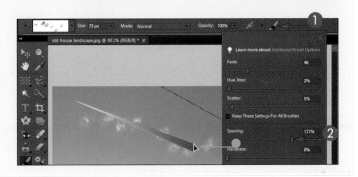

Add Color with the Paint Bucket Tool

The Paint Bucket tool lets you fill areas in your image with solid color. You can use this technique to change the color of clothes, the sky, backgrounds, and more. By default, when you apply the Paint Bucket tool, it affects adjacent pixels in the image. You can set the Paint Bucket's tolerance value to determine the range of colors the paint bucket affects when you apply it.

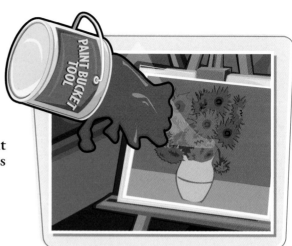

Add Color with the Paint Bucket Tool

Select the Paint Bucket Tool

① In the Editor, click the **Paint Bucket** tool (🪣).

Note: For more on opening the Editor, see Chapter 1.

② Click the **Foreground Color** box (■) to select a color for painting.

Note: For more, see the section "Set the Foreground and Background Colors."

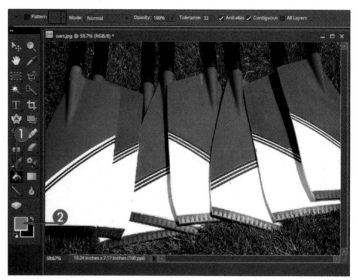

Set the Tolerance

③ Type a tolerance value from 0 to 255.

Tolerance is the amount by which neighboring pixels can differ from the selected pixel and still be affected.

To paint over a narrow range of colors, type a small value; to paint over a wide range of colors, type a large value.

④ Click inside the image.

Photoshop Elements fills an area of the image with the foreground color.

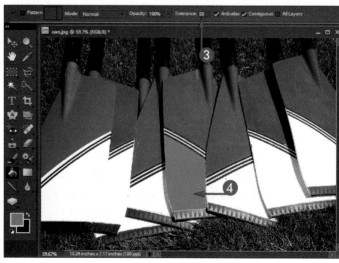

Set Image Opacity

⑤ To fill an area with semi-transparent color, type a percentage value of less than 100% in the opacity field.

⑥ Click inside the image.

Photoshop Elements fills an area with see-through paint.

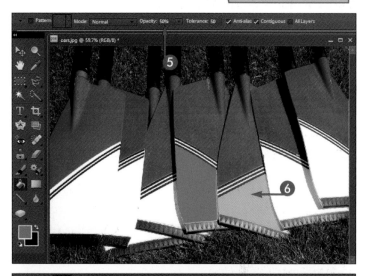

Fill Noncontiguous areas

⑦ To fill noncontiguous but similar areas throughout the image, deselect the **Contiguous** check box (☑ changes to ■).

⑧ Click inside the selection.

Photoshop Elements fills similar areas of the image, even if they are not contiguous with the clicked pixel.

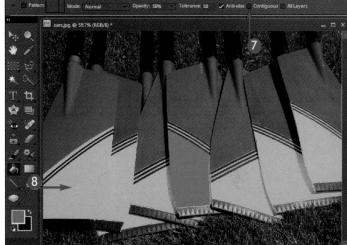

 TIP

How can I reset a tool to the default settings?
You can reset a tool by using a command in the Options bar:

① Click the tool you want to select in the Toolbox.

② Click **Reset** (■) on the far-left side of the Options bar.

③ Click **Reset Tool** from the menu that appears.

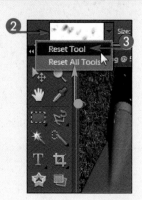

For painting tools, this resets the opacity to 100%, the blending mode to Normal, and other attributes to their startup values.

● You can click **Reset All Tools** from the menu to reset all the Photoshop Elements tools to their default settings.

Replace a Color with a Brush

You can replace colors in your image with the current foreground color by using the Color Replacement tool. This gives you a free-form way of recoloring objects in your image while keeping the shading on the objects intact.

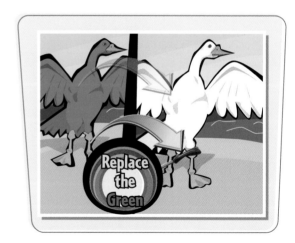

① In the Editor, right-click on the **Brush** tool (🖌).

Note: For more on opening the Editor, see Chapter 1.

② From the list that appears, click the **Color Replacement** tool (🖌).

③ Click the **Foreground Color** box to select a color for painting.

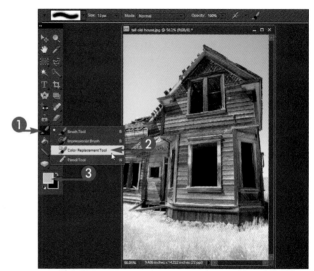

④ Click here to choose a brush size and type.

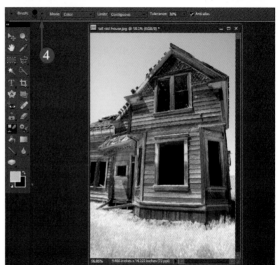

5 Type a tolerance from 1% to 100%.

The greater the tolerance, the greater the range of colors the tool replaces.

6 Click and drag in your image.

Photoshop Elements replaces the color.

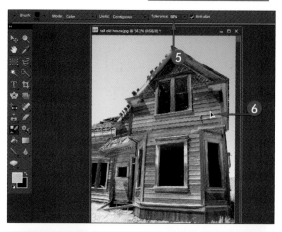

7 Continue to click and drag in your image.

Photoshop Elements replaces more color.

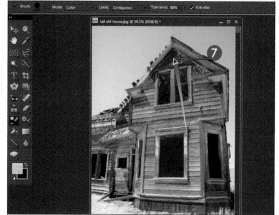

 TIP

How do I fill a selection with a color?

You can use the Fill command to fill a selection with a solid or semi-transparent color. Filling is an easy way to change the color of an object in your image.

1 Make a selection with a selection tool. See Chapter 6 for more on making selections.

2 Click **Edit**.

3 Click **Fill Selection**. The Fill Layer dialog box opens.

4 Select the color you want to fill with and then set an opacity for the fill color.

5 Click **OK**.

● Photoshop Elements fills the selection.

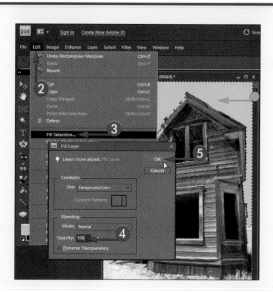

Adjust Colors with the Smart Brush

You can simultaneously select objects in your photo and apply color adjustments to them with the Smart Brush tool. Different tool options enable you to increase, decrease, remove, or transform color in the objects.

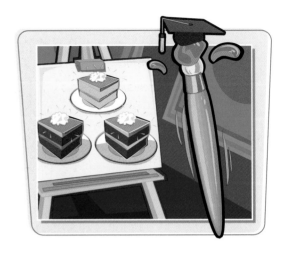

① In the Editor, click the **Smart Brush** tool (⬛).

Note: *For more on opening the Editor, see Chapter 1.*

● The Smart Paint menu opens.

② Click here to choose a category.

Photoshop Elements lists the painting effects in that category.

● A thumbnail image shows an example of each painting effect.

③ Click an effect.

④ Press Enter to close the Smart Paint menu.

⑤ Click here to choose a brush style and size.

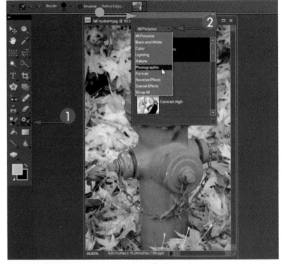

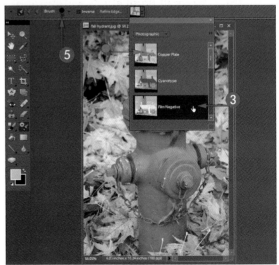

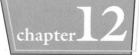

6 Click and drag over objects in your image to apply the tool.

Photoshop Elements selects the objects and applies the effect.

● You can make multiple selections with the tool. Each selection is marked with a different icon.

● The effect is stored as a new adjustment layer.

Note: *For more on adjustment layers, see Chapter 8.*

● You can click **Inverse** (■ changes to ✓) to invert your selection and apply the effect to the other pixels in your image.

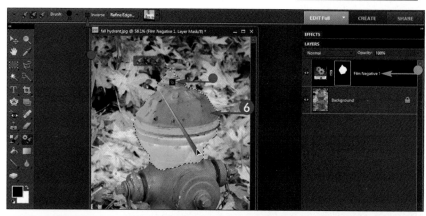

Undo the Smart Brush Effect

1 Click the Smart Brush adjustment layer to activate the selection.

2 Click the **Subtract from Selection** option (🔳).

3 Click and drag over the selection.

Photoshop Elements deselects the area and reverts the effect.

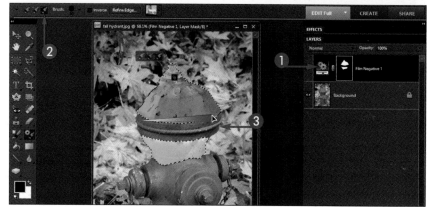

 TIP

How do I decrease the effect of the Smart Brush so that it is only partially applied?
Because Smart Brush effects are applied as adjustment layers, you can decrease a Smart Brush effect by reducing the opacity of its layer.

1 In the Layers panel, click the adjustment layer created by the Smart Brush. For more on layers, see Chapter 8.

2 Type a value less than 100% in the opacity field.

● Photoshop Elements decreases the Smart Brush effect.

● You can click the visibility icon (👁) to turn off the adjustment layer and hide the effect.

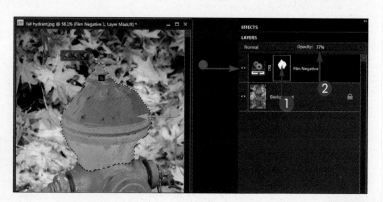

Draw a Shape

You can create solid shapes in your image by using the many shape tools in Photoshop Elements. Shapes offer an easy way to add whimsical objects, labels, or buttons to an image.

When you add a shape to an image, Photoshop Elements places the shape in its own layer. This makes it easy to move and transform the shape later on. Because shape objects are vector graphics in Photoshop Elements, they can be resized without a loss in quality. For more on layers, see Chapter 8.

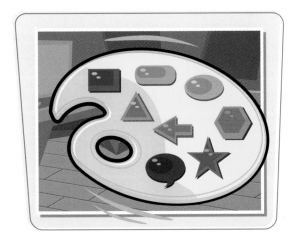

Draw a Shape

① In the Editor, right-click the **Rectangle** tool (■).

Note: For more on opening the Editor, see Chapter 1.

② Click the **Custom Shape** tool (♥) in the menu that appears.

The Custom Shape tool shares space in the Toolbox with the other shape tools.

Note: See Chapter 1 for more on the Toolbox tools.

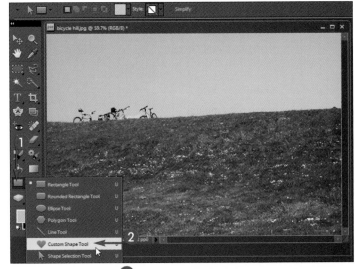

③ Click here to open the Custom Shapes menu.

④ Click a shape.

⑤ Press Enter to close the menu.

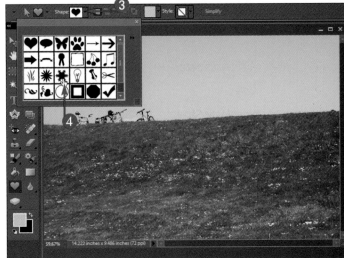

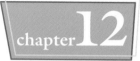

6 Click here to choose a color for your shape.

7 Press Enter to close the menu.

● You can click here to select a style, such as a 3-D style, for your shape.

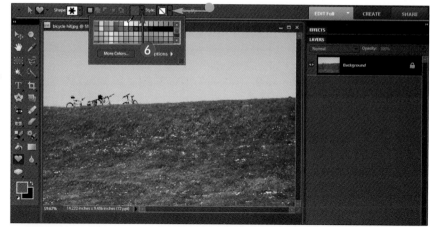

8 Click and drag your mouse pointer (+) to draw the shape.

● Photoshop Elements places the shape in its own layer.

Note: *For more on layers, see Chapter 8.*

You can click and drag multiple times to create more than one shape.

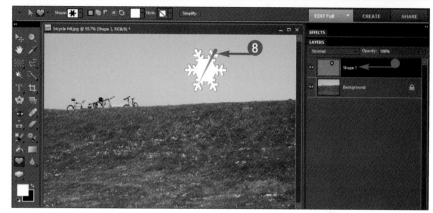

TIP

How do I resize a shape after I draw it?

1 Click the shape's layer.

2 Click the **Custom Shape** tool (♥).

3 Click **Image**.

4 Click **Transform Shape**.

5 Click a transform command.

You can then resize the shape just like you would a selection. See Chapter 7 for more on transformations.

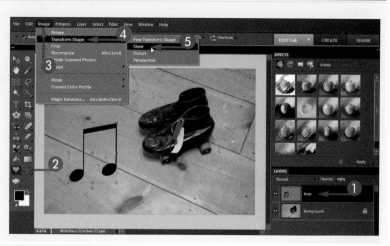

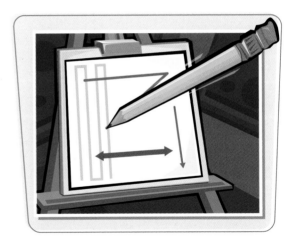

You can use the Line tool in Photoshop Elements to draw straight lines in your image. You can customize the line with arrows, giving you an easy way to point out elements in your image.

When you add a line to an image with the Line tool, Photoshop Elements places the line in its own layer. This makes it easy to move and transform the line later on. Because line objects are vector graphics in Photoshop Elements, they can be resized and otherwise transformed without a loss in quality. For more on layers, see Chapter 8.

Draw a Line

1. In the Editor, right-click on the **Rectangle** tool (▣).

Note: For more on opening the Editor, see Chapter 1.

2. Click the **Line** tool (◥).

    The Line tool shares space in the Toolbox with the other shape tools.

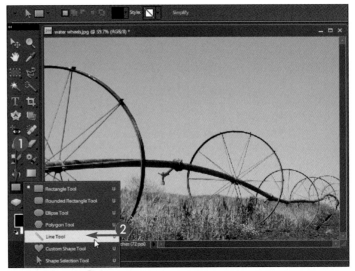

3. Click here and then click **Start** or **End** to include arrowheads on your line (■ changes to ✓).

● You can also specify the shape of the arrowheads by typing values here.

4. Press Enter to close the menu.

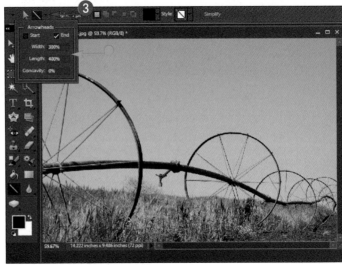

5 Type a line weight.

6 Click here to choose a different line color.

● You can click here to set a style for your line. Styles such as 3-D and shadow are available.

7 Press **Enter** to close the menu.

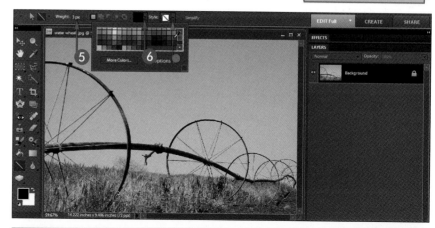

8 Click and drag your mouse pointer (+) to draw the line.

● Photoshop Elements places the line in its own layer.

Note: For more on layers, see Chapter 8.

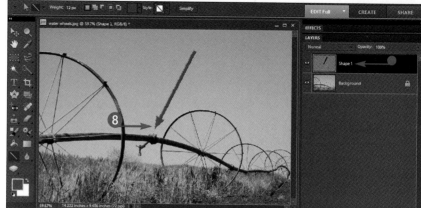

TIP

How can I add an outline along a selection in my image?

1 Click **Edit**.

2 Click **Stroke (Outline) Selection**.

3 In the Stroke dialog box, type a width for the line.

● You can click here to choose a color for the line.

4 Click a location (● changes to ○).

5 Click **OK**.

● Photoshop Elements applies the stroke.

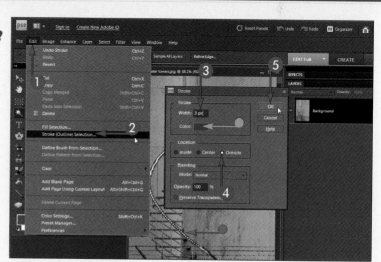

Erase an Area

You can use the Eraser tool to erase unwanted areas of your photo. When you apply the Eraser tool in the Background layer, the erased pixels are replaced with the current background color. When you erase in other layers, the Eraser tool turns the pixels transparent, revealing any underlying layers.

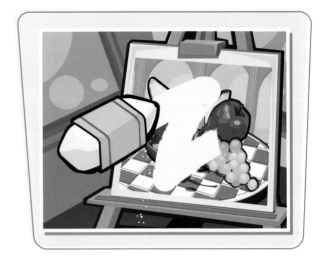

Erase an Area

1 In the Editor, click the **Eraser** tool (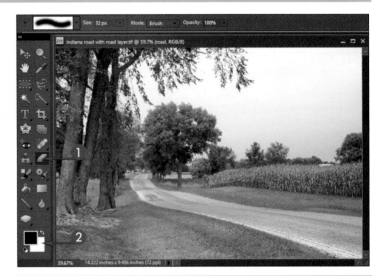).

Note: For more on opening the Editor, see Chapter 1.

2 Click the **Background Color** box (☐) to choose a color to appear in place of the erased pixels.

Note: For more, see the section "Set the Foreground and Background Colors."

3 Click here to choose an eraser size and type.

● You can also click here and adjust a slider to set an eraser size.

Erase the Background Layer

④ Click the Background layer.

⑤ Click and drag the mouse pointer
(○) to erase.

Portions of the Background layer
are erased and filled with the
background color.

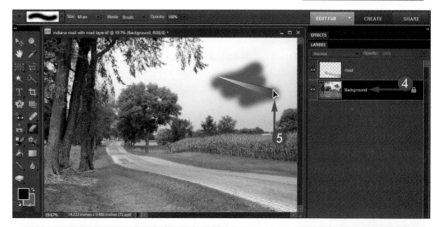

Erase a Normal Layer

⑥ Click a normal layer.

⑦ Click and drag the mouse pointer
(○) to erase.

Portions of a layer are erased to
reveal the underlying layer.

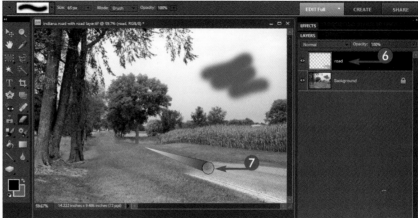

 TIPS

What eraser shapes are available?

You can right-click on the
Eraser tool (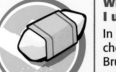) to access
other eraser types. You can
use the Background Eraser
tool (🔲) to sample a color in
your image and erase only
that color as you drag the tool over your
image. The Magic Eraser tool (🔲) erases all
the adjacent, similarly colored pixels when
you click it.

Which eraser mode should I use?

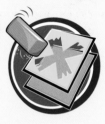

In the Options bar, you can
choose from three eraser modes:
Brush, Pencil, and Block. Brush
mode, which is the default mode,
enables you to apply the eraser to
your image similar to the Brush
tool. The Pencil mode acts like the
Pencil tool while erasing, with the strokes having a
harder edge. The Block mode turns the eraser mouse
pointer into a hard-edged square shape for erasing.

Apply a Gradient

You can apply a *gradient*, which is a blend from one color to another, to give objects in your image a radiant or 3-D look. You can apply a gradient to a selected portion of an image or the entire image.

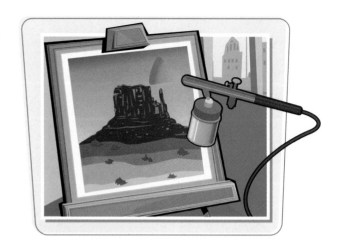

Apply a Gradient

1 In the Editor, make a selection.

Note: *For more on opening the Editor, see Chapter 1. See Chapter 6 for more on making selections.*

If you do not make a selection, the gradient is applied to the entire image.

2 Click the **Gradient** tool (■).

● A linear gradient (■) is the default. You can select different geometries in the Options bar.

3 Click the gradient swatch.

The Gradient Editor dialog box opens.

4 Click a preset gradient type from the top box.

● You can define a custom gradient by changing these settings.

5 Click **OK**.

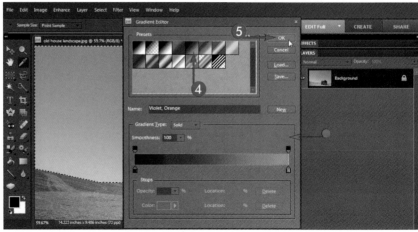

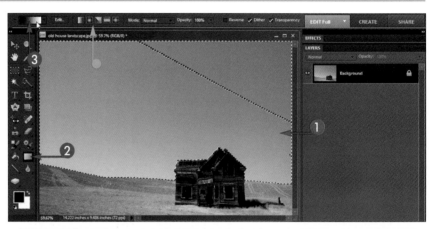

6 Click and drag the mouse pointer (+) inside the selection.

This defines the direction and transition of the gradient.

Dragging a long line with the tool produces a gradual transition.

Dragging a short line with the tool produces an abrupt transition.

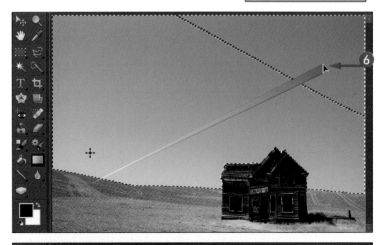

Photoshop Elements generates a gradient inside the selection.

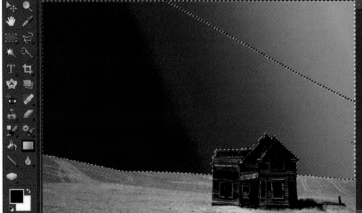

TIP

How can I highlight an object in my image by using a gradient?

1 Place the object in its own layer.

2 Create a new layer below the object and then select the new layer.

3 Click the **Gradient** tool (▨).

4 Click the **Radial Gradient** button (▨).

5 Click and drag the mouse pointer (+) from the center of the object outward to create the gradient.

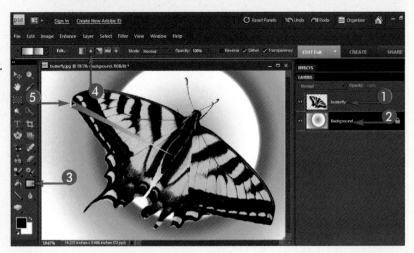

Applying Filters

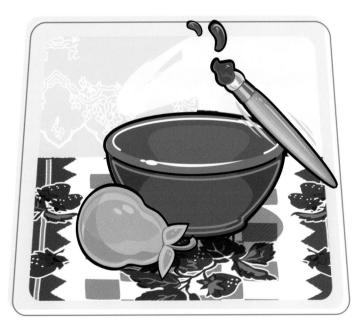

You can use the filters in Photoshop Elements to quickly and easily apply enhancements to your image, including artistic effects, texture effects, and distortions. Filters can help you correct defects in your images or let you turn a photograph into something resembling an impressionist painting. This chapter highlights a few of the more than 100 filters available in Photoshop Elements. For more on all the filters, see the Help documentation.

Blur an Image

You can use the Blur filters to apply a variety of blurring effects to your photos. For example, you can use the Gaussian Blur filter to obscure background objects while keeping foreground objects in focus.

Blurring a busy background makes an image look as if it has a short depth of field. A short depth of field keeps the foreground subject in focus while placing the background out of focus.

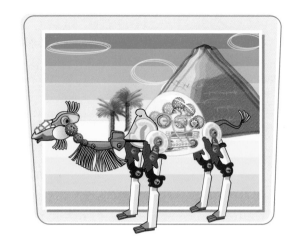

Blur an Image

① In the Editor, select the layer to which you want to apply the filter.

Note: *For more on opening the Editor, see Chapter 1. For more on layers, see Chapter 8.*

In this example, the scenery around the flower has been selected.

② Click **Filter**.

③ Click **Blur**.

④ Click **Gaussian Blur**.

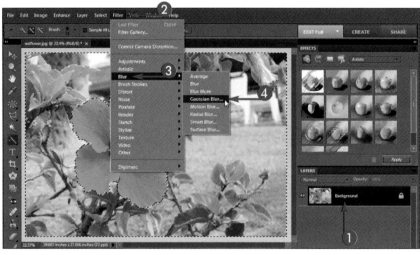

The Gaussian Blur dialog box opens, displaying a preview of the filter's effect.

⑤ Click the minus sign (⊖) or plus sign (⊕) to zoom out or in.

⑥ Click the **Preview** check box to preview the effect in the image window (■ changes to ✓).

⑦ Click and drag the **Radius** slider (▥) to control the amount of blur added. In this example, boosting the Radius value increases the amount of blur.

⑧ Click **OK**.

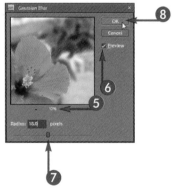

Photoshop Elements applies the filter.

Note: To apply the filter to just part of your image, select an element by using a selection tool. For more on selection tools, see Chapter 6.

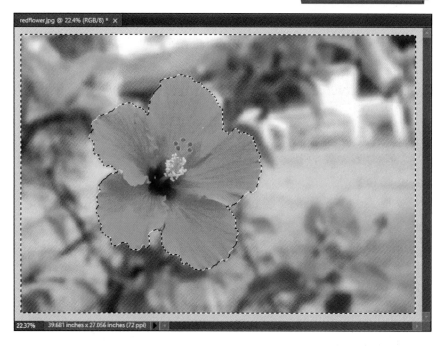

TIP

How do I add directional blurring to an image?

1 Select the layer to blur.

2 Click **Filter**.

3 Click **Blur**.

4 Click **Motion Blur**.

The Motion Blur dialog box opens, displaying a preview of the filter's effect.

5 In the Motion Blur dialog box, click and drag the **Angle** dial to define the direction of the blur.

6 Click and drag the slider (■) to adjust the distance, or the amount of blur.

7 Click **OK** to apply the filter.

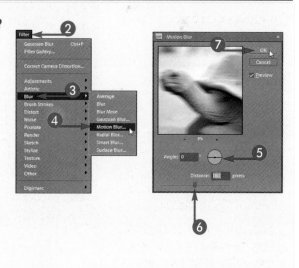

Distort an Image

You can use any of the Distort filters to stretch and squeeze your image, creating the appearance of waves, glass, swirls, and more. For example, the Twirl filter turns the image into a swirl of colors, and the Ripple filter adds wavelike effects.

To apply the filter to just part of your image, select that portion by using a selection tool. For more on selection tools, see Chapter 6.

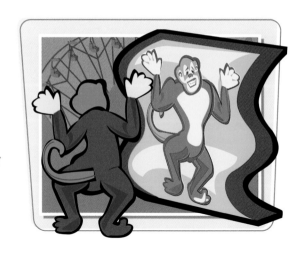

Distort an Image

1 In the Editor, select the layer to which you want to apply a filter.

Note: For more on opening the Editor, see Chapter 1. For more on layers, see Chapter 8.

2 Click **Filter**.

3 Click **Distort**.

4 Click a filter.

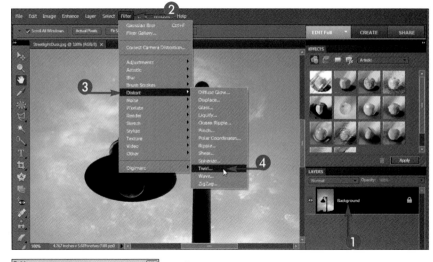

The filter's dialog box opens.

5 Make adjustments to the filter's settings to fine-tune the effect.

With some filters, you can preview the effect before applying it to the image.

6 Click **OK**.

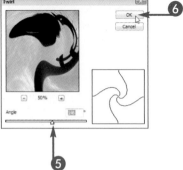

Photoshop Elements applies the filter.

In this example, the Twirl distortion filter is applied.

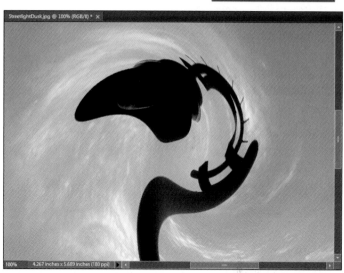

In this example, the Ripple distortion filter is applied.

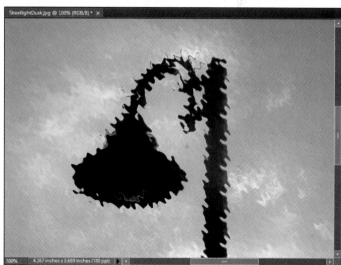

How many filters does Photoshop Elements offer?

Photoshop Elements has 106 filters grouped into 14 categories. You can experiment with each one to find out what effect it has on your image. Two of the more popular filters are Unsharp Mask (used for sharpening an image's focus) and Lighting Effects (which creates the illusion of spotlights and other specialized lights in your photos). See Chapters 9 and 10 for more on using these two filters. You can also download additional filters from third-party companies. Some of these filters are free, while others must be purchased.

Is there another way to distort a selection?

Yes. You can use the Distort command to reshape a selected element in your photo. After selecting the element, click **Image**, **Transform**, and then **Distort**. Photoshop Elements surrounds the selection with handles, which you can drag to distort the element. See Chapter 7 for more on distorting selections.

Turn an Image into a Painting

You can use many of the Artistic filters in Photoshop Elements to make your image look as if you created it with a paintbrush or other art media. The Watercolor filter, for example, applies a painted effect by converting similarly colored areas in your image to solid colors.

To apply the filter to just part of your image, select that portion by using a selection tool. For more on selection tools, see Chapter 6.

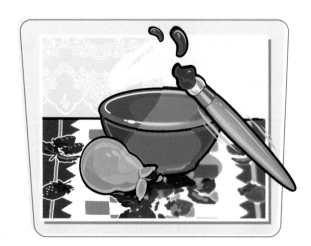

Turn an Image into a Painting

① In the Editor, select the layer to which you want to apply a filter.

Note: *For more on opening the Editor, see Chapter 1. For more on layers, see Chapter 8.*

In this example, the image has a single Background layer.

② Click **Filter**.

③ Click **Artistic**.

④ Click a filter.

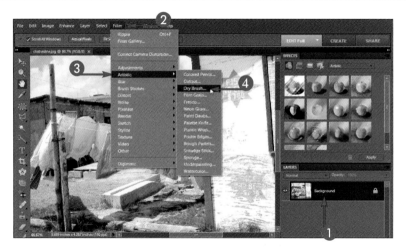

The Filter Gallery dialog box opens, displaying a preview of the filter's effect.

⑤ Adjust the filter's settings to fine-tune the effect.

● With some filters, you can preview the effect before applying it to the image. Click the minus sign (⊟) or the plus sign (⊞) to zoom out or in.

● You can select a different filter by clicking ⊡ in the right pane.

⑥ Click **OK**.

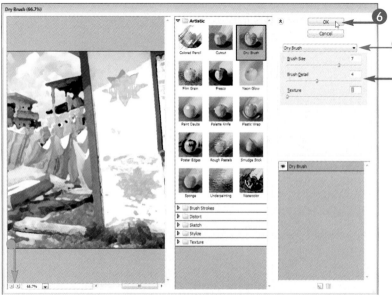

Photoshop Elements applies the filter. In this example, the Dry Brush filter is applied.

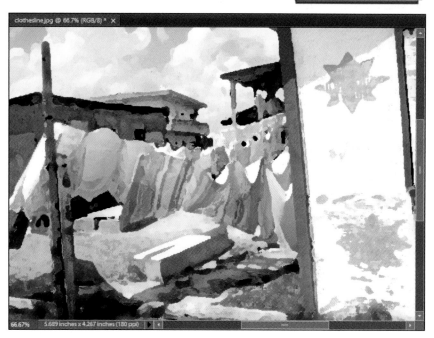

TIP

How do I make my image look like a sponge painting?

You can use the Sponge filter to reduce details and modify the image's shapes:

1. Follow steps **1** to **4** in this section, but select **Sponge** in step **4**.

2. In the Filter Gallery dialog box, click and drag the sliders (⊡) to define the size and contrast of the sponge strokes.

3. Click **OK**.

   Photoshop Elements applies the filter.

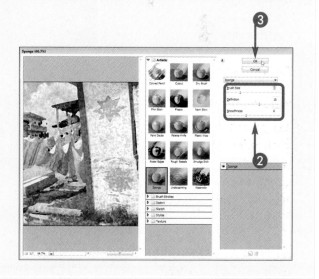

Turn an Image into a Sketch

The Sketch filters add outlining effects to your image. The Charcoal filter, for example, makes an image look as if you sketched it by using charcoal.

The Charcoal filter uses the foreground as the charcoal color and the background as the paper color. Changing these colors alters the filter's effect. For more on adjusting colors, see Chapter 11.

To apply the filter to just part of your image, select that portion by using a selection tool. For more on selection tools, see Chapter 6.

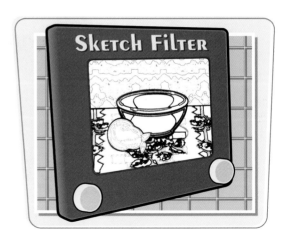

Turn an Image into a Sketch

① In the Editor, select the foreground and background colors that you want to apply with the sketch filter.

Note: *For more on opening the Editor, see Chapter 1. For more on how to select colors, see Chapter 11.*

② Select the layer to which you want to apply the filter.

Note: *For more on layers, see Chapter 8.*

In this example, the image has a single Background layer.

③ Click **Filter**.

④ Click **Sketch**.

⑤ Click **Charcoal**.

The Filter Gallery dialog box opens, displaying a preview of the filter's effect.

⑥ Click the minus sign (◻) or plus sign (◻) to zoom out or in.

⑦ Click and drag the sliders (▭) to control the filter's effect.

⑧ Click **OK**.

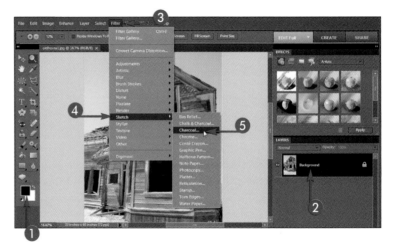

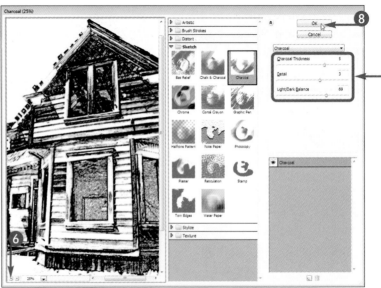

258

Photoshop Elements applies the filter.

In this example, the thickness of the charcoal strokes increases and the detail decreases.

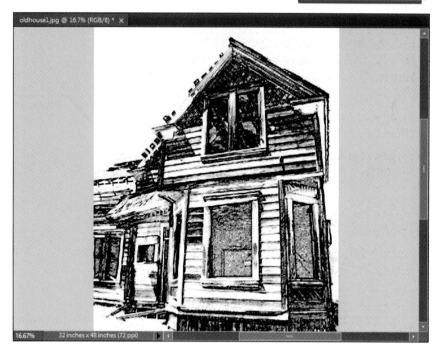

16.67%   32 inches x 48 inches (72 ppi)

TIP

What does the Photocopy filter do?

The Photocopy filter converts your image's shadows and midtones to the foreground color and converts highlights to the background color to make the image look like a photocopy.

① Follow steps **1** to **4** in this section, selecting **Photocopy** in step **4**.

② In the Filter Gallery dialog box, click and drag the sliders (🖾) to control the detail and darkness of the colors.

③ Click **OK**.

Photoshop Elements applies the filter.

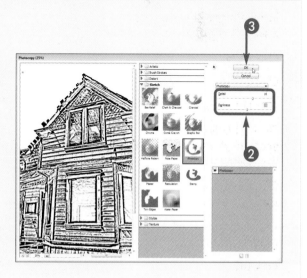

Add Noise to an Image

Filters in the Noise menu add graininess to or remove it from your image. You can add graininess with the Add Noise filter.

To apply the filter to just part of your image, select that portion by using a selection tool. For more on selection tools, see Chapter 6.

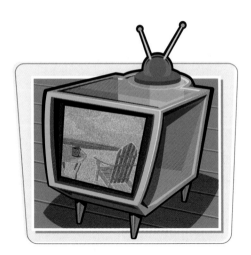

Add Noise to an Image

① In the Editor, select the layer to which you want to apply the filter.

Note: For more on opening the Editor, see Chapter 1. For more on layers, see Chapter 8.

In this example, the Background layer is selected. Above it are layers with text and an astronaut.

② Click **Filter**.

③ Click **Noise**.

④ Click **Add Noise**.

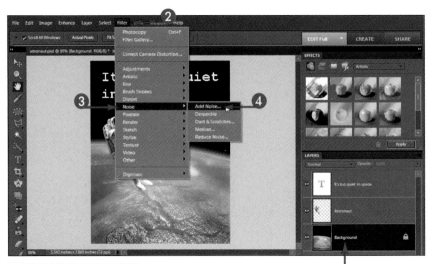

The Add Noise dialog box opens, displaying a preview of the filter's effect.

⑤ Click the minus sign (⊟ or plus sign (⊞) to zoom out or in.

⑥ Click the **Preview** check box to preview the effect in the main window (■ changes to ✓).

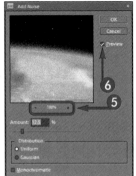

7. Click and drag the **Amount** slider (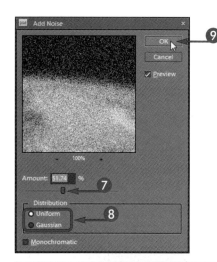) to change the noise.

   In this example, the Amount value is increased.

   You can also type the amount of noise you want to apply to an image.

8. Click a Distribution radio button to select how you want the noise distributed (● changes to ○).

   The Uniform option spreads the noise more evenly than Gaussian.

9. Click **OK**.

   Photoshop Elements applies the filter.

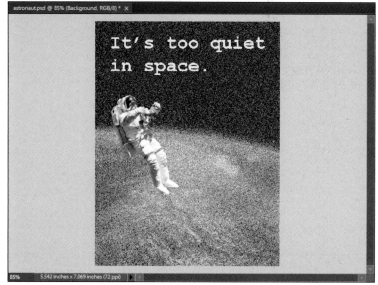

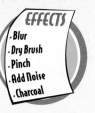

TIPS

What does the Monochromatic setting in the Add Noise dialog box do?

If you click to select **Monochromatic** (■ changes to ✓), Photoshop Elements adds noise by lightening or darkening pixels in your image. Pixel hues stay the same. At high settings with the Monochromatic setting on, the filter produces a television-static effect.

Can you apply filters from the Photoshop Elements Effects panel?

Yes. If you open the Effects panel and click **Filters** (■), you can access most of the filters that are also found under the Filter menu. You can choose different filter categories from the panel menu.

EFFECTS
- Blur
- Dry Brush
- Pinch
- Add Noise
- Charcoal

Pixelate an Image

The Pixelate filters divide areas of your image into solid-colored dots or shapes. The Crystallize filter, one example of a Pixelate filter, re-creates your image by using colored polygons.

To apply the filter to just part of your image, select a portion by using a selection tool. For more on selection tools, see Chapter 6.

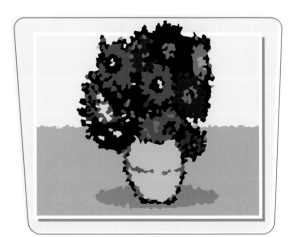

Pixelate an Image

① In the Editor, select the layer to which you want to apply the filter.

Note: *For more on opening the Editor, see Chapter 1. For more on layers, see Chapter 8.*

In this example, the image has a single Background layer.

② Click **Filter**.

③ Click **Pixelate**.

④ Click **Crystallize**.

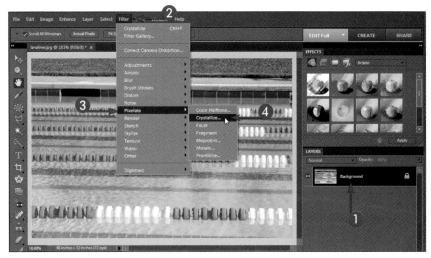

The Crystallize dialog box opens, displaying a preview of the filter's effect.

⑤ Click the minus sign ( ) or plus sign ( ) to zoom out or in.

⑥ Click and drag the **Cell Size** slider ( ) to adjust the size of the shapes.

The size can range from 3 to 300.

In this example, the Cell Size has been increased.

⑦ Click **OK**.

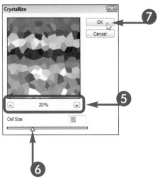

Photoshop Elements applies the filter.

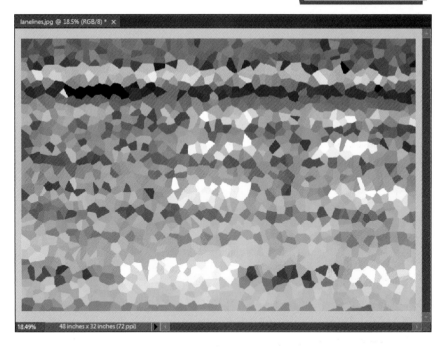

TIP

What does the Mosaic filter do?

The Mosaic filter converts your image to a set of solid-color squares.

1 Click **Filter**.

2 Click **Pixelate**.

3 Click **Mosaic**.

The Mosaic dialog box opens.

4 Click and drag the slider ( ) to specify the mosaic square size.

5 Click **OK** to apply the filter.

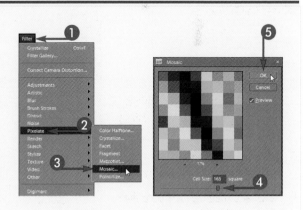

Emboss an Image

You can achieve the effect of a three-dimensional shape pressed into paper with the Emboss filter. You may find this filter useful for generating textured backgrounds.

To apply the filter to just part of your image, select that portion by using a selection tool. For more on selection tools, see Chapter 6.

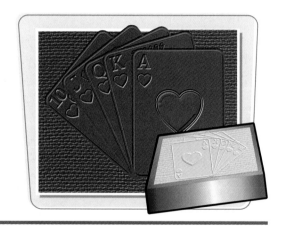

Emboss an Image

① In the Editor, select the layer to which you want to apply the filter.

Note: *For more on opening the Editor, see Chapter 1. For more on layers, see Chapter 8.*

In this example, the image has a single Background layer.

② Click **Filter**.

③ Click **Stylize**.

④ Click **Emboss**.

The Emboss dialog box opens, displaying a preview of the filter's effect.

⑤ Click the minus sign (🔍) or the plug sign (🔍) to zoom out or in.

⑥ Type an angle value to specify the direction of the shadow.

⑦ Click and drag the **Height** slider (🔲) to set the strength of the embossing.

⑧ Click and drag the **Amount** slider (🔲) to set the number of edges the filter effects.

You can also type in a number for the amount of height or embossing.

⑨ Click **OK**.

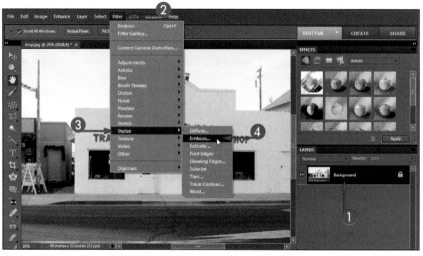

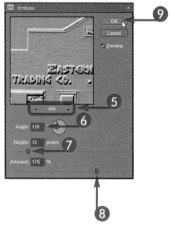

Photoshop Elements applies the filter.

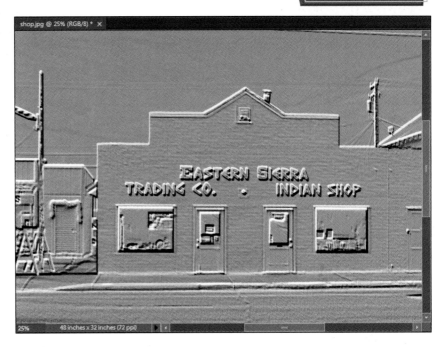

Do I have another way to create an embossed effect in an image?

Yes. You can use the Bas Relief filter to get a similar effect.

1 Follow steps **1** to **4** in this section, clicking **Sketch** in step **3** and **Bas Relief** in step **4**.

2 In the Filter Gallery dialog box, click and drag the slider (⊟) to control the detail.

3 Click and drag the slider (⊟) to control the smoothness.

4 Click **OK**.

Photoshop Elements applies the filter.

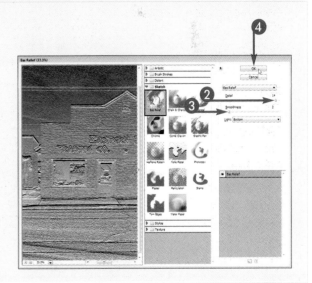

Apply Multiple Filters

You can apply more than one filter to an image by using the Filter Gallery interface. The interface enables you to preview a variety of filter effects and apply them in combination.

Many filters open the Filter Gallery interface when you apply them, including the Charcoal Sketch filter, which is covered earlier in this chapter. Not all the effects listed under the Photoshop Elements Filter menu appear in the Filter Gallery. Ones not shown can be accessed in the Filter menu.

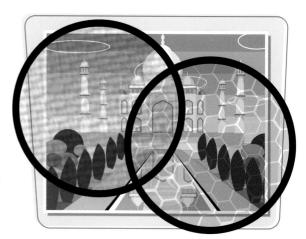

Apply Multiple Filters

① In the Editor, select the layer to which you want to apply the filters.

Note: For more on opening the Editor, see Chapter 1.

In this example, the image has a single Background layer.

Note: To apply the filters to just part of your image, make a selection with a selection tool. For more on selection tools, see Chapter 6.

② Click **Filter**.

③ Click **Filter Gallery**.

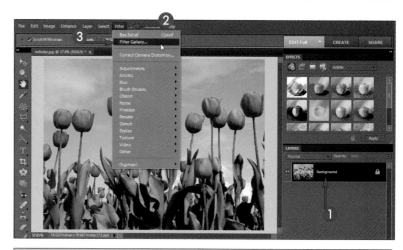

The Filter Gallery dialog box opens, with the most recently applied filter selected.

The left pane displays a preview of the filtered image.

④ Click an arrow to display filters from a category (▷ changes to ▽).

⑤ Click a thumbnail to apply a filter.

● The filter appears in the filter list.

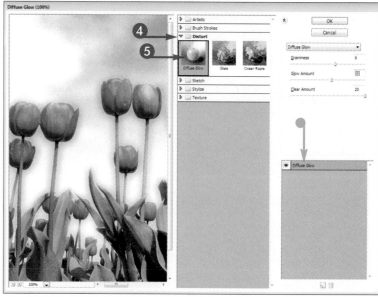

6 Click the **New Effect Layer** button (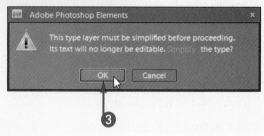).

● The new effect appears in the filter list.

You can click and drag effects in the list to change their order and change the look of your image.

Note: For more on rearranging layers, see Chapter 8.

7 Click a different triangle to display filters from another category (▶ changes to ▾).

8 Click a thumbnail to apply another filter.

You can repeat steps **6** to **8** to apply additional filters.

9 Click **OK**.

Photoshop Elements applies the filters.

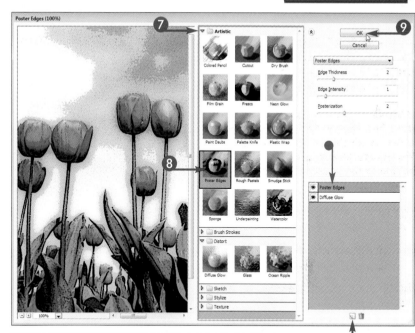

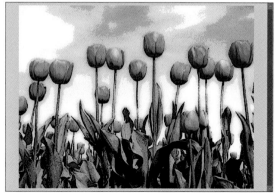

How can I apply filters to text?

You can apply filters to a type layer in your image, but you must first simplify the layer. *Simplifying* converts your type layer to a regular Photoshop Elements layer. After simplifying, you can no longer edit the type with the type tools.

1 Select a type layer.

2 Select a filter under the Filter menu.

A dialog box opens, asking if you want to simplify the type layer.

3 Click **OK**. Photoshop Elements converts the type layer to a regular layer.

4 Apply the filter as you would to any other layer.

Adding Text Elements

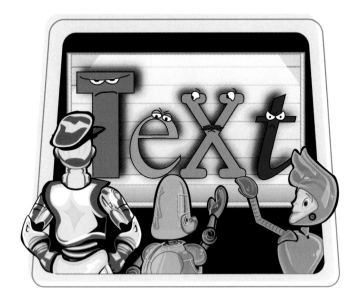

Do you want to add letters and words to your photos and illustrations? Photoshop Elements lets you add text to your images and precisely control the appearance and layout of text. You can also stylize your text by using effects and other tools in Photoshop Elements.

Add Text

Adding text enables you to label elements in your image or use letters and words in artistic ways. When you add text, it appears in its own layer. You can manipulate text layers in your image to move or stylize text.

Photoshop Elements comes with a number of expensive typefaces that are not typically preinstalled on computers.

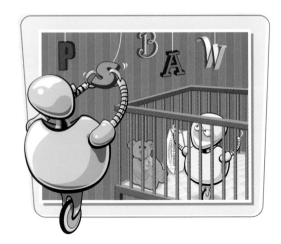

Add Text

① In the Editor, click the **Horizontal Type** tool ( ).

Note: *For more on opening the Editor, see Chapter 1.*

② Click in the image where you want the text to begin.

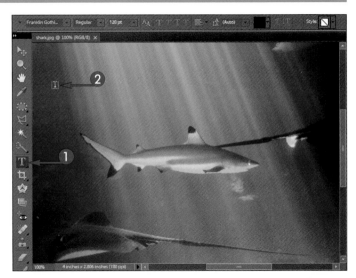

③ Select a font, style, and size for your text from these menus.

④ Click the **Color** drop-down arrow ( ).

⑤ Click a color for your text.

When you position your mouse pointer ( ) over a color, it changes to an eyedropper ( ).

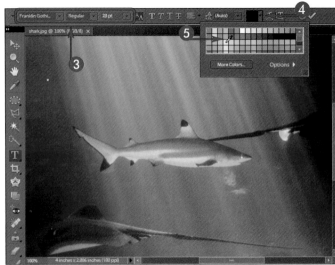

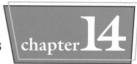

6 Type your text.

To create a line break, press
Enter.

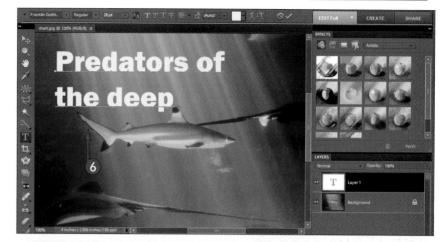

7 When you finish typing your text,
click ✓ or press Enter on your
keyboard's number pad.

● You can click ⊘ or press Esc to
cancel.

● Photoshop Elements places the
text in its own layer.

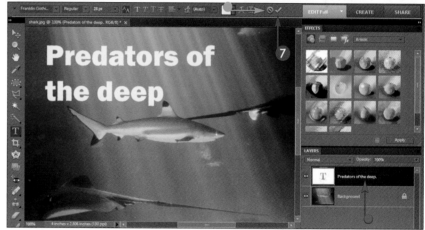

How do I reposition my text?

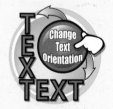

You can move the
layer that contains
the text with the
Move tool (⊹).
Click the layer of
text, click the **Move**
tool, and then click and drag to reposition
your text. For more on moving a layer, see
Chapter 8.

How do I add vertical text to my image?

Right-click on the **Horizontal Type**
tool (T) and then click the **Vertical
Type** tool (IT) in the menu that
appears. You can also click the Vertical
Type tool on the Options bar. Your text
appears with a vertical orientation, and
lines are added from right to left. You can change the
orientation of existing text in your image by selecting a text
layer and then clicking the **Change the Text Orientation**
button (IT). This converts horizontal text to vertical text and
vice versa.

Change the Formatting of Text

You can change the font, style, size, and other characteristics of your text. This can help emphasize or de-emphasize your text.

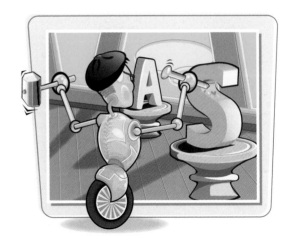

Change the Formatting of Text

① In the Editor, click the **Horizontal Type** tool (T).

Note: For more on opening the Editor, see Chapter 1.

② Click the text layer that you want to edit.

Note: For more on how to open the Layers panel, see Chapter 1.

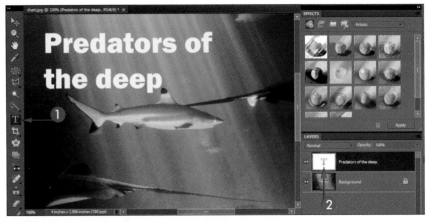

③ Click and drag to select some text from the selected layer.

● You can double-click the layer thumbnail to select all the text.

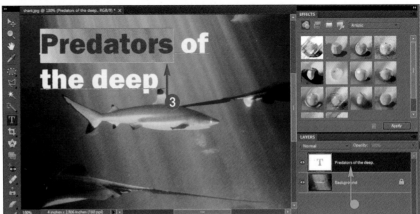

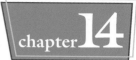

4️⃣ Click here to choose a font.

5️⃣ Click here to choose the text's style.

6️⃣ Click here to choose the text's size.

7️⃣ Click the **Anti-Aliased** button (🔠) to control the text's anti-aliasing.

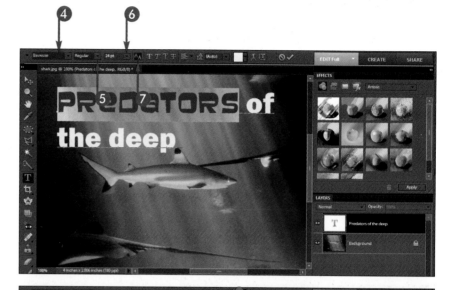

8️⃣ When you finish formatting your text, click ✅ or press **Enter** on your keyboard's number pad.

● You can click 🚫 or press **Esc** to cancel.

Photoshop Elements applies the formatting to your text.

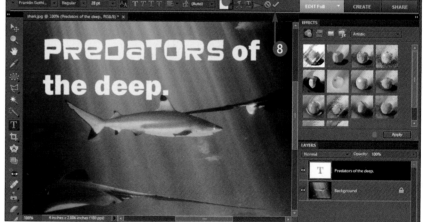

TIPS

What is anti-aliasing?
Anti-aliasing is the process of adding semi-transparent pixels to curved edges in digital images to make the edges appear smoother. You can apply anti-aliasing to text to improve its appearance. Text that you do not anti-alias can sometimes look jagged.
You can control the presence and style of your text's anti-aliasing with the Options bar. At very small text sizes, anti-aliasing can be counterproductive and cause blurring.

How do I change the alignment of my text?
When creating your text, click one of the three alignment buttons in the Photoshop Elements Options bar: Left Align Text (▤), Center Text (▤), or Right Align Text (▤). You may find these options useful when you create multi-line passages of text.

Change the Color of Text

You can change the color of your text to make it blend or contrast with the rest of the image. You can change the color of all or just part of your text.

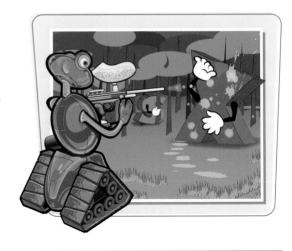

1 In the Editor, click the **Horizontal Type** tool (![T]).

Note: For more on opening the Editor, see Chapter 1.

2 Click the text layer that you want to edit.

Note: For more on how to open the Layers panel, see Chapter 1.

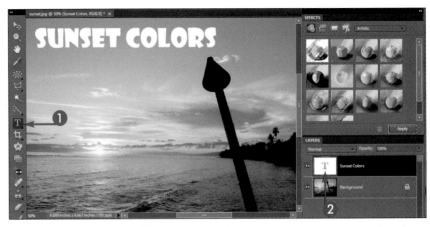

3 Click and drag to highlight some text.

● You can double-click the layer thumbnail to highlight all the text.

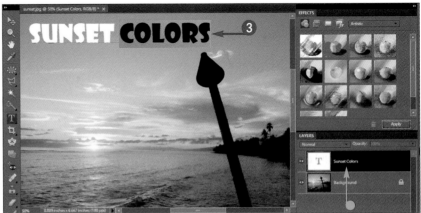

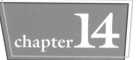

④ Click here to choose a color.

When you position your mouse pointer (🖑) over a color, it changes to an eyedropper (🖋).

● You can click **More Colors** to open the Color Picker for more color options.

● You can click here to open the Select Color dialog box.

⑤ Press Enter on your keyboard's number pad to close the color menu.

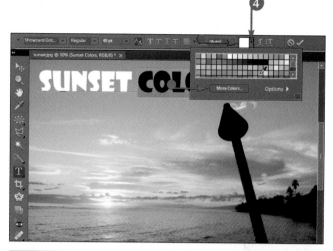

⑥ Click ✓ or press Enter on your keyboard's number pad again.

● You can click 🚫 or press Esc to cancel.

Photoshop Elements changes the text to the new color.

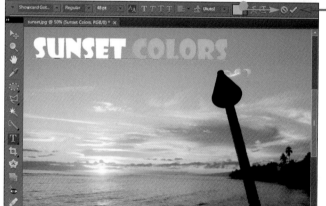

 TIP

How do I change type color by using the Color Swatches panel?

① Click **Window** and then **Color Swatches** to open the panel.

② Click the text layer in the Layers panel.

③ Click and drag in the image window to highlight the text you want to recolor.

④ Click a color in the Color Swatches panel.

The text changes color. To see the actual new color, click away from the type in the image window to deselect it.

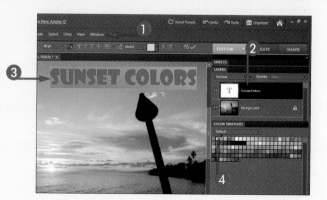

Create Warped Text

You can easily bend and distort layers of text by using the Warped Text feature in Photoshop Elements. This can help you stylize your text to match the theme of your image.

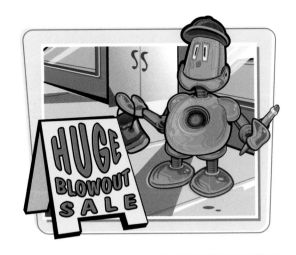

Create Warped Text

① In the Editor, click the **Horizontal Type** tool (📷).

Note: For more on opening the Editor, see Chapter 1.

② Click the text layer that you want to warp.

Note: For more on how to open the Layers panel, see Chapter 1.

③ Click the **Create Warped Text** button (📷).

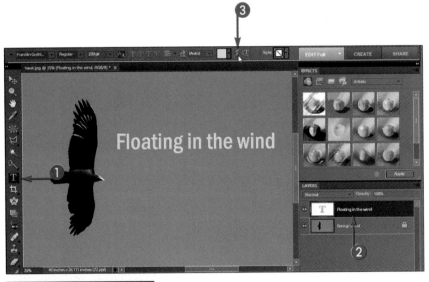

The Warp Text dialog box opens.

④ Click here to choose a warp style.

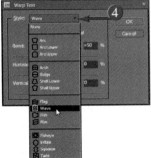

5 Click a radio button to select an orientation for the warp effect (● changes to ○).

6 Adjust the Bend and Distortion values by clicking and dragging the sliders (▭).

You can also type Bend and Distortion values.

The Bend and Distortion values determine how Photoshop Elements applies the warp.

For all settings, a value of 0% means Photoshop Elements does not apply that aspect of a warp.

7 Click **OK**.

Photoshop Elements warps the text.

You can still edit the format, color, and other characteristics of the type when you apply a warp. See the other tasks in this chapter for more.

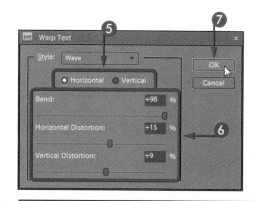

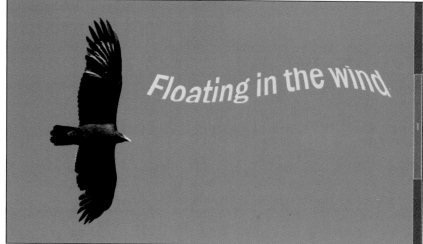

TIP

How do I unwarp text?

1 Follow steps **1** to **3** in this section.

2 In the Warp Text dialog box, click here and then choose **None**.

3 Click **OK**.

Your text unwarps.

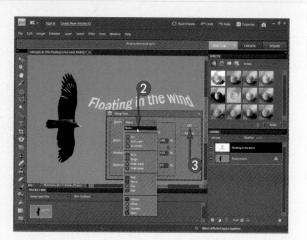

You can give your text a raised look by adding a beveled effect. Photoshop Elements offers several beveled options in the Effects panel.

For more on effects in Photoshop Elements, see Chapter 15.

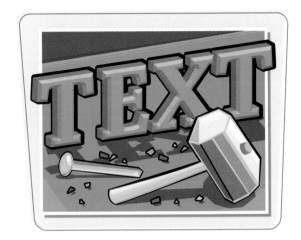

Create Beveled Text

① In the Layers panel, click a text layer.

② In the Effects panel, click the **Layer Styles** button (■).

Note: *For more on how to open the Layers and Effects panels, see Chapter 1.*

③ Click here and then choose **Bevels**.

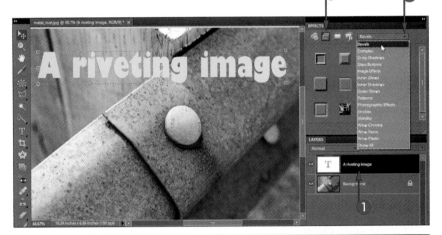

Photoshop Elements displays the bevel effects.

④ Click a bevel effect.

⑤ Click **Apply**.

Photoshop Elements applies the beveling to the text.

● Photoshop Elements adds an icon (■) to the layer to show that the layer includes an effect. You can double-click the icon to edit the effect.

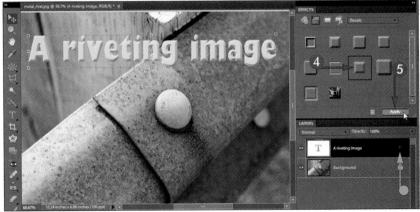

Add a Shadow to Text

You can cast a shadow behind your text to give the letters a 3-D look. Photoshop Elements offers several shadow options in the Effects panel.

For more on effects in Photoshop Elements, see Chapter 15.

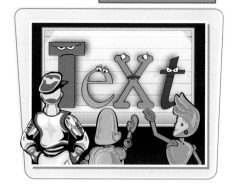

1 In the Layers panel, click a text layer.

2 In the Effects panel, click the **Layer Styles** button ( ).

Note: For more on how to open the Layers and Effects panels, see Chapter 1.

3 Click here to choose **Drop Shadows**.

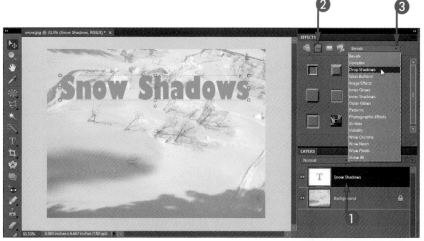

Photoshop Elements displays the Drop Shadows effects.

4 Click a shadow effect.

5 Click **Apply**.

Photoshop Elements applies the shadow to the text.

● Photoshop Elements adds an icon ( ) to the layer to show that the layer includes an effect. You can double-click the icon to edit the effect.

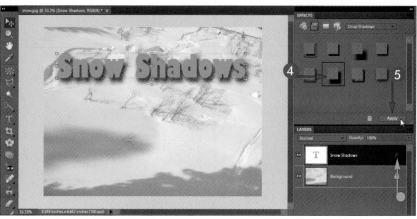

Applying Styles and Effects

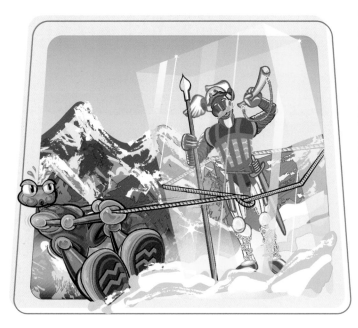

You can apply special effects to your images by using the built-in styles and effects in Photoshop Elements. The effects let you add shadows, glows, and a 3-D appearance to your art. You can also add special effects to your layers with layer styles.

Frame a Photo with a Drop Shadow

You can apply a drop shadow to make your photo look like it is floating above the image canvas.

You can also apply a drop shadow to just a layer. See the section "Add a Drop Shadow to a Layer" for more. To add shadowing to text, see Chapter 14.

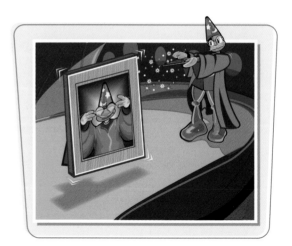

Frame a Photo with a Drop Shadow

① In the Editor, open the Effects panel.

Note: For more on opening the Editor or panels, see Chapter 1.

② Click the **Photo Effects** button (▣).

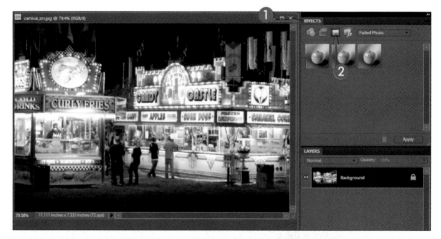

③ Click here and then choose **Frame**.

The Frame effects appear.

④ Double-click the **Drop Shadow Frame** effect.

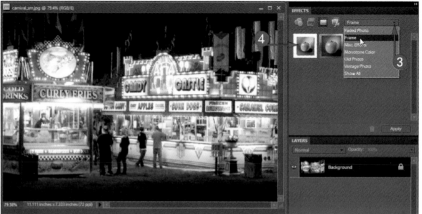

● Photoshop Elements duplicates the selected layer, adds extra space around the photo, and then applies the effect.

● Photoshop Elements applies the drop shadow over a canvas with the current background color, which is white in this example.

Note: For more on setting the background color, see Chapter 12.

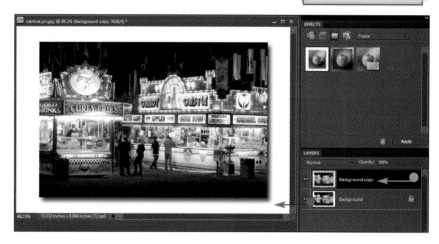

TIP

How do I change the color of a drop shadow?

You can change the color of a drop shadow in the Style Settings dialog box.

❶ After applying the drop shadow style, double-click the **Style** icon (◼) to open the Style Settings dialog box for the style.

❷ Click here to open the Select Shadow Color dialog box to select a shadow color.

❸ Click **OK**.

● Photoshop Elements changes the shadow color.

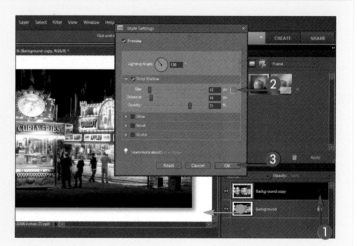

Add a Drop Shadow to a Layer

You can add a drop shadow to a layer to give objects in your photo a 3-D look. Style settings enable you to control the shadow's placement.

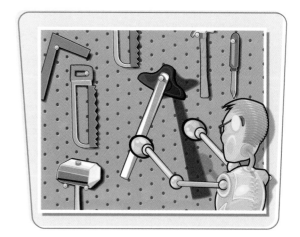

1. In the Editor, open the Layers panel.

   Note: *For more on opening the Editor, see Chapter 1.*

2. Open the Effects panel.

3. Click the **Layer Styles** button (▣).

4. Click the layer to which you want to add a drop shadow.

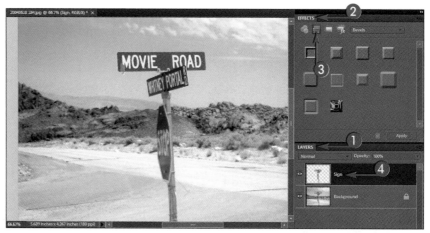

5. Click here to choose **Drop Shadows**.

   The Drop Shadow styles appear.

6. Click a drop shadow style.

7. Click **Apply**.

   Photoshop Elements applies the drop shadow to the layer.

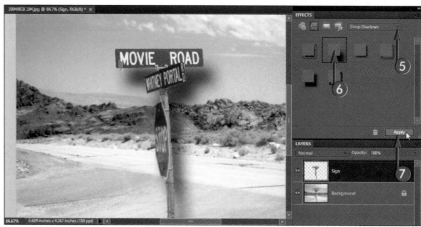

⑧ Double-click the **Style** icon ( ) in the affected layer.

The Style Settings dialog box opens.

⑨ Click and drag the **Lighting Angle** dial to specify the direction of the shadowing.

You can also type in an angle.

⑩ Click and drag the **Distance** slider ( ) to increase or decrease the distance of the shadow from your layer.

You can also type a distance.

⑪ Click **OK**.

Photoshop Elements applies the style settings.

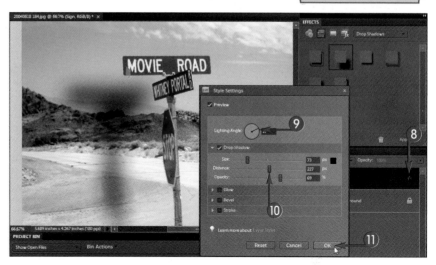

How can I add color shading to a layer by using layer styles?

You can add color shading to a layer by using the Photographic Effects styles.

① Click a layer.

② Open the Effects panel.

③ Click the **Layer Styles** button ( ).

④ Click here and then choose **Photographic Effects**.

⑤ Double-click an effect.

Photoshop Elements applies the shading.

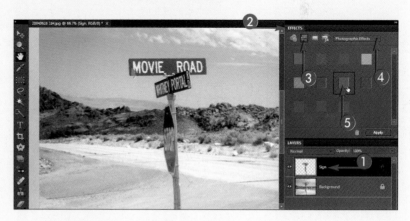

Create a Vintage Photo

You can apply an effect that removes color and adds a wrinkled texture to your photo, creating the look of an older snapshot.

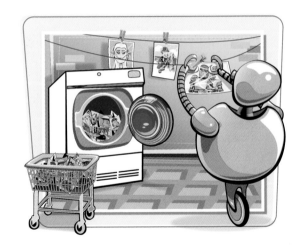

① In the Editor, open the Effects panel.

Note: *For more on opening the Editor or panels, see Chapter 1.*

② Click the **Photo Effects** button (▦).

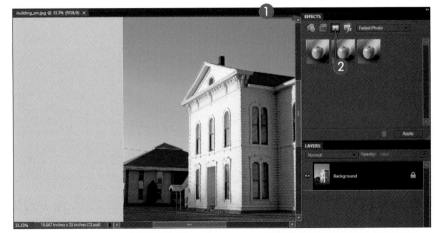

③ Click here and then choose **Vintage Photo**.

An Old Paper effect appears.

④ Double-click the Old Paper effect.

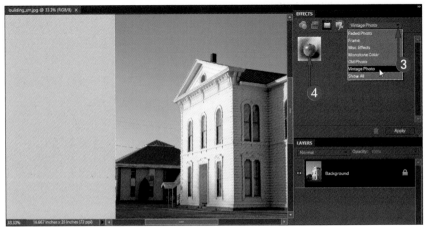

- Photoshop Elements duplicates the selected layer and then applies the effect.

- You can reduce the opacity of the new layer to make the effect more subtle.

Note: See Chapter 8 for more on layer opacity.

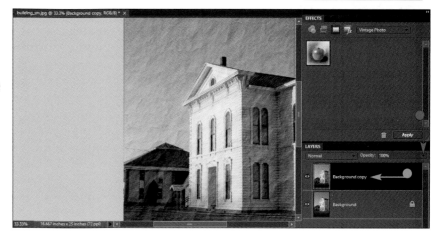

How can I add the vintage effect to just part of a photo?
You can add the vintage effect to just part of your photo by making a selection before applying the effect.

1. Make a selection by using one of the selection tools. See Chapter 6 for more on making selections.

2. In the Effects panel, double-click the Old Paper effect.

Photoshop Elements applies the effect to the selected area.

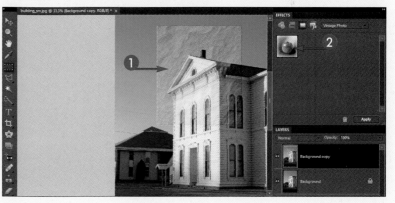

Add a Fancy Background

You can add a fancy background to your image by using one of several color or texture effects available in Photoshop Elements.

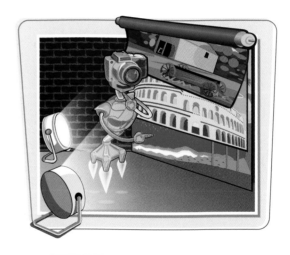

① In the Editor, open the Layers panel.

② Open the Effects panel.

Note: *For more on opening the Editor or panels, see Chapter 1.*

③ Click the **Layer Styles** button (■).

④ Click the layer to which you want to add the fancy background.

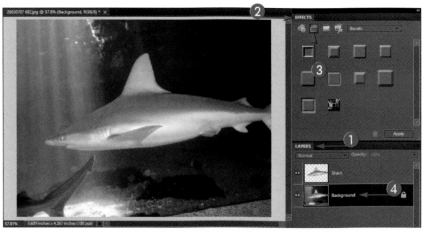

⑤ Click here and then choose **Patterns**.

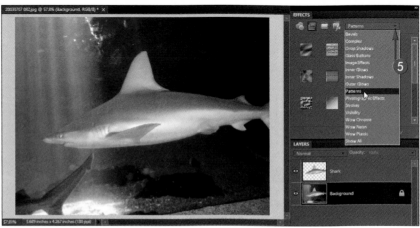

The Pattern styles appear.

⑥ Double-click a style.

If you selected the Background layer in step 4, a dialog box opens, asking if you want to make your background a normal layer.

⑦ Click **OK** and then click **OK** again in the dialog box that follows.

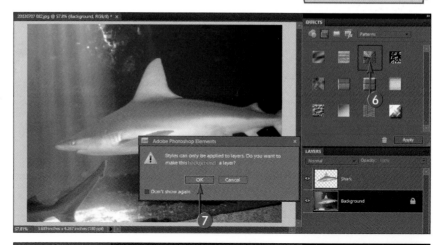

Photoshop Elements applies a pattern to the selected layer, creating a background behind the other layers.

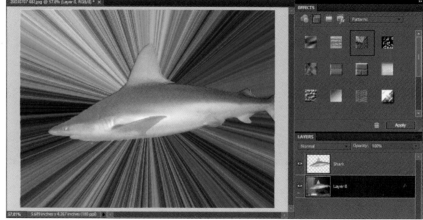

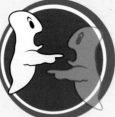

How can I reduce the strength of an effect that I just applied?

In cases where the effect is applied to a duplicate layer, you can reduce the opacity of the new layer to lessen the effect. Reducing the opacity to less than 100% allows the original content underneath to show through.

How can I customize the Effects panel?

Clicking the Effects menu arrows (▦) in the Effects panel opens a menu that allows you to tailor the Effects panel to your liking. You can select different thumbnail sizes for each effect and display the names of the effects. Selecting **Styles and Effects Help** opens a Web browser with information about the different effects.

Add an Outline to a Layer

You can add a color outline to a layer in your image. You can make the objects in the layer stand out by adding an outline that contrasts with the background.

To add a fancy coloring to the outer edge of a layer, see the section "Add an Outer Glow to a Layer."

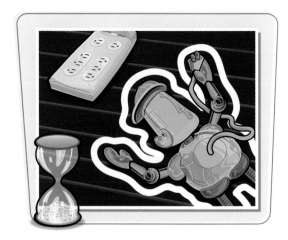

Add an Outline to a Layer

1 In the Editor, open the Layers panel.

2 Open the Effects panel.

Note: For more on opening the Editor or panels, see Chapter 1.

3 Click the layer to which you want to apply the outline.

In this example, a text layer is outlined.

Note: For more on using text, see Chapter 14.

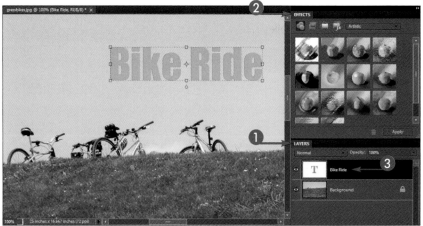

4 Click the **Layer Styles** button (🔲).

5 Click here and then choose **Strokes**.

The Stroke styles appear.

6 Double-click a stroke style.

Photoshop Elements applies the outline to the layer.

7 Double-click the **Style** icon (🔳) in the affected layer.

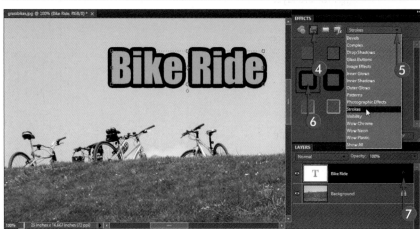

The Style Settings dialog box opens.

⑧ Click and drag the slider (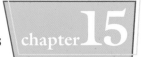) to adjust the size of the outline.

You can also type a size.

⑨ Click here to open the Select Stroke color dialog box.

⑩ Click to select a color.

You can also type in values to create a color.

⑪ Click **OK**.

⑫ Click **OK**.

Photoshop Elements applies the style settings.

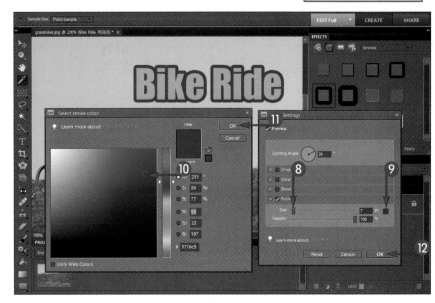

TIP

How do I add beveling to the layer that I have outlined?
You can add a second effect, such as beveling, to a layer by using the Style Settings dialog box.

① Double-click the **Style** icon (■) for the layer to open the Style Settings dialog box.

② Click the **Bevel** check box (■ changes to ☑).

③ Click and drag the slider (■) to adjust the size of the beveling.

You can also type a size for the bevel.

④ Click **OK**.

● Photoshop Elements applies beveling to the layer.

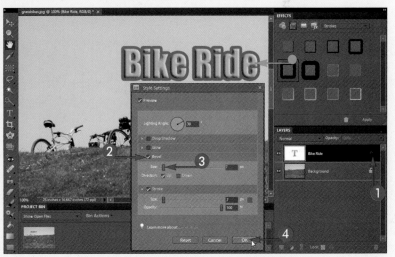

Add an Outer Glow to a Layer

The outer glow style adds fancy coloring to the outside edges of a layer's content, which can help highlight the layer.

To add a solid color to the edge of a layer, see the section "Add an Outline to a Layer."

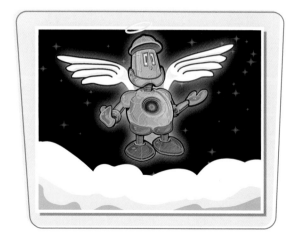

1. In the Editor, open the Layers panel.

   Note: For more on opening the Editor or panels, see Chapter 1.

2. Open the Effects panel.

3. Click the layer to which you want to apply the outer glow.

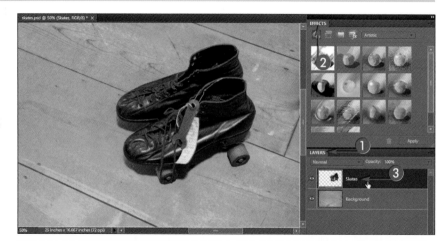

4. Click the **Layer Styles** button (■).

5. Click here and then choose **Outer Glows**.

   Photoshop Elements displays the Outer Glow styles.

6. Double-click an outer glow style.

   Photoshop Elements applies the outer glow to the layer.

7. Double-click the **Style** icon (■) in the affected layer.

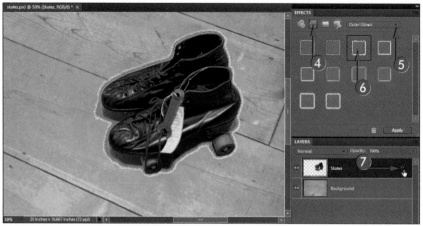

The Style Settings dialog box opens.

⑧ Click and drag the slider (▦) to increase or decrease the outer glow size.

You can also type a size.

⑨ Click **OK**.

Photoshop Elements applies the style settings.

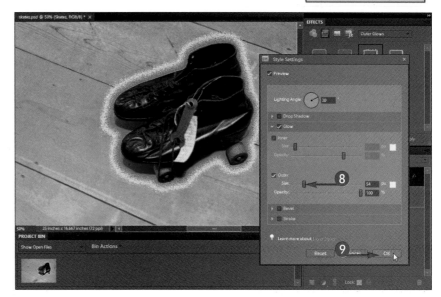

TIP

Can I add an inner glow to layer objects?
Yes. An inner glow adds color to the inside edge of a layer object.

① Click a layer.

② Open the Effects panel.

③ Click the **Layer Styles** button (▦).

④ Click here and then choose **Inner Glows** from the menu that appears.

⑤ Double-click an inner glow style.

Photoshop Elements applies the inner glow.

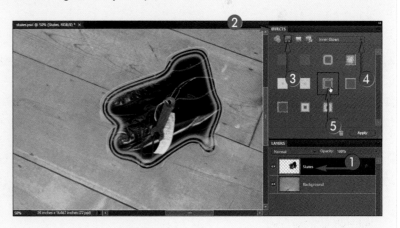

Add a Fancy Covering to a Layer

You can apply any of a variety of layer effects that can make a layer look as if it is covered in colorful glass or metal.

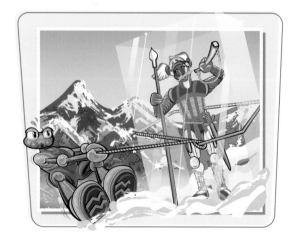

Cover with Glass

1. In the Editor, open the Layers panel.

2. Open the Effects panel.

Note: For more on opening the Editor and panels, see Chapter 1.

3. Click the layer that you want to cover.

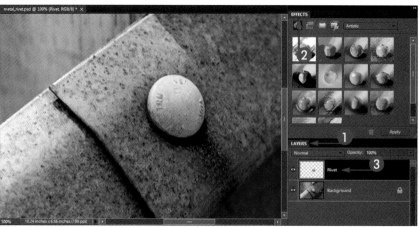

4. Click the **Layer Styles** button (🔲).

5. Click here to choose **Glass Buttons**.

Photoshop Elements displays a number of glass styles.

6. Double-click a style.

Photoshop Elements applies the style to the layer.

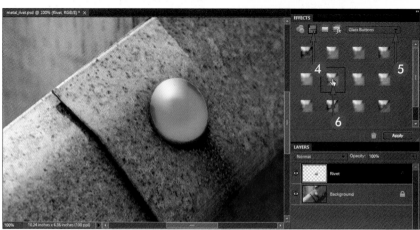

Cover with Metal

1 Click the layer that you want to cover.

2 Click here to choose **Complex**.

Photoshop Elements displays various styles.

3 Double-click the Diamond Plate style.

Photoshop Elements applies the style to the layer.

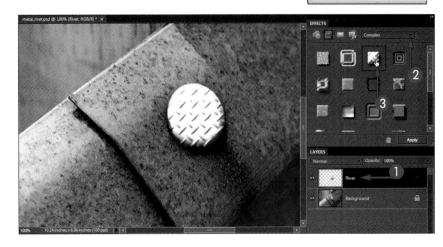

TIP

How do I remove a style from a layer?

1 Click a layer that has a style applied. Such layers are marked with a Style icon ( ).

2 Click **Layer**.

3 Click **Layer Style**.

4 Click **Clear Layer Style**.

Photoshop Elements removes the style from the layer.

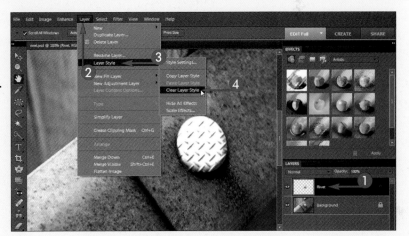

Add a Watermark

Photoshop Elements can automatically add watermarks to a collection of photos. Watermarks are semi-opaque words or designs overlaid on images to signify ownership and discourage illegal use.

Before you can begin, you need to create a source folder and a destination folder for your images. To work with folders, see your operating system's documentation.

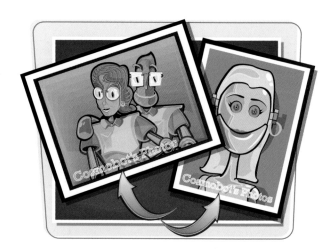

Add a Watermark

1. Place the images to which you want to add watermarks into a source folder.

2. Create an empty destination folder in which to save your watermarked files.

3. In the Photoshop Elements Editor, click **File**.

Note: For more on opening the Editor, see Chapter 1.

4. Click **Process Multiple Files**.

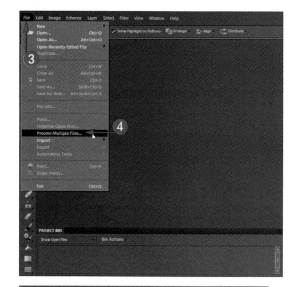

The Process Multiple Files dialog box opens.

5. Click **Browse** next to the Source box.

The Browse for Folder dialog box opens.

6. Click the source folder containing your images.

7. Click **OK**.

8. Click **Browse** next to the Destination box and then repeat steps **6** to **7** for the destination folder.

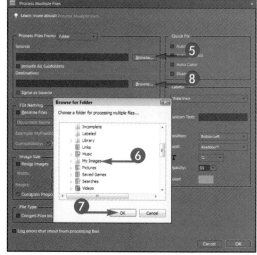

9️⃣ Click here to choose **Watermark**.

🔟 Type your watermark text.

1️⃣1️⃣ Select the position, font, and size for the text.

1️⃣2️⃣ Click here to specify an opacity from 1 to 100. The lower the opacity, the more transparent the watermark will be.

You can also type an opacity value.

1️⃣3️⃣ Click the color box and then choose a watermark color.

You may want to select a color that contrasts with the colors in your photo.

1️⃣4️⃣ Click **OK**.

Photoshop Elements adds watermarks to the photos in the source folder and saves them in the destination folder.

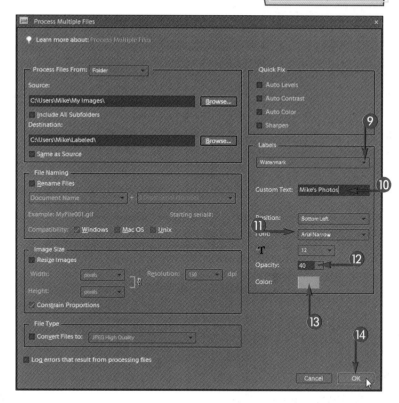

TIPS

How can I automatically add captions to my photos?

In the Process Multiple Files dialog box, you can select **Caption** under the top menu in the Labels panel. With Caption chosen, Photoshop Elements applies text that is associated with the photo to the top of the photo. Similar to applying a watermark, you can specify the positioning, font, size, opacity, and color of the caption.

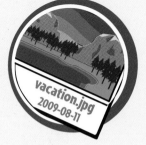

What kinds of captions can I add to my photos?

You can add the file name, date modified, and description as a caption. You can add this information by itself — for example, just the file name — or in combination by clicking one or more check boxes (■ changes to ✓).

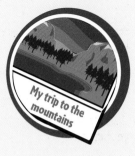

Presenting Photos Creatively

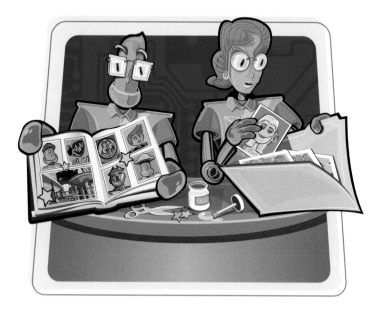

You can use photos that you have edited in Photoshop Elements in a variety of creative projects. Some of the projects, such as the greeting card and the photo collage, can be output on your printer. Others, such as PhotoStamps, must be purchased online through Adobe Photoshop Services. This chapter introduces you to some of the more interesting creative projects in Photoshop Elements.

Create a Slide Show

You can use the Create feature in Organizer to make a variety of projects by using the photos in your Organizer catalog. For example, you can create slide shows and share them with others or turn your photos into album pages, calendars, and even Web galleries.

Slide shows are easy to share with others by copying the finished file onto a disk or e-mailing it.

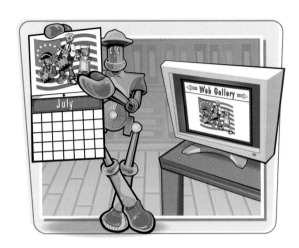

Create a Slide Show

① In the Organizer, **Ctrl** + click the images you want to put in your slide show.

Note: For more on using the Organizer, see Chapter 3.

② Click **Create**.

③ Click **Slide Show**.

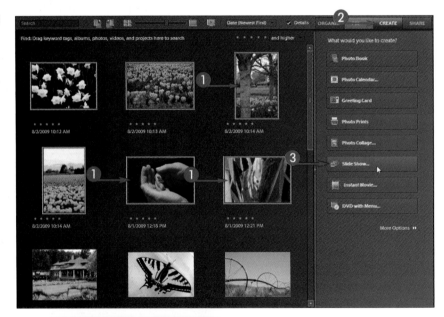

The Slide Show Preferences dialog box opens.

④ Choose a duration, transition, and other options.

⑤ Specify the quality of the preview photos. Choosing a lower quality results in a smaller file size.

⑥ Click **OK**.

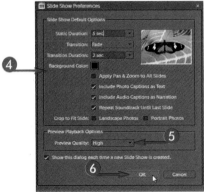

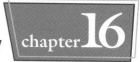

The Slide Show Editor dialog box opens.

● To add more photos to your slide show, you can click **Add Media**.

● Photoshop Elements displays thumbnails for the slides and icons for the transitions along the bottom of the Slide Show Editor.

⑦ Click the slide to which you want to add text.

⑧ Click **Add Text**.

The Edit Text dialog box opens.

⑨ Type your text.

⑩ Click **OK**.

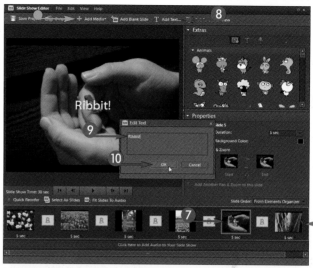

Photoshop Elements adds the text to the selected slide.

The text properties appear.

⑪ Click and drag inside the text to position it.

⑫ Choose formatting options for your text.

⑬ Repeat steps **7** to **12** for the other slides in your slide show.

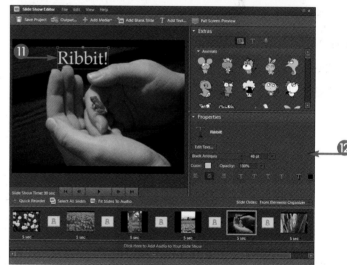

TIPS

How do I rearrange the photos in my slide show?

In the Slide Show Editor dialog box you can click and drag the photo thumbnails at the bottom to change their order in the slide show. To remove a slide entirely, right-click on it and then choose **Delete Slide**. If you have a lot of slides, you can click **Quick Reorder** to view and rearrange them in a larger window.

How do I add music to my slide show?

To add music or narration to a slide show, click **Add Media** and then choose one of the audio options in the Slide Show Editor. Or click the audio timeline located below the slide and transition thumbnails. You can add an audio file that plays in the background while the slide show runs. Organizer supports MP3, WAV, WMA, and AC3 audio file formats. You can click **Fit Slides To Audio** located below the Play button (▶) to sync your slide show with the audio.

continued

When creating a slide show, you can control the transition effects and slide duration as well as set the show to loop continuously. Transition effects control how one slide flows to the next.

Organizer saves your slide show as either a WMV file or a PDF file. You can view WMV files with Windows Media Player. You can view PDFs with a variety of applications, including the free Adobe Reader.

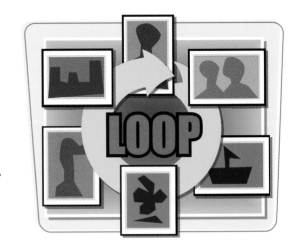

⑭ If the Extras panel is closed, click **Extras** to open it.

⑮ Click the slide to which you want to add clip art.

⑯ Click and drag the clip art to the slide.

You can click and drag the clip art to reposition it.

● Choose options here to resize or recolor the clip art.

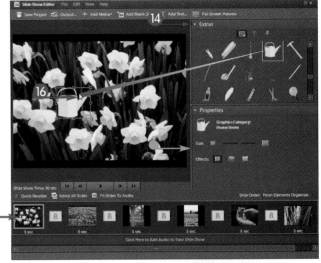

⑰ Click a transition icon between the slides.

The transition properties appear.

⑱ Click here to choose a transition duration.

⑲ Click here to choose a transition style.

⑳ Click the **Play** button (▶) to preview your slide show.

Photoshop Elements cycles through the slides.

You can click the **Pause** button (❚❚) to pause the preview.

● You can click **Full Screen Preview** to preview the slide show at maximum size.

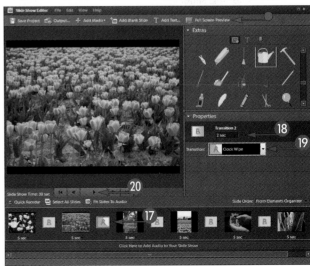

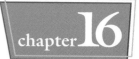

㉑ Click **Save Project**.

A dialog box opens, asking you to name your slide show.

㉒ Type a name.

㉓ Click **Save**.

Photoshop Elements saves your slide show to the Organizer.

㉔ Click here to close the Slide Show Editor and return to the Organizer.

● You can click **Output** to save the slide show as a PDF file or movie or burn it to a CD or DVD.

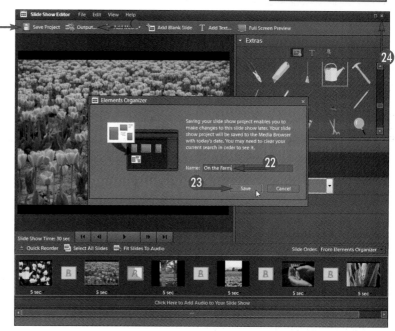

TIP

How do I add a title page to my slide show?

① Click a slide thumbnail. Your title page will be inserted after this slide.

② Click **Add Blank Slide**.

● Photoshop Elements adds a blank slide to your slide show.

③ Click **Add Text**.

④ In the dialog box that opens, type a title for your page.

⑤ Click **OK**.

You can click and drag the new title page to reposition it (for example, to before the first slide in your slide show).

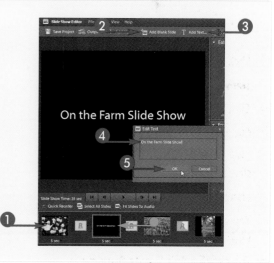

Create a Collage

Photoshop Elements lets you combine photos into a set of pages, which it calls a collage. You can customize the appearance of the photos and add artwork to the pages.

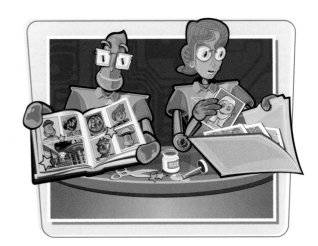

1 In the Organizer, Ctrl + click the images you want to include in your collage.

Note: For more on using the Organizer, see Chapter 3.

2 Click **Create**.

3 Click **Photo Collage**.

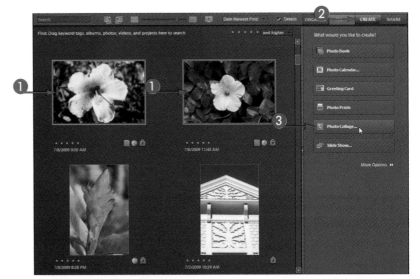

The Editor opens and displays your images in the Project Bin.

4 Click here to choose a page size for your collage.

● You can choose a theme for your collage.

5 Choose a layout for your collage.

● Photoshop Elements displays a preview of the layout.

6 Click **Done**.

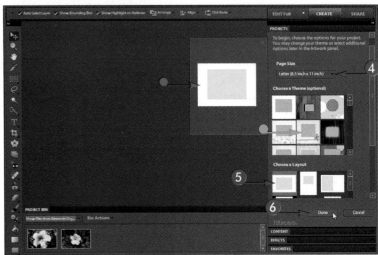

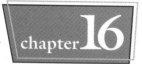

Photoshop Elements creates a collage from the photos you selected.

To reposition your photo, click and drag inside it.

● To resize your photo, click and drag a corner handle.

● To crop your photo, click and drag a side handle.

⑦ Click the **Next** button (▶) to view and edit the next photo.

You can also click a page in the Project Bin to go directly to that page.

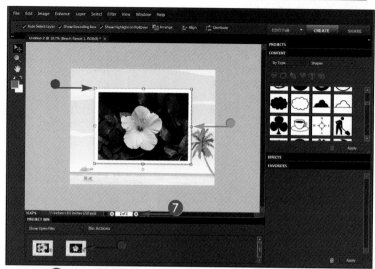

⑧ Click **File**.

⑨ Click **Save**.

The Save As dialog box opens.

⑩ Choose a destination folder.

⑪ Type a file name.

⑫ Click the **Include in the Organizer** check box (☐ changes to ☑) to add your collage to the Organizer.

⑬ Click **Save**.

Photoshop Elements saves your collage.

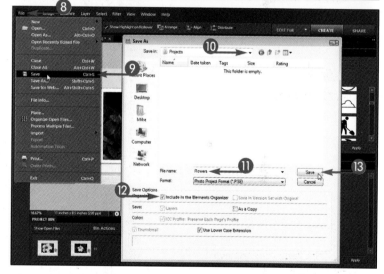
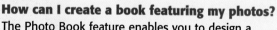

TIPS

How do I apply additional artwork to my collage?
You can add artwork by clicking and dragging items from the Content panel. After you complete step **6** above, Photoshop Elements opens the Content panel in the Panel Bin. You can display text, shapes, and other types of art by using the panel drop-down menus.

How can I create a book featuring my photos?
The Photo Book feature enables you to design a custom book with one or more of your photos on each page. Similar to the collage, you can choose a theme and layout for the book pages. You can order a hard- or softcover version of the book through printing services such as Shutterfly and Kodak Gallery or print book pages on your local printer. To start creating such a book from the Organizer, click the **Create** tab and then click **Photo Book**.

Create a Greeting Card

You can design a printable greeting card by using one of your Photoshop Elements photos. Photoshop Elements lets you decorate your card with a variety of border styles and photo layouts. You can also add custom text.

A Photoshop Elements greeting card is more like a postcard than a foldable card. This feature creates a single image that you can print out.

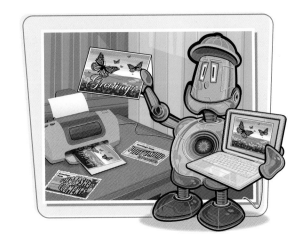

Create a Greeting Card

① In the Editor, open an image to use in your greeting card.

Note: See Chapter 1 for more on opening an image.

② Click **Create**.

③ Click **Greeting Card**.

④ In the panel that appears, click **Print with Local Printer**.

To order professionally printed cards, you can click the Shutterfly or Kodak Gallery buttons.

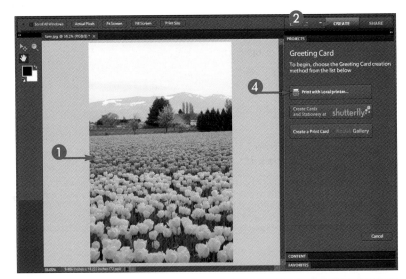

The Greeting Card options appear.

⑤ Click here to choose a page size.

⑥ Choose a theme here.

● A pop-up preview of the theme appears.

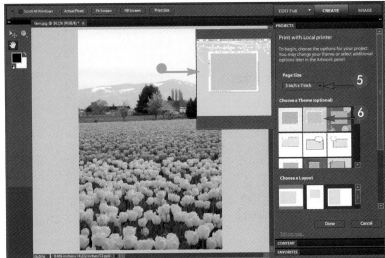

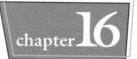

7 Click here to scroll down and view the other options.

8 Click a layout option.

● A pop-up preview of the layout appears.

9 Click the **Auto-Fill** check box to automatically add the open photo to your card (■ changes to ☑).

10 Click **Done**.

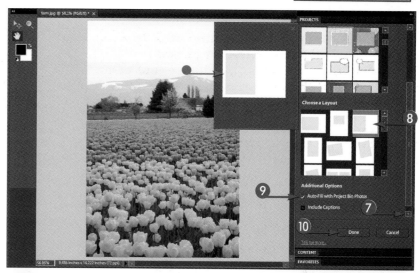

Photoshop Elements displays the greeting card in a new image window.

11 To save the greeting card, click **File** and then **Save**.

Note: For more on saving, see Chapter 1. For more on printing the card, see Chapter 17.

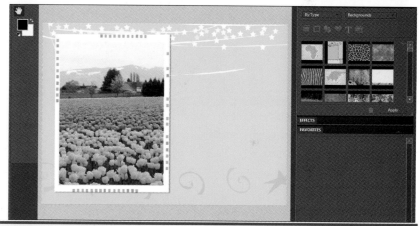

TIP

How do I add text to my greeting card?

After completing step **10** above, follow these steps:

1 Click here and then choose **Text**.

2 Click a type style and drag it onto the greeting card.

3 Type your text and then press Enter.

4 In the bounding box, click and drag the handles to change the size of the text. You can click and drag inside the text to reposition it.

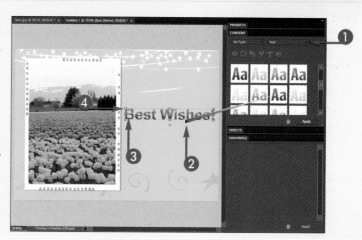

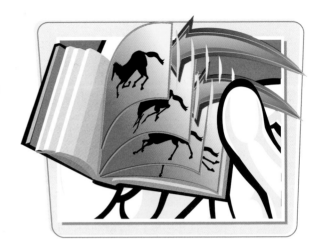

Create a Flipbook

You can take a sequence of action photos and turn them into a flipbook, which is similar to a short movie. You can specify the frame rate of the movie as well as the dimensions.

Create a Flipbook

1 In the Organizer, **Ctrl** + click to select the photos you want to include in your flipbook.

Note: For more on using the Organizer, see Chapter 3.

2 Click **Create**.

3 Click **More Options**.

4 Click **Flipbook**.

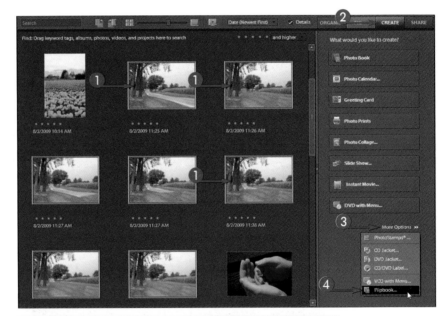

The Flipbook dialog box opens.

5 Type a playback speed between 1 and 30. *Fps* stands for frames per second.

● You can also click and drag the slider (⬚) to set a playback speed.

● Your photos are ordered as they were in the Organizer. You can click the **Reverse Order** check box (■ changes to ✓) to reverse the order.

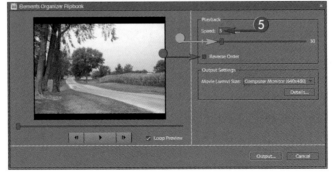

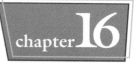

⑥ Choose an output setting based on how the flipbook will be viewed. The setting determines the dimensions of the movie.

● You can click **Details** for an explanation of the current setting.

⑦ Click the **Play** button (▶) to preview your flipbook.

⑧ Click **Output**.

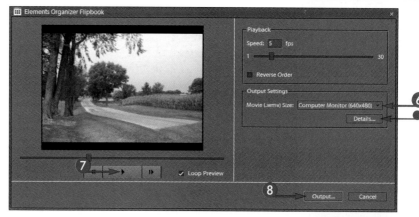

The Save dialog box opens.

⑨ Type a file name for your flipbook.

● Only the Windows Media type is supported.

⑩ Click here to choose where to save the flipbook.

⑪ Click **Save**.

Photoshop Elements saves the flipbook.

The flipbook is also added to the Organizer.

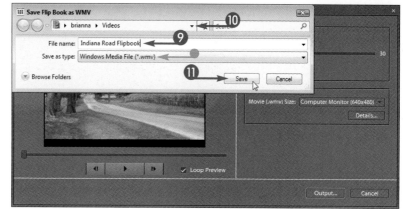

 TIP

What are my options for previewing a flipbook?
Besides clicking the **Play** button (▶) to play the flipbook, you can do the following:

● Click and drag the slider (▮) to the left and right to cycle back and forth through the flipbook photos.

● Click the **Previous** button (◀) to go to the previous photo.

● Click the **Next** button (▶) to go to the next photo.

● Click to deselect the **Loop Preview** check box (☑ changes to ▮) to stop the preview from looping.

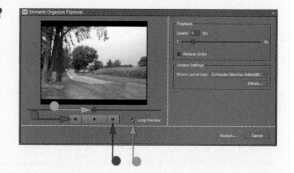

Create PhotoStamps

You can turn an image into U.S. Postal Service–approved stamps by using the PhotoStamps feature. After you upload the photo you want displayed on the stamp to the service, you can customize the stamp and then purchase a set.

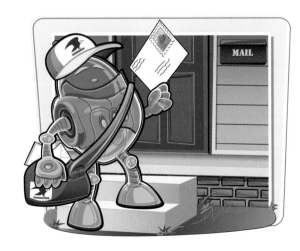

① From the Organizer, click the photo you want to use on your stamps.

Note: *For more on using the Organizer, see Chapter 3.*

You can **Ctrl** + click to select multiple photos.

② Click **More Options**.

③ Click **PhotoStamps**.

④ In the PhotoStamps dialog box that opens, click **Upload My Photos**.

Photoshop Elements uploads the photo(s) to the PhotoStamps Web site.

⑤ In the confirmation dialog box that opens, click **Continue**.

The Adobe Photoshop Services page opens in a browser window.

⑥ Click the **Create Product** link beneath your photo.

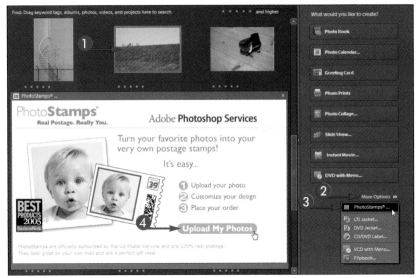

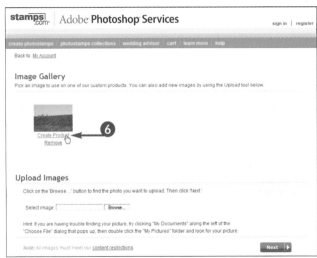

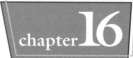

7 On the Image Details page that appears, click the **PhotoStamps** link under Create Products.

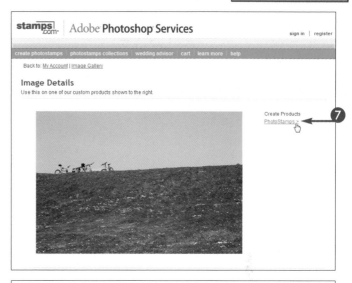

The Customize Your PhotoStamps page appears.

8 Click options to customize your stamps.

You can zoom into or out of your photo, rotate it, add a border, or change the color of the postage amount.

9 Click **Continue**.

Your stamps are added to your shopping cart.

On the pages that follow, you can enter payment and shipping information to purchase the stamps.

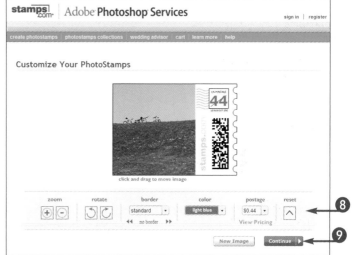

TIPS

How can I order prints of my Photoshop Elements photos?

You can obtain prints of your photos by clicking the **Create** tab and then **Photo Prints**. A panel appears that enables you to order prints through Shutterfly or Kodak Gallery. You need an Internet connection to use these services. The panel also lets you print your photos on a local printer or create a picture package that arranges multiple photos on a single page.

How can I create a calendar featuring my images?

You can create a calendar by clicking the **Create** tab and then **Photo Calendar**. A panel appears that lets you design and order calendars through Shutterfly or Kodak Gallery. With both services, you use tools on external Web sites to build the calendar pages. You need an Internet connection to do this.

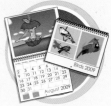

Create a Photo Panorama

You can use the Photomerge feature in Photoshop Elements to stitch several sequential images together into a single panoramic image. This enables you to capture more scenery than is usually possible in a regular photograph.

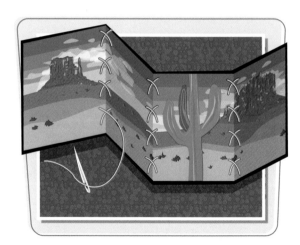

Create a Photo Panorama

① In the Editor, click **File**.

Note: For more on opening the Editor, see Chapter 1.

② Click **New**.

③ Click **Photomerge Panorama**.

The Photomerge dialog box opens.

④ Click **Auto** (● changes to ○).

With the Auto setting, Photoshop Elements automatically chooses the best method for stitching your photos together.

⑤ Click **Browse**.

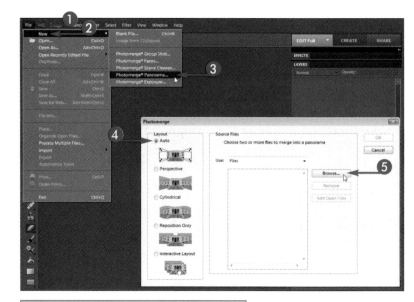

The Open dialog box opens.

⑥ Click here to choose the folder that contains the images you want to merge.

⑦ Ctrl + click the images you want to merge into a panoramic image.

⑧ Click **OK**.

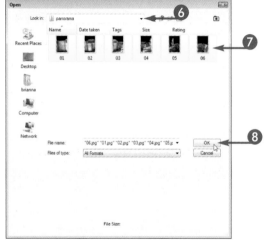

● The file names of the images appear in the Source Files list.

9 Click **OK** to build the panoramic image.

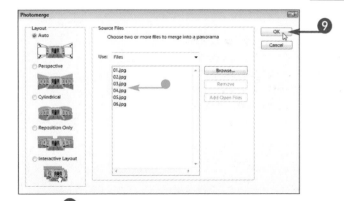

Photoshop Elements merges the images into a single panoramic image.

● Parts of each image appear in separate layers in the Layers panel.

Note: For more on layers, see Chapter 8.

● You can use the **Crop** tool ( ) to remove extra space around the panorama.

Note: For more on cropping, see Chapter 5.

10 Click **File** and then **Save** to save the panorama.

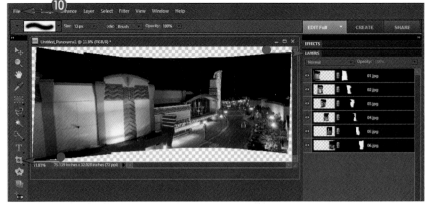

How can I create photos that merge successfully?

To merge photos successfully, you need to align and overlap the photos as you shoot them. Here are a few hints:

● Use a tripod to keep your photos level with one another.
● Experiment with the different layout modes in the Photomerge dialog box.
● Refrain from using lenses that distort your photos, such as fisheye lenses.
● Shoot your photos so they overlap at least 30%.

For more tips, see the Photoshop Elements Help documentation.

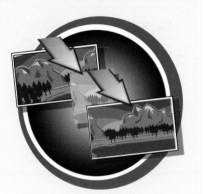

CHAPTER 17

Saving and Sharing Your Work

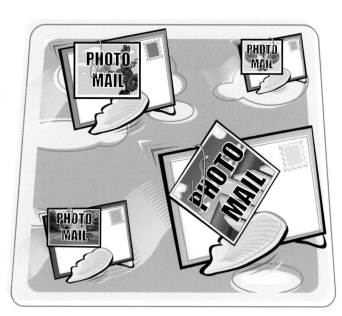

Photoshop Elements lets you save your images in different file formats for use on the Web and in other applications. You can also share your photos by e-mailing them, putting them in an online gallery, or printing them. For safekeeping, you can export your photos to a separate folder on your computer, back them up to a CD or DVD, or back them up online.

Save a JPEG for the Web

You can save a file in the JPEG — Joint Photographic Experts Group — format and then publish it on the Web. JPEG is the preferred Web format for saving images.

Photoshop Elements saves JPEG images at 72 dpi.

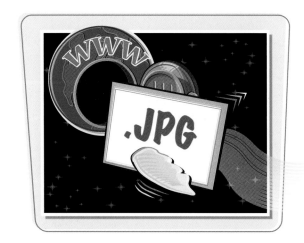

Save a JPEG for the Web

1. In the Editor, click **File**.

Note: For more on opening the Editor, see Chapter 1.

2. Click **Save for Web**.

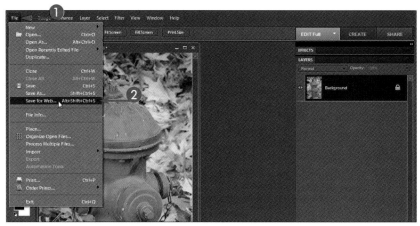

The Save For Web dialog box opens.

Your original image appears on the left and a preview of the JPEG version is on the right.

3. Click here to choose **JPEG**.

4. Click here to choose a quality setting.

● Alternatively, you can select a numeric quality setting from 0 (low quality) to 100 (high quality).

The higher the quality, the larger the resulting file size.

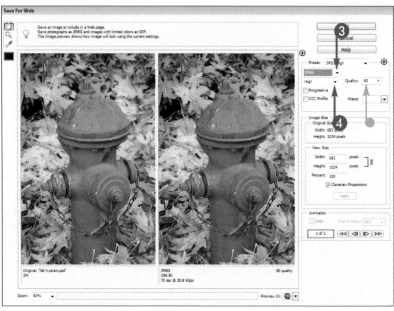

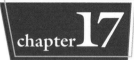

⑤ Use the preview area to verify that the file quality and size are acceptable.

● You can resize the resulting image by typing dimensions or a percentage and then clicking **Apply**.

⑥ Click **OK**.

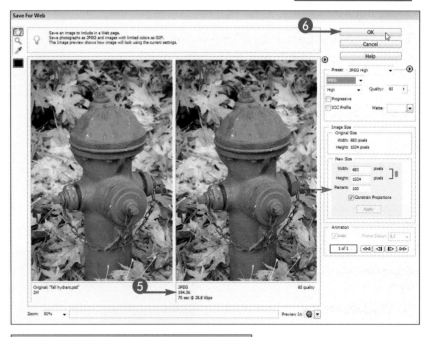

The Save Optimized As dialog box opens.

⑦ Click here to choose a folder in which to save the file.

⑧ Type a file name. Photoshop Elements automatically assigns a .jpg extension if you do not specify an extension.

⑨ Click **Save**.

The original image file remains open.

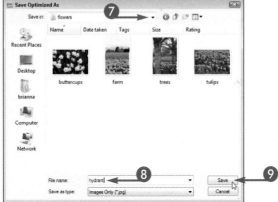

 TIPS

What is image compression?

Image compression involves using mathematical techniques to reduce the amount of information required to describe an image. This results in smaller file sizes, which is important when transmitting information on the Web. Some compression schemes, such as JPEG, reduce image quality somewhat, but the loss is usually negligible compared to the savings in file size.

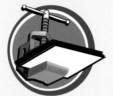

How can I adjust the view of my image in the Save For Web dialog box?

You can use the Hand tool ( ) in the upper-left corner to shift the position of your image in the Save For Web dialog box or use the Zoom tool ( ) to zoom in or out.

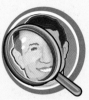

Save a GIF for the Web

You can save an image as a GIF — Graphics Interchange Format — file and then publish it on the Web. The GIF format is good for saving illustrations that have a lot of solid color. The format supports a maximum of 256 colors.

Photoshop Elements saves GIF images at 72 dpi. Unlike JPEG images, GIF images can include transparency.

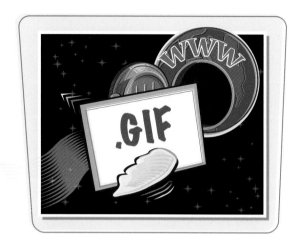

Save a GIF for the Web

1 In the Editor, click **File**.

Note: For more on opening the Editor, see Chapter 1.

2 Click **Save for Web**.

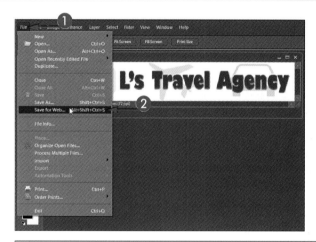

The Save For Web dialog box opens.

3 Click here to choose **GIF**.

4 Click here to choose the number of colors to include in the image.

GIF allows a maximum of 256 colors.

● You can click here to choose the method Photoshop Elements uses to select the GIF colors.

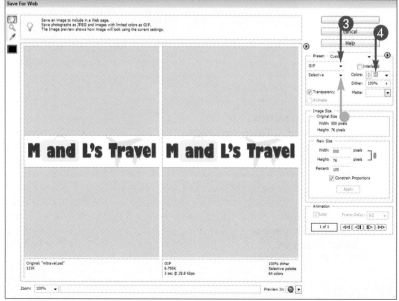

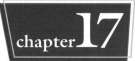

⑤ Use the preview area to verify that the file quality and size are acceptable.

● You can resize the resulting image by typing dimensions or a percentage and then clicking **Apply**.

● Click the **Transparency** check box (☐ changes to ☑) to ensure that any transparent areas of your image remain that way in your final GIF image.

⑥ Click **OK**.

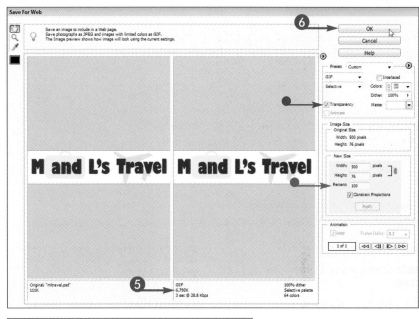

The Save Optimized As dialog box opens.

⑦ Click here to choose a folder in which to save the file.

⑧ Type a file name. Photoshop Elements automatically assigns a .gif extension if you do not specify an extension.

⑨ Click **Save**.

The original image file remains open.

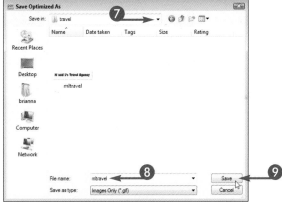

TIPS

How do I minimize the file sizes of my GIF images?

The most important factor in creating small GIFs is limiting the number of colors in the final image. GIF files are limited to 256 colors or fewer. In images that have just a few solid colors, you can often reduce the total number of colors to 16 or even 8 without any noticeable reduction in quality. See step **4** on the previous page to set the number of colors in your GIF images.

How can I use GIF transparency in my Web images?

GIF images that include transparency allow the background of a Web page to show through. Transparent GIFs enable you to add nonrectangular elements to your Web projects. Because Background layers cannot contain transparent pixels, you need to work with layers other than the Background layer to create transparent GIFs. See Chapter 8 for more on layers.

You can save an image as a PNG — Portable Network Graphics — file and then publish it on the Web.

PNG was devised as a high-quality alternative to GIF and JPEG. PNG can support more than 256 colors. However, it is not as universally supported as GIF and JPEG are by Web browsers.

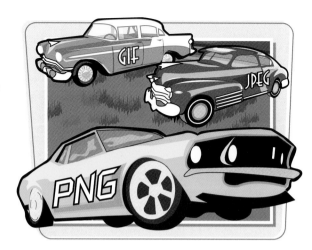

Save a PNG for the Web

1 In the Editor, click **File**.

Note: For more on opening the Editor, see Chapter 1.

2 Click **Save for Web**.

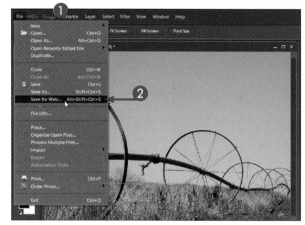

The Save For Web dialog box opens.

3 Click here to choose **PNG-8** or **PNG-24**.

Note: See the tip on the next page for more on the different PNG settings.

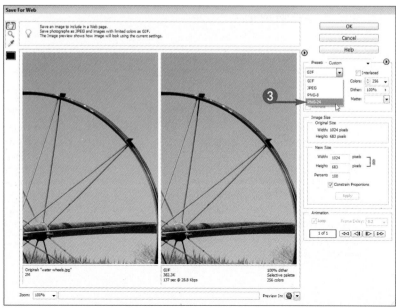

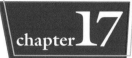
④ Use the preview area to verify that the file quality and size are acceptable.

● You can resize the resulting image by typing dimensions or a percentage and then clicking **Apply**.

● Click the **Transparency** check box (☐ changes to ☑) to ensure that any transparent areas of your image remain that way in your final PNG image.

⑤ Click **OK**.

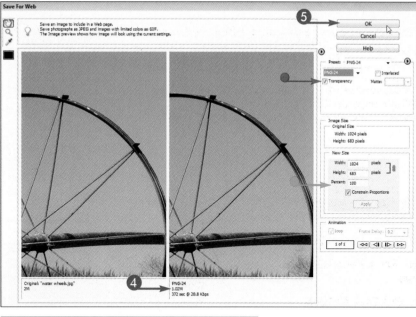

⑥ Click here to choose a folder in which to save the file.

⑦ Type a file name. Photoshop Elements automatically assigns a .png extension if you do not specify an extension.

⑧ Click **Save**.

The original image file remains open.

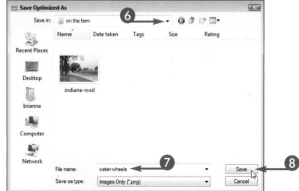

What is the difference between the PNG-8 and PNG-24 settings?
PNG-8 stands for PNG 8-bit. With it, you can limit the number of colors in the final PNG image and thereby decrease the resulting file size. Similar to GIF, PNG-8 can include a maximum of 256 colors. PNG-24 stands for PNG 24-bit. This format includes a wider range of colors than 8-bit and leads to better image quality, but it generally results in much larger file sizes.

How does the PNG format support transparency?
Like GIF files, PNG files can include transparency. But unlike GIFs, the PNG format supports a more advanced feature called alpha-channel transparency, which allows a background behind an image to partially show through. You can add partial transparency to your image by decreasing the opacity of a layer. For more on layers and opacity, see Chapter 8.

Convert File Types

You can quickly and easily convert images from one file type to another in Photoshop Elements by using the Process Multiple Files feature. This makes it easy to convert a collection of PSD files to the JPEG format for sending by e-mail or posting on the Web.

For more on file types supported by Photoshop Elements, see Chapter 2.

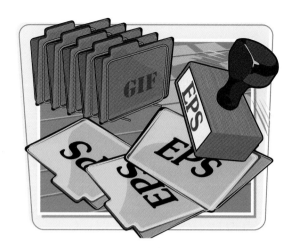

Convert File Types

① Place the images that you want to convert in a folder.

Note: *To work with folders, see your operating system's documentation.*

② In the Editor, click **File**.

Note: *For more on opening the Editor, see Chapter 1.*

③ Click **Process Multiple Files**.

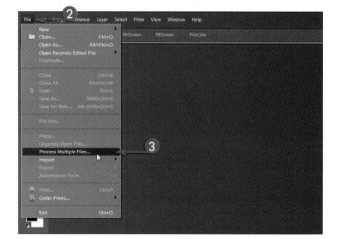

The Process Multiple Files dialog box opens.

④ Click **Browse**.

The Browse for Folder dialog box opens.

⑤ Click here to open folders on your computer (□ changes to ◢).

⑥ Click the folder containing your images.

⑦ Click **OK**.

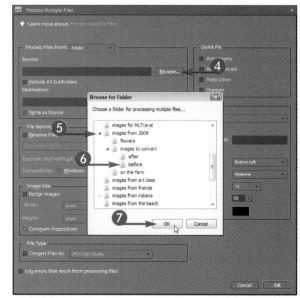

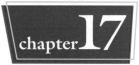

8 Click **Browse** and then repeat steps **5** to **7** to specify a destination folder where you want your processed images to save.

● You can optionally click the **Resize Images** check box (■ changes to ✓), type a new width and height, and then Photoshop Elements resizes the images before saving.

Note: For more on resizing images, see Chapter 5.

9 Click the **Convert Files to** check box (■ changes to ✓).

10 Click here to choose a file format to convert to.

11 Click **OK**.

Photoshop Elements processes the images and then saves them in the destination folder.

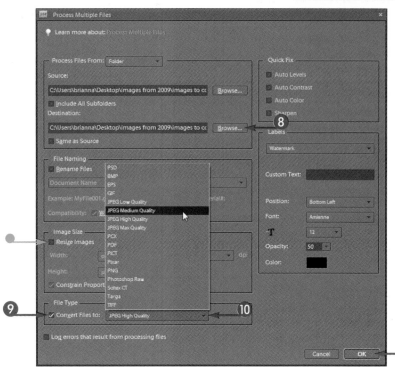

How can I automatically fix color and lighting problems in my converted photos?

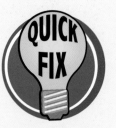

There are automatic optimization settings under the Quick Fix heading in the Process Multiple Files dialog box. You can select them to have Photoshop Elements improve the color, contrast, and sharpness of your photos before they are converted. For more on these settings, see Chapter 10.

How can I quickly add labels to my converted photos?

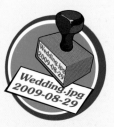

Under the Labels heading in the Process Multiple Files dialog box, there are tools for adding captions and watermarks to your converted photos. You can automatically add file name, description, and date information as captions as well as specify the size and style of the caption font. For more on adding watermarks, see Chapter 15.

E-mail Images with Photo Mail

You can embed your images in an e-mail message and then send them to others by using the Photo Mail feature. With Photo Mail, you can select custom stationery that inserts colors, graphics, and captions next to your images.

This feature requires that you already have an e-mail program, such as Microsoft Outlook, set up on your computer. Photoshop Elements does not come with e-mail capability.

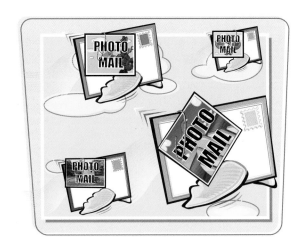

E-mail Images with Photo Mail

① In the Organizer, click **Share**.

Note: For more on using the Organizer, see Chapter 3.

② Click **Photo Mail**.

Note: Photoshop Elements may display a dialog box asking you to choose your e-mail client. If so, choose the software with which you prefer to send e-mail and then click **Continue**.

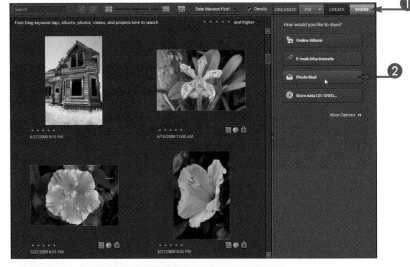

The Photo Mail pane opens.

③ Click and drag images you want to mail from the main Organizer window into the Photo Mail pane.

● Photoshop Elements totals the file sizes and estimates how long they will take to send.

④ Click **Next**.

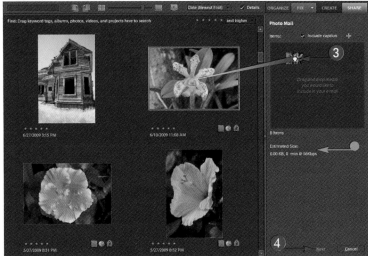

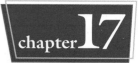

chapter 17

5 Type a message to accompany your images.

6 Click the **Contact Book** button (📖) to define your recipient.

The Contact Book dialog box opens.

7 Click **New Contact**.

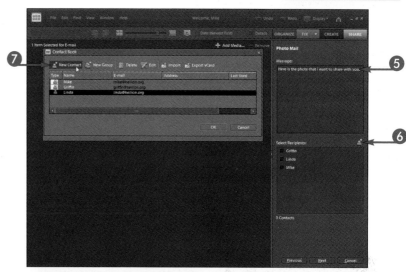

The New Contact dialog box opens.

8 Type the contact details for your recipient.

9 Type an e-mail address for your recipient.

10 Click **OK**.

● The recipient appears in the Contact Book.

11 Click **OK** in the Contact Book dialog box.

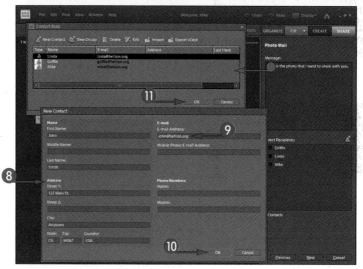

 TIPS

Can I send my images as e-mail attachments?

If you want to send your photos as plain e-mail attachments rather than as embedded items in an e-mail message, click the **E-mail Attachments** option in the Organizer's Share pane. Sending attachments is similar to sending Photo Mail but without the steps where you select stationery and a layout.

How can I keep the file sizes of my images small when e-mailing them?

If you are worried about the file sizes of your images when e-mailing, choose the **E-mail Attachments** option rather than the Photo Mail option in the Organizer's Share pane. In the E-mail Attachments option, you can adjust both the dimensions of your photos and the JPEG compression that is applied prior to sending.

E-mail Images with Photo Mail *(continued)*

Photo Mail includes more than 50 stationery designs that you can apply to the photos that you e-mail. You can select stationery with animal, seasonal, or party themes. Photoshop Elements embeds your images and the stationery into the e-mail message by using HTML.

Some e-mail programs do not display HTML that is embedded in e-mail. Recipients using such e-mail programs will not be able to see the styles and graphics offered in the Photo Mail feature.

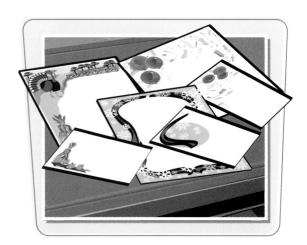

E-mail Images with Photo Mail *(continued)*

The new contact appears in the Select Recipients list.

⑫ Click the check box for each intended recipient (▇ changes to ✅).

⑬ Click **Next**.

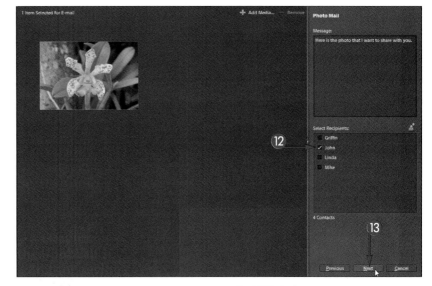

The Stationery & Layouts Wizard opens with the Choose a Stationery options.

● You can click a category to open stationery options.

⑭ Click a stationery with which to style your e-mail.

● You can click text inside the stationery design to caption your images.

⑮ Click **Next Step**.

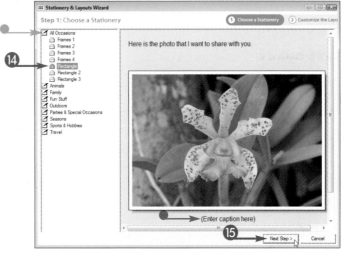

326

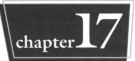

The Customize the Layout options appear.

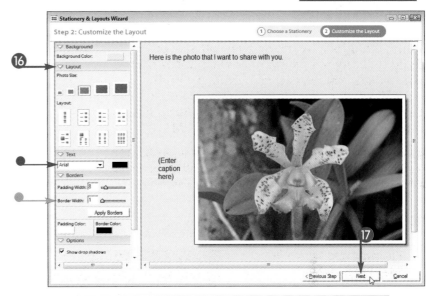

16 Click the layout options to organize and size your images.

● You can optionally customize your text.

● You can click here to set other options. The available options will vary depending on the stationery selected in step **14**.

17 Click **Next**.

Photoshop Elements opens a new message in your e-mail client.

● The recipient is added to the To field.

● Your message text, layout design, and images are included in the body of the message.

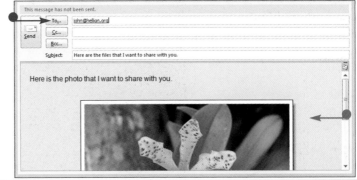

Note: For more on sending your message, see the documentation for your e-mail application.

TIP

How can I view a history of what I have e-mailed?

1 Click **Find**.

2 Click **By History**.

3 Click **E-mailed to**.

● A dialog box opens, showing a history of e-mail messages sent through Photoshop Elements. You can double-click an entry to view the photos that were sent.

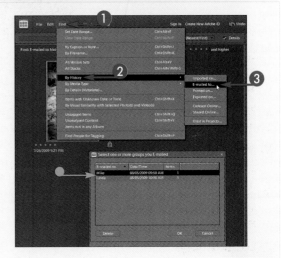

Print a Photo

You can print your Photoshop Elements images to create hard copies of your work. You can then add your photos to a physical photo album.

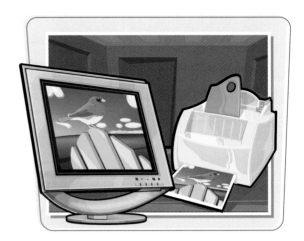

① Make sure the layers you want to print are visible.

Note: An eye icon (👁) means that a layer is visible. To read more on layers, see Chapter 8.

② Click **File**.

③ Click **Print**.

This example shows printing from the Editor. You can also select an image and follow steps from **2** forward to print from the Organizer.

Note: See Chapter 1 for more on the Editor and Organizer.

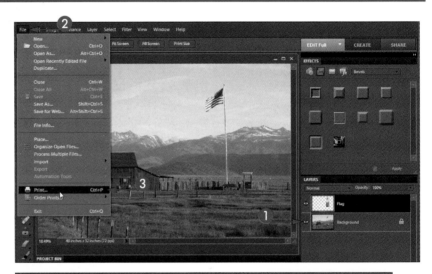

The Print dialog box opens.

④ Select your printer and paper settings. These will vary depending on the make and model of your printer.

⑤ Select a print type.

Note: See the section "Print a Picture Package" for more on print types.

⑥ Select a print size. You can select from popular photo sizes or specify custom dimensions.

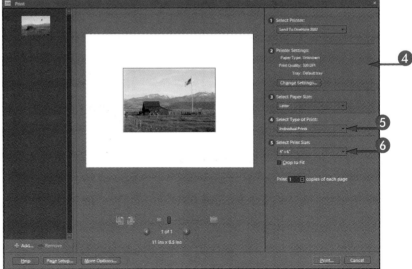

- You can click and drag the slider (▦) to zoom the photo.

- You can click here to rotate the photo.

- You can click and drag your photo within the print size boundary.

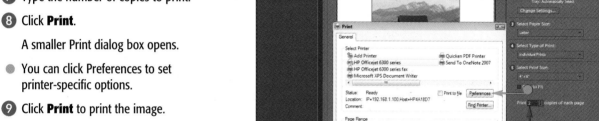

7️⃣ Type the number of copies to print.

8️⃣ Click **Print**.

A smaller Print dialog box opens.

- You can click Preferences to set printer-specific options.

9️⃣ Click **Print** to print the image.

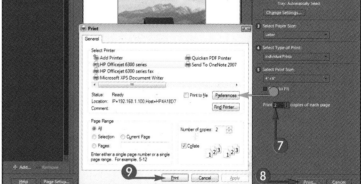

How can I add captions and other text to my printed photo?

1️⃣ In the Print dialog box, click **More Options**.

2️⃣ Click **Printing Choices**.

3️⃣ Click here to print a caption if your photo has one (■ changes to ✓). For more on captions, see Chapter 3.

- You can click here to print the date the photo was taken or the file name.

- You can use these settings to print a solid border around the photo.

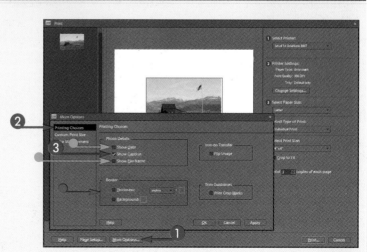

Print Multiple Photos

Photoshop Elements makes it easy to print more than one photo from your photo catalog. You can choose from a variety of standard photo sizes and then print each photo multiple times.

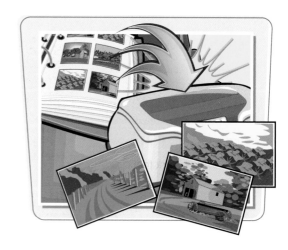

Print Multiple Photos

① In the Organizer, **Ctrl** + click to select the photos you want to print.

Note: For more on using the Organizer, see Chapter 3.

If no photos are selected, Photoshop Elements includes all the photos currently displayed.

② Click **File**.

③ Click **Print**.

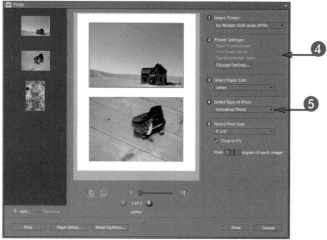

The Prints dialog box opens, showing the selected photos in the left column.

④ Select your printer and paper settings. These will vary depending on the make and model of your printer.

⑤ Click here to choose **Individual Prints**.

Note: For details on using the Picture Package option, see the section "Print a Picture Package."

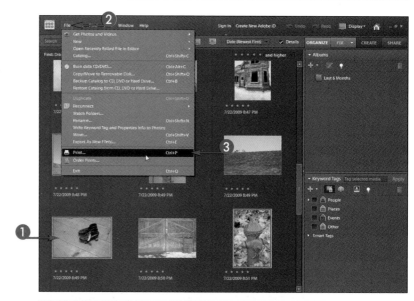

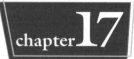

⑥ Click here to choose a print size.

Photoshop Elements displays a preview of the photos to be printed — on multiple pages if necessary.

● Click here to go to the next page.

● Click here to go back to the previous page.

⑦ Type a number here to specify how many times each photo is to be printed.

⑧ Click **Print**.

Photoshop Elements prints the photos.

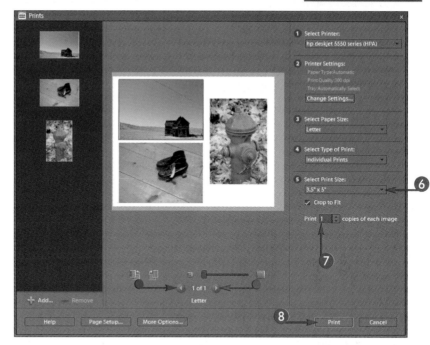

How do I print multiple photos from the Editor?

① Open the photos you want to print in the Editor.

② In the Project Bin, click **Bin Actions**.

③ Click **Print Bin Files**.

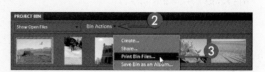

Photoshop Elements opens the Print dialog box for printing multiple photos.

See Chapter 5 for more on managing images with the Project Bin.

Print a Picture Package

You can automatically create a one-page layout with one or more photos at various sizes to create a picture package. You may find this useful when you want to print pictures as gifts for friends or family.

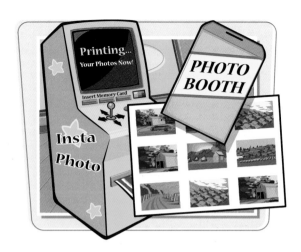

Print a Picture Package

1 In the Organizer, **Ctrl** + click to select the photos you want to display in your picture package.

Note: *For more on using the Organizer, see Chapter 3.*

If no photos are selected, Photoshop Elements includes all the photos currently displayed.

2 Click **File**.

3 Click **Print**.

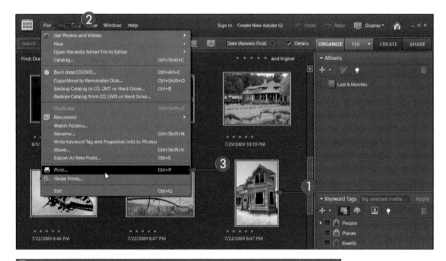

The Prints dialog box opens, showing the selected photos in the left column.

4 Select your printer and paper settings. These will vary depending on the make and model of your printer.

5 Click here and to choose **Picture Package**.

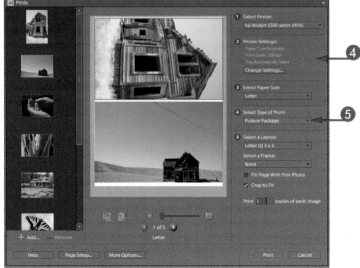

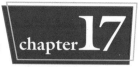

6 Click here to choose a layout.

● Photoshop Elements automatically adds your photos to the layout.

To replace a photo, click and drag a photo from the left column to the layout.

● You can click here to add a custom frame to your photos in the picture package.

● You can click here to create a separate picture package layout for each selected photo (☑ changes to ■).

7 Click **Print**.

Photoshop Elements prints your picture package.

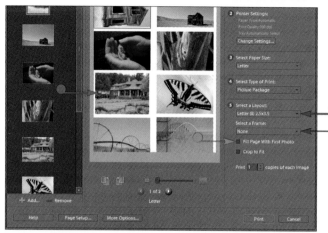

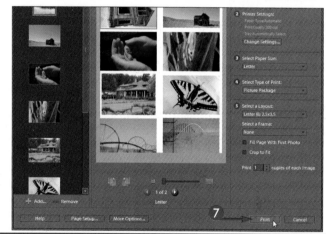

TIP

How do I create a contact sheet?

You can create a printout that displays your photos as a grid of *thumbnails*, or miniature images. This is known as a *contact sheet* in photography.

1 In the Organizer, select your photos, click **File**, and then click **Print**.

2 Click here to choose **Contact Sheet**.

● Photoshop Elements arranges the photos in a grid.

3 Select the layout and caption information.

4 Click **Print**.

Photoshop Elements prints the contact sheet.

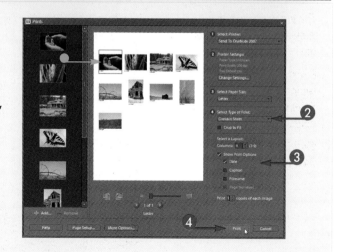

Export Photos

You can export the photos in the Organizer to a folder. Photoshop Elements lets you export your photos in a variety of file formats.

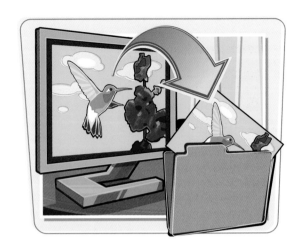

Export Photos

1 **Ctrl** + click to select the photos you want to export in the Organizer.

Note: For more on using the Organizer, see Chapter 3.

2 Click **File**.

3 Click **Export As New File(s)**.

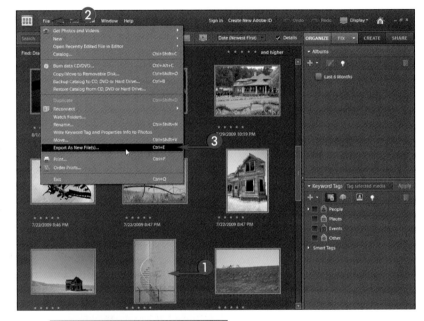

The Export New Files dialog box opens, showing the selected photos listed.

4 Click a radio button to choose a file type (● changes to ○).

● Some file types allow you to specify a size or quality.

5 Click **Browse** to choose a destination folder for the images.

6 To select more images to export, click **Add**.

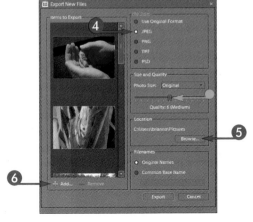

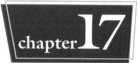

The Add Media dialog box opens.

7 Click the check box next to the photos you want to add (■ changes to ✓).

● You can limit the photos displayed by using the Add Media From settings.

8 Click **Done**.

Photoshop Elements adds the photos.

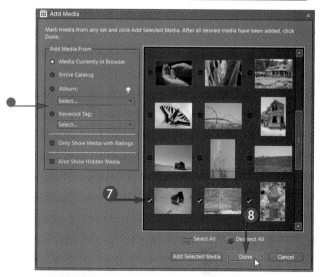

● To remove a photo from the export list, click the photo and then click **Remove**.

9 Click **Export**.

Photoshop Elements exports your images.

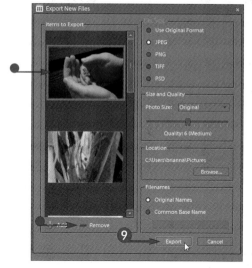

How do I customize the names of my exported images?
You can customize the file names of your exported images in the Export New Files dialog box.

1 Click the **Common Base Name** check box (● changes to ○).

2 Specify a base name for your photo file names.

3 Click **Export**.

Photoshop Elements exports your images.

Photoshop Elements appends a hyphen and number to your base name to create each file name.

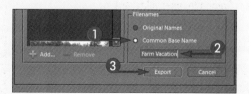

Back Up Photos

You can back up your collection of photos by using the Organizer's backup tool. This feature walks you through the steps for backing up your photo files to a CD, a DVD, or another storage device.

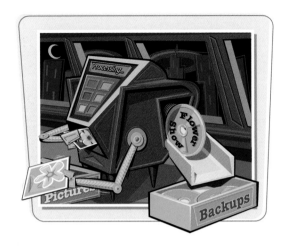

Back Up Photos

① In the Organizer, open the catalog you want to back up.

Note: For more on catalogs, see Chapter 3.

② Click **File**.

③ Click **Backup Catalog to CD, DVD or Hard Drive**.

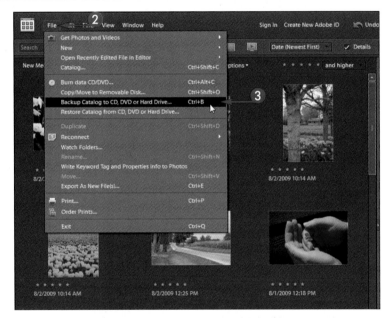

Photoshop Elements may display a warning about missing files. If this happens, click **Reconnect** to perform a check.

The Backup Catalog to CD, DVD, or Hard Drive dialog box opens.

④ Click the **Full Backup** radio button (● changes to ○).

● For subsequent backups, you can select the **Incremental Backup** option. Incremental Backup backs up files that have changed or have been added since the last backup.

⑤ Click **Next**.

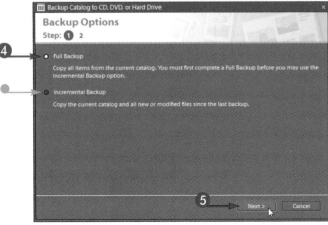

6 Click the drive to which you want to copy the backup files.

● You can type a name for the backup in this text box.

● Depending on your backup drive selection, the wizard may display an estimated file size and creation time.

7 Click **Done**.

Photoshop Elements backs up your photos.

A prompt box alerts you when the procedure is complete.

Depending on the media you used, you may have the option of verifying your backup when the backup is finished.

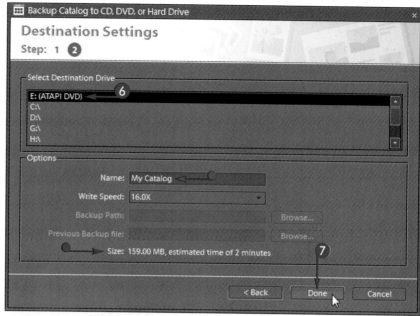

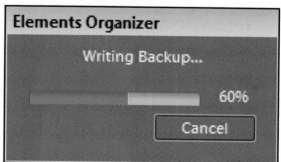

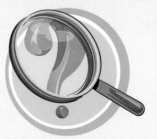

TIPS

The Organizer prompts me to find missing files before backing up my photos. What do I do?

If any of the catalog photos no longer contain valid links to original files, the backup tool displays a prompt box, asking you to reconnect any missing files. A file can appear to be missing if you move it after adding the photo to the Organizer or if you rename the file outside the Organizer. You can click **Reconnect** to allow Photoshop Elements to look for the missing links and then continue with the backup.

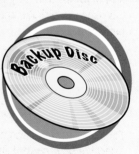

How do I restore my backed-up files?

You can click **File** and then **Restore Catalog from CD, DVD or Hard Drive** to restore backups of your photos to your computer. The Restore dialog box offers options for restoring backed-up photos and catalogs to their original location or to a new location of your choosing.

Sign Up for Online Services

Photoshop Elements lets you sign up for an online account at Photoshop.com. With this service, you can create online galleries of your photos to share with friends. You can also back up your photos online for safekeeping.

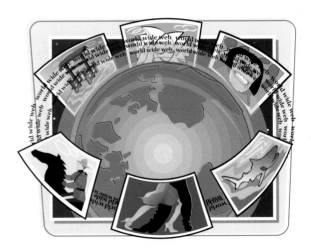

1 In the Organizer, click **Create New Adobe ID**.

Note: For more on using the Organizer, see Chapter 3.

You can also click **Create New Adobe ID** on the welcome screen or in the Editor to sign up.

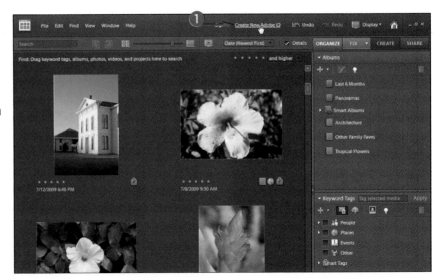

A Create your Adobe ID dialog box opens.

2 Type your signup information.

3 Create a personalized Web address, or URL, for accessing your account.

You can use letters, numbers, and underscores to create your Web address but no other special characters.

4 Click **Create Account**.

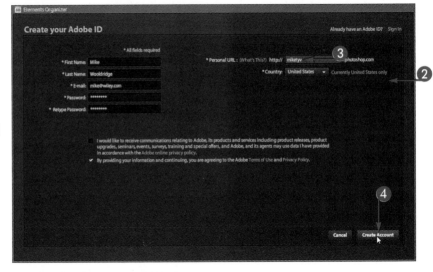

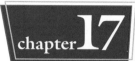

An Account Benefits dialog box opens.

● You can click **Plus** to sign up for a premium account, which offers more storage space and other premium features.

⑤ To continue with a free account, click **Free**.

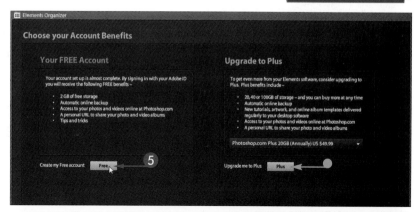

An Account Verification dialog box opens.

Adobe sends a verification message to your e-mail address.

⑥ To complete the signup, you must access the Web address contained in the verification e-mail.

● After you verify the e-mail address, you can sign in here.

⑦ Click **Done** to close the dialog box.

To sign in to your account from Photoshop Elements, see the tip below.

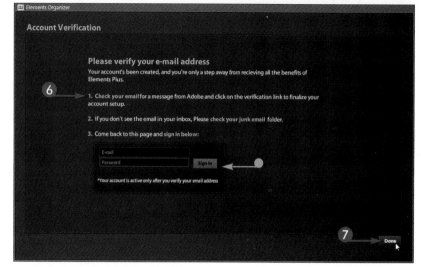

TIP

How do I sign in to my Photoshop.com account from Photoshop Elements?

To use the online sharing and backup features in Photoshop Elements, you must sign in to your Photoshop.com account.

① In the Organizer or Editor, click **Sign In**.

You can also sign in by using the form on the welcome screen.

A sign-in dialog box opens.

② Type the e-mail address associated with your account.

③ Type your password.

④ Click **Sign In**.

A confirmation dialog box opens, and welcome text appears in the menu bar.

To sign out, you can click the welcome text and then click **Sign Out** in the dialog box that opens.

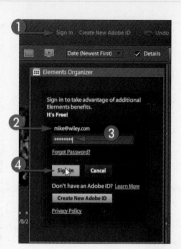

You can share an album that you created in the Organizer on Photoshop.com. Photoshop Elements uploads the album photos to your Photoshop.com account and then displays them in a custom template. You can announce the album via e-mail to your contacts.

Contacts can view your online photo albums at the personalized Web address for your account. See the section "Sign Up for Online Services" for more. Because sharing albums involves uploading photos, the feature works best with a fast Internet connection.

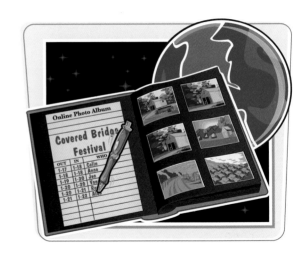

Share a Photo Gallery Online

1 Sign in to your Photoshop.com account in Photoshop Elements.

Note: *See the section "Sign Up for Online Services" for more.*

2 In the Organizer, click **Organize**.

3 Click here to open the Albums panel.

4 Click an album to share.

5 Click **Share** (■).

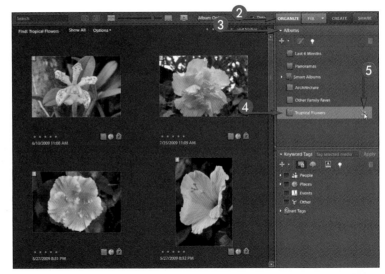

The Album Details panel appears, showing a preview of the album.

6 Type a name for the online album. Photoshop Elements uses the current name as the default.

● You can click here to choose a different template for your gallery.

7 Click here to share your album to Photoshop.com (■ changes to ✓).

● You can click here to feature the album in the My Gallery section of your account.

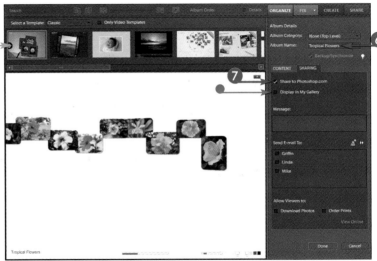

8 Type a message to send to your contacts.

9 Click here to select the contacts (■ changes to ☑).

Note: *See the section "E-mail Images with Photo Mail" for more on adding contacts.*

● You can optionally allow viewers to download photos or order prints from within the gallery.

10 Click **Done**.

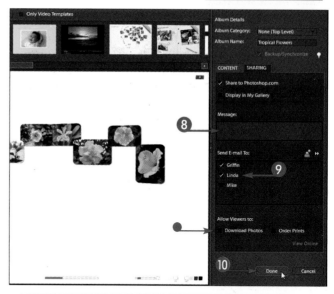

● Photoshop Elements uploads the album photos to your gallery at Photoshop.com for sharing. This may take a few minutes or more, depending on the size of your album and your upload speed.

An e-mail is sent to each contact, inviting the recipient to view the gallery.

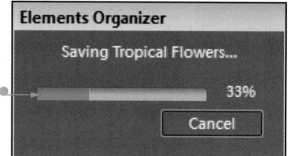

How do I stop an album from being shared?

1 In the Albums pane in the Organizer, click **Stop Sharing** (▣).

A Stop Sharing icon appears next to each shared album.

Photoshop Elements displays a confirmation dialog box.

2 Click **OK**.

Photoshop Elements changes the status of the photos so that they are no longer accessible online.

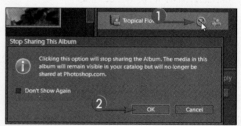

Back Up and Synchronize Photos Online

You can automatically back up albums that you create in the Organizer at your Photoshop.com account. This safeguards your photos in case you lose them on your local computer. Backed-up albums are also synchronized, which means any changes you make to the albums in Photoshop Elements are also made to the backed-up copies.

Because backing up and synchronizing albums involves uploading photos to Photoshop.com, the features work best with a fast Internet connection.

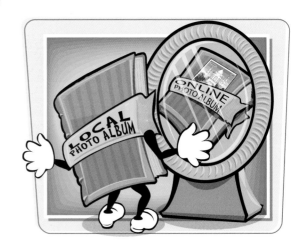

Back Up and Synchronize Photos Online

1 Sign in to your Photoshop.com account in Photoshop Elements.

Note: See the section "Sign Up for Online Services" for more.

2 In the Organizer, click **Edit**.

3 Click **Preferences**.

4 Click **Backup/Synchronization**.

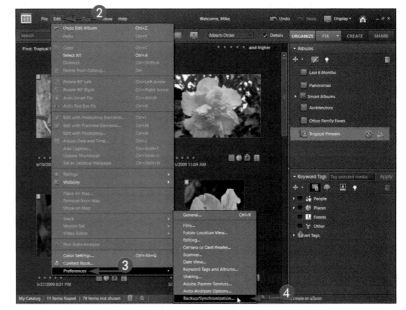

The Backup/Synchronization Preferences dialog box opens.

● You can click here to turn on Backup/Synchronization (■ changes to ✓).

● Albums that are shared on Photoshop.com are automatically backed up and synchronized.

Note: See the section "Share a Photo Gallery Online" for more.

5 Click here to back up and synchronize an album (■ changes to ✓).

6 Click here to view advanced options.

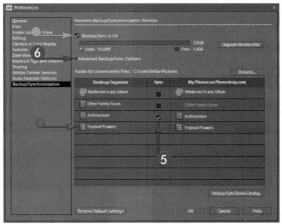

- You can click here to automatically back up and synchronize new albums (■ changes to ☑).

- You can click here to limit the types of files that are backed up and synchronized.

⑦ Click **OK**.

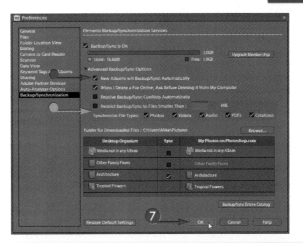

Photoshop Elements backs up and synchronizes the selected albums at Photoshop.com. It may take some time for the files to transfer from your computer to Photoshop.com.

- Photoshop Elements marks the selected albums with a Backup/Synchronize icon (▣).

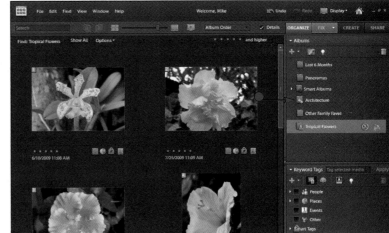

 TIP

How do I check my Photoshop.com account details from within Photoshop Elements?

① Sign in to your Photoshop.com account in Photoshop Elements. See the section "Sign Up for Online Services" for more.

② Click **Welcome** on the menu bar.

③ Type your password in the dialog box that opens.

④ Click **My Account**.

Your account details appear.

- A graph shows you how much storage space you are using.

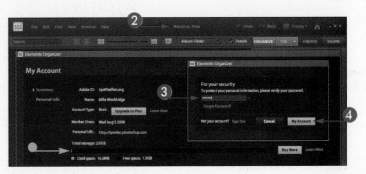

Index

Index

Index

Index

Index

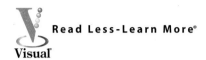
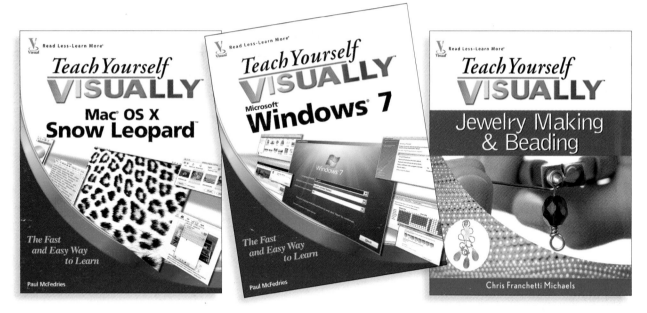